Greenscapes

Greenscapes
Olmsted's Pacific Northwest

Joan Hockaday

Washington State University Press
Pullman, Washington

Washington State University Press
PO Box 645910
Pullman, Washington 99164-5910
Phone: 800-354-7360
Fax: 509-335-8568
E-mail: wsupress@wsu.edu
Web site: wsupress.wsu.edu

Library of Congress Cataloging-in-Publication Data
Hockaday, Joan.
  Greenscapes : Olmsted's Pacific Northwest / Joan Hockaday.
    p. cm.
  Includes bibliographical references and index.
  ISBN 978-0-87422-298-2 (alk. paper)
 1. Olmsted, John Charles, 1852-1920. 2. Landscape architects--United States--Biography. 3. Landscape archi-
tects--Northwest, Pacific--Biography. 4. Olmsted, John Charles, 1852-1920--Influence. 5. Olmsted, John Charles,
1852-1920--Travel--Northwest, Pacific. 6. Landscape architecture--Northwest, Pacific--History. 7. Landscape
design--Northwest, Pacific--History. 8. City planning--Northwest, Pacific--History. 9. Parks--Northwest, Pacific--History.
10. Northwest, Pacific--History, Local. I. Title.

SB470.O53H634 2009
712.092--dc22
[B]

Cover image: Lake Washington Boulevard through Colman Park, June 1913. *Don Sherwood Collection, Seattle Municipal Archives*

Fine Quality Books from the Pacific Northwest

Table of Contents

To all dutiful sons—
Including "JCO"
and to "Somes" and "BC"
and to other sons and daughters
today carrying on family traditions.

Acknowledgments

A prolific writer of letters, John Charles Olmsted sent hundreds home to his wife Sophia in Brookline, Massachusetts, while he fulfilled numerous Pacific Northwest commissions in the early 20th century. Discovering these daily letters proved the deciding factor for my writing of *Greenscapes*.

I especially thank Mary Daniels, the special collections librarian at the Frances Loeb Library, Harvard Graduate School of Design (GSD), in Cambridge, Massachusetts. She processed and serves as the curator of the John Charles Olmsted Papers, donated to Harvard University by John and Sophia's daughter, Carolyn, in 1977. Mary Daniels is a most astute observer of the Olmsted legacy. Her humor and institutional memory proved invaluable during my years of research.

My appreciation also goes to Amy S. Brown, who shared her Harvard GSD research, and to Jerry McCue, dean emeritus of the Harvard GSD, for small favors that loom large in a researcher's busy day. Also at Harvard, I extend gratitude to Lisa Pearson of the Arnold Arboretum Horticultural Library for tracking down family history regarding Fred Dawson, one of Olmsted's assistants.

In the small community of Lee, in southwest Massachusetts, thanks goes to the Bed & Breakfast proprietors who directed me to the Sam Hill family's fine summer home near Stockbridge in the Berkshire Hills, where Olmsted provided services.

Close to Boston, I extend my gratitude to the Wellesley College Club's Mary Martin Holliday, who heard about this book earlier than most and who, of course, has waited for it longer. Up the hill in Wellesley, Judith S. Hull provided local and family history during a month's retreat for my research.

At the Olmsteds' former summer home, Felsted, on the Maine coast, both the curators and keepers, especially Michele Clark and Michael Dosch, provided many courtesies despite a rush to close the old house before major renovation. Also at Deer Isle, an Olmsted family invitation resulted in a few days' visit, which was among the most memorable of my entire research project. To walk the same shoreline, to see the same view, and to take the "Binnacle" cabin path that John Charles Olmsted and the family enjoyed a century ago was a priceless gift—I thank Stephen and Margaret Gill for my special time with them.

The Deer Isle-Stonington Historical Society provided me with their last two copies of Carolyn and Margaret Olmsted's nostalgic little book, *Penobscot Bay Treasures*. I greatly appreciate these reminders indicating that the Olmsted daughters grew to love the same Maine landscape that their father admired.

At the Library of Congress in Washington, D.C., the good cheer and expertise of Bruce Kirby and the staff assisted me in long days of microfilm research. Also, luncheons with old Maine friend Valerie Lester and visits with Olmsted scholar Jonathan Powell in the nearby Folger Shakespeare Library garden are remembered highlights.

Visiting the National Association of Olmsted Parks (NAOP) office near the White House likewise proved of special interest, and increased my appreciation of the many scholars who came before me, studying the legacy of Frederick Law Olmsted Sr. and the Olmsted Brothers.

To the late Dr. Charles C. McLaughlin, the first editor of the Olmsted Papers project published at Johns Hopkins University (a multi-volume effort, still in progress), all succeeding Olmsted scholars remain indebted. Thanks also go to Charles E. Beveridge—and to other past, current, and future editors focusing on Frederick Law Olmsted Sr.'s career—for keeping the series coming off the presses. With the series arranged chronologically, later volumes will increasingly include the work of John Charles Olmsted, and, of course, are of great interest to Pacific Northwest readers.

On the West Coast, the Portland, Oregon, supporters of this venture—Chet Orloff, Bill Hawkins, and Mike Houck, all park board members at one time or another—deserve my thanks for keeping *Greenscapes* alive between 2003 and 2008 centennial celebrations. Our joint Seattle-Portland parks centennial in 2003 brought us together again, commemorating Olmsted's Portland and Seattle visits in 1903.

Chet Orloff, director-emeritus of the Oregon Historical Society, agreed to read the first draft and provided, along with Mike Houck, excellent comments on weaving chapters closer together and adding more history apart from Seattle. Chet's long association with the Oregon Historical Society helped sort historical priorities, and his presentation on Portland's 1905 Lewis and Clark Exposition during our modern centennial in Seattle was enjoyed by all.

Bill Hawkins is a descendent of 1903 park commissioner Lester L. Hawkins, one of Olmsted's most important contacts in Portland a century ago. Also, by great coincidence, Bill was a classmate of my husband, Peter, at the Yale Architecture School and an usher in our wedding many years ago.

Mike Houck's co-edited book, *Wild in the City*, presents Olmsted's Portland story in walk-able segments and is recommended for Olmsted followers. Both Mike and Bill also serve on the National Association of Olmsted Parks' board of directors. Their encouragement—especially for noting the 18 park principles from Olmsted's 1903 Portland park report—was most appreciated. The principles are included in *Greenscapes*.

A most willing thank-you likewise goes to Kenneth J. Guzowski for sharing his Oregon based research.

At the Oregon Historical Society, Marianne Keddington-Lang invited me to expand on my chapter regarding Olmsted's work at Oregon colleges, which appeared in the *Oregon Historical Quarterly* (summer 2007). It is a rare treat to find such a fine, patient, and interested editor.

At Pacific University in Forest Grove, librarian Alex Toth proved especially helpful, and trustee emeritus Bryce Seidl of Seattle graciously paved my way. In Corvallis, archivists Erika Castano, Elizabeth Nielsen, and others at Oregon State University likewise provided much appreciated favors.

Also in Oregon, I thank antiquarian booksellers Ginny and John McCormac for my rare two-volume edition of Theodora Kimball and Frederick Law Olmsted Jr.'s *Forty Years of Landscape Architecture: Frederick Law Olmsted Senior.*

In California, Maggie Kimball of Stanford University Libraries graciously sent an old worn copy of *The Founders and the Architects: The Design of Stanford University*, which told the Frederick Law Olmsted Sr. and Leland Stanford story. Archivists at Stanford also searched for sketches and other historical material with great success.

At the University of California, Berkeley, the papers of architect John Galen Howard held by the Bancroft Library revealed much detail about Seattle's 1909 Alaska-Yukon-Pacific Exposition (AYPE). My gratitude goes to the staff for assembling materials outlining John Charles Olmsted and Howard's involvement at the AYPE.

In the state of Washington, Betty Long-Schleif at the Maryhill Museum supplied a portrait of Sam Hill. The photo depicts Hill in his later years, after Olmsted provided advice regarding his fine new Seattle property atop "Volunteer Hill."

During Spokane's 2008 parks centennial, Marsha Rooney at the Museum of Arts and Culture (MAC) put together a wonderful exhibit of Olmsted's park and garden accomplishments in the Inland Northwest a century ago. The Spokane artwork also came to Seattle. During the long planning process, she gained a lifelong friend and my utmost respect for her detailed museum work. My appreciation also goes to Rose Krause at the MAC's Joel Ferris Library, Spokane parks expert Sally Reynolds, and Taylor Bressler of Spokane Parks.

In Walla Walla, Colleen McFarland and other archivists at Whitman College searched for—and found—Olmsted's original letters sent from Seattle (on Rainier Club stationery) to President Stephen Penrose regarding campus and Walla Walla park work. I also thank them for providing a portrait of President Penrose.

At the University of Idaho in Moscow, archivist Julie Monroe proved most helpful in accessing old alumni magazines and books. Thanks to her, a copy of Keith C. Petersen's *This Crested Hill: An Illustrated History of the University of Idaho* (1988) now sits on my library shelf.

Also in Moscow, the Bookpeople store provided invaluable advice, and instant connection, to historians, including Edwin P. Garretson, editor of the Whitman County Historical Society's *Bunchgrass Historian*. He remembered a published piece regarding Washington State University's former president Enoch A. Bryan, which confirmed Olmsted's favorable interest in Bryan when they both attended Oregon State University graduation ceremonies at Corvallis in 1909.

In British Columbia, Professor Larry McCann requested my John Charles' travel itinerary while researching his own book on Olmsted's work in Canada. Within weeks, a box of Rogers' Chocolates Ltd. creams arrived on my doorstep, a reminder that interest in Olmsted unites friends across the international border. Rogers' chocolates were a favorite of Olmsted's during his time in Victoria,

At Victoria, thanks also are extended to Lynn Milnes, author of *In a Victoria Garden*, who a decade ago provided a tour of Olmsted's Uplands residential development. At the time, a Guerilla Gardener film crew from Toronto interviewed and taped a good gardener there. The Uplands neighborhood indeed remains as Olmsted envisioned—handsome and natural.

Orcas Island historian Christopher M. Peacock, author of *Rosario Yesterdays*, also willingly shared his Olmsted research. On Bainbridge Island, appreciation goes to Andrew Price Jr. for allowing us to sketch the Country Club's "Little Clubhouse," where Olmsted shared a picnic with clients a century ago. The Bainbridge Island Historical Society's Lorraine Scott found a most beautiful turn-of-the-century image of Restoration Point, as it appeared about the time of Olmsted's visitation.

In Olympia, Dave Hastings of the Secretary of State's office provided a portrait of early Seattle parks board member Charles Saunders and access to the Olmsted Brothers' State Capitol plan and papers.

At the University of Washington in Seattle, Carla Rickerson and the staff in Special Collections were extremely helpful in retrieving the most pertinent Olmsted and Board of Regents documents.

Regarding photographers who transfer old images onto CDs and into other modern forms, I am indebted to the people at Ballard Camera—the Cozens and Monica Schippers—above all. Also, appreciation goes to the University of Washington photo lab experts—Christina Olsen Burtner, and others—in the windowless basement of Kane Hall.

Ed Breen's walkabout at Seattle's Discovery Park was full of history and anecdotes, which brought Olmsted's lengthy interaction with military officers at Fort Lawton alive again. Ed's daughter has her own history of the park, living proof of the park's preservation success.

In West Seattle at the Log House Museum, Andrea Mercado, Judy Bentley, and Alan Schmitz—grandson of early park board member Ferdinand Schmitz—were especially helpful and enthusiastic.

On Fourth Avenue in downtown Seattle, three repositories provided wonderful archives—and gracious archivists. At City Hall, Anne Frantilla helped find files for Olmsted and park historian Don Sherwood, and then arranged for photography. Just north of City Hall at the venerable Rainier Club—Olmsted's base for months at a time—executive director Michael Troyer shared Edward Curtis photographs of early club members whom Olmsted encountered. A short distance north at the Central Library, Jodee Fenton and the staff also keep excellent track of Seattle's past.

Near the northern border of Seattle, Dunn Garden archivist Beth Dodrill-Rezghi provided materials for the Dunn family, who were private clients of the Olmsted Brothers. Farther north in Shoreline, the history of The Highlands residential development came alive thanks to Carol Wilder and the late Lucia Lawrence.

Finally, appreciation goes to the board of directors of the Friends of Seattle's Olmsted Parks (FSOP), who produced a fine parks centennial week in 2003. It sparked an interest in extending the *Greenscapes* focus beyond Seattle's border to other parts of the Pacific Northwest. Thanks also to the first FSOP board in the 1980s (Donald Harris, Doug Jackson, and others still active) and again to the board today, with special appreciation to Brice Maryman.

Thanks especially to FSOP art keepers Anne Knight and Jerry Arbes who provided favors in many ways. The two also agreed to travel east with me in the summer of 2004 to digitally photograph, at my request, Olmsted materials that I unearthed beyond Seattle's borders. I appreciate their patience while waiting five years to see this book into print. Hopefully, *Greenscapes* is every Olmsted follower's reward.

March 2009

The Harvard Letters of John Charles Olmsted

Mary Daniels

Special Collections, Frances Loeb Library,
Harvard Design School

John Charles Olmsted (1852–1920), sequentially nephew, stepson, and business partner of Frederick Law Olmsted Sr. (1822–1903), trained at the Yale Sheffield Scientific School, graduating in 1875. He apprenticed with the elder Olmsted in professional practice as a landscape architect. During the subsequent three decades, the Olmsted firm became securely established as the premier landscape design office in America—their hundreds of commissions and projects ranged from private gardens to large-scale institutional planning and municipal park systems.

Throughout this period, John Charles Olmsted assumed responsibility for the administration of the office while also traveling extensively for design work in the United States and Canada. By the time of his death in 1920, the firm's clients numbered more than 3,500 since its founding—a figure due, in no small measure, to John Charles' skills as a designer and meticulous administrator.

The John Charles Olmsted Papers, donated to Harvard by his daughter Carolyn in 1977, include some 5,000 letters exchanged with his wife, Sophia White Olmsted (1862–1956), in the years 1898–1920. During this time, John Charles traveled for lengthy periods on Olmsted firm business and the letters provide insight into the realities of both business and domestic concerns. There also are files containing correspondence with professional colleagues, various materials of professional interest, as well as family papers, ephemera, and photographs.

In 1899, Olmsted made a late marriage with Sophia B. White, long a Brookline, Massachusetts, neighbor, whose family home stood next door to famed architect H.H. Richardson's residence on a hill above John Charles' own house and office. Given the demands of his career, the fact that Olmsted had any time for courtship is noteworthy (even of a woman living a few blocks distant).

Within a very few years, John and Sophia had two daughters. The parents then were subjected to the strains of prolonged absences on his part, of the hitherto unknown demands of child-raising and household man-agement, and of the circumstances encountered by living in proximity to the firm's office and a tangle of blood relatives and in-laws.

Within days of ending their six-week honeymoon, John Charles left Brookline on a series of professional consultations, setting a familiar pattern of absences in the years ahead. He intricately calibrated these trips—juggling railroad schedules and appointments to guarantee the greatest productive use of his time. The most carefully prepared itinerary, however, was frequently upset by unexpected complications or by the promise of a new commission.

In addition to visiting sites and attending innumerable planning meetings with local clients, Olmsted also drafted plans and prepared reports while on the road. The telegraph and mails kept him in touch with the Brookline office. Overscheduled, yet fearful of being under-employed, he would pick up new commissions en route, further increasing the work-load.

His script in many letters testifies to his frequent exhaustion—the correspondence is rife with descriptions of fatigue. His digestion might be assaulted by hotel and boardinghouse cuisine; the vagaries of climate entail obsessive concern with proper clothing; fresh air is extolled, yet exposure to inclement weather during fieldwork causes bouts of flu—resulting in John Charles sitting in a hotel rocking chair, fully-dressed (including overcoat and hat) and shrouded in blankets.

The letters written to his wife from Brookline—during the warm months when Sophia and their daughters spent time at the family's summer home in Maine—reflect, however, the relative ease of an over-burdened man who, at least, was "home" in Massachusetts with predictable creature comforts and congenial relatives.

In *Greenscapes*, John Charles' letters present an extraordinary portrait of his professional days on the road, as well as glimpses of his domestic home life and marriage—all within the social and class framework of American life in the first decade of the last century.

John Charles Olmsted (September 14, 1852–February 24, 1920).

Introduction

A Life Led in the Shadow

It seems I now have three unusually important visits to make on the Pacific Coast and may have more. Things seem to be booming. I wish we had another energetic partner!
—From the Hotel Aragon, Atlanta, March 14, 1903

By his own design, John Charles Olmsted remained in the shadow of his famous stepfather, Frederick Law Olmsted Sr., for nearly three decades until the latter passed away in 1903. By coincidence, Portland and Seattle park commissioners first summoned the younger Olmsted west in April of that year, just four months before Olmsted Sr.'s death.

Great fame already had come Frederick Law Olmsted Sr.'s way after winning a competition in 1857 to design Central Park in New York with partner and architect Calvert Vaux. Frederick Law Olmsted Sr. (1822–1903), nicknamed "FLO," almost single-handedly shaped the new profession of landscape architecture during the last decades of the 19th century and instilled in his sons—John Charles Olmsted (1852–1920) and Frederick Law Olmsted Jr. (1870–1957)—the duty to carry on. Despite the fact that Olmsted Sr. had never graduated from college, as few young men did in the mid 19th century, both college-educated sons admitted lesser capabilities than their father.[1]

John Charles Olmsted actually was born to Olmsted Sr.'s beloved brother, John Hull Olmsted, who died in November 1857, five years after the birth of his son and two other children. Young John Charles and his sisters, however,

Central Park Mall, New York.

soon found a new home when his widowed mother, Mary Perkins Olmsted, and his uncle, Frederick Law Olmsted Sr., married to seal the family ties.

Shy and content to watch his stepfather take the limelight, young John Charles after his 1875 Yale graduation apprenticed with his "father," as he affectionately called Olmsted Sr. Young John Charles, then and for the rest of his life, was affectionately called JCO to distinguish him from his father, FLO.

After moving their office from New York to Brookline, Massachusetts, near Boston in the 1880s, the Olmsted firm found public and private work increasing at a rapid rate. John Charles kept his father's growing office on a solid footing, while the increasingly elderly Olmsted Sr. traveled the country answering growing client demands, all clamoring for attention. Stanford University, the Washington, D.C. zoo, the Chicago World's Fair, and the Biltmore Estate, along with Atlantic seaboard park systems and a growing Boston client base, all needed attention, which young John Charles helped channel throughout the 1880s and 1890s.

The expanding client list around Boston and elsewhere in New England included the indefatigable botanist, Charles Sprague Sargent, at Harvard University's famed Arnold

Arboretum. Sargent's vast botanical planning was matched by Olmsted Sr.'s grand design, but the details in the project, as often the case, were left to John Charles back at the Brookline office.[2]

In a long letter on September 26, 1891, to his roaming father, John Charles wrote in part: "Dear Father: We have felt a little in the dark here as to your movements & yesterday telegraphed & learned you were to be in Biltmore Monday…I sent a print of the Zoo Park map in order that you may look it over in connection with my letter & also that you may study upon it, if you have time, before going to Washington. I am expecting you to telegraph me when to meet you there. I shall assume that we will meet at Hotel Normandie…I presented a revised plan of East Boston Park yesterday. It is a better and cheaper one. No action was taken upon it…Mr. Sargent has persuaded Mr. Ames not to build on our site…I haven't had time to get on with this plan nor Sherwood Land Co. but almost everything else is in good shape. Affly, J.C.O."

John Charles waited expectantly for his younger half-brother (by 18 years), Frederick Law Olmsted Jr., to graduate from Harvard in 1894 and take on duties in the office. In this period, John Charles experienced aching setbacks when two promising assistants suddenly died—29-year-old Henry Sargent Codman in 1893, and 37-year-old Charles Eliot succumbed to spinal meningitis in 1897. John Charles and his half brother would be left to shoulder even more burdens without these capable colleagues.

Olmsted Sr., too, started to fail mentally during the Biltmore Estate planning, and quit active work in 1895. New college graduate Frederick Law Olmsted Jr. (called "Rick" by associates and family) admitted his botany skills were weak. However, John Charles had spent two decades working with Olmsted Sr., absorbing FLO's love of the outdoors and the necessary disciplines of park design, botany, and plantsmanship. These proved to be exactly the talents that

"FLO"—Frederick Law Olmsted Sr.

the Olmsted firm would need for projects out west after the turn of the century.

The brothers and their mother, Mary, were reluctant to announce Olmsted Sr.'s failing condition to the public. Consequently in 1898, they fixed on "Olmsted Brothers" when dropping the firm's then previously temporary identification as "F.L. and J.C. Olmsted," and the earlier "Olmsted, Olmsted and Eliot" in 1893–97. Years passed before outsiders generally knew that the brothers were indeed FLO's sons and that they were leading the projects. The name "Olmsted Brothers" would be retained for the firm well past the mid 20th century.

Meanwhile, the two brothers themselves broke new ground in the profession of landscape architecture. In 1899, the American Society of Landscape Architects was formed, with John Charles serving as its first president. Beginning in 1900, Rick taught the new landscape architecture curriculum at Harvard, gaining much fame like his father, who was by then totally incapacitated.

Against this backdrop, Northwest park and garden clients entered the picture as the City Beautiful movement gained ground in the new century. Easterners moving out west longed for civilizing influences taken for granted in cities on the Atlantic seaboard. John Charles, with a Yale education and carefully trained in restraint, observation, and punctuality (the latter, however, often of little interest to westerners), was the ideal person in the eyes of those city fathers aiming to tame ragged urban landscapes.

Many eastern transplants held important social, economic, and government positions out west. These clients often were members of city boards, giving of their time to make rough edged cityscapes more civilized and attractive. In Seattle, for example, park commissioner Charles Saunders (an architect), and university trustee Alden J. Blethen (a prominent newspaper editor), hailed originally from New England. In Walla Walla, Whitman College president

Stephen Penrose, too, brought his eastern sensibilities to bear on a rugged campus. In the years ahead, the Olmsted firm was destined to open office files for more than 60 public and 150 private commissions throughout the Northwest.[3]

By the time 50-year-old John Charles arrived out west in the spring of 1903, he had been married for only four years and now had two young daughters, Carolyn and Margaret. In 1899, he had married his Brookline neighbor, Sophia B. White, relatively late in life when he was 46. Sophia was a decade younger. When traveling, his letters to and from home each day frequently revealed how trying his absences were for him and his family.

He sometimes wrote heartbreaking apologies when missing family milestones and other important moments together, as in this letter from Buffalo, New York, in May 1906. "I am sorry to be away so much and leave you alone, but as long as Rick continues professoring I suppose I shall have to keep up the western end of our business. When Charles Eliot was with us he objected to being away so much and [as] I was then the bachelor of the firm it fell to me… I made a good reputation on the Chicago and Louisville parks so people knew me and wanted me personally. However, I think Rick may give up the professorship in a few years & then if he isn't married he can do some of the longer trips. I must go to my train now. Ever lovingly your husband."

Three years earlier, when wrapping up his Grant Park work in Atlanta, Olmsted confided to Sophia on March 17, 1903, about newfound western work in California, Portland, and Seattle. Word about new projects often came by telegram from the office while Olmsted traveled. "I am resolved to leave tomorrow. I could spend a few days more on Grant Park here [in Georgia] but I would rather have the topographical map…before I spend much time on it. It seems I now have three unusually important visits to make on the Pacific Coast & may have more. Things seem to be booming. I wish we had another energetic partner!…Love to the babies!"

Sophia playfully replied on the 31st: "I hope you have had good weather for the scenery part of your trip, but I hope you will not be so fascinated with Seattle when you arrive there that you will wish to stay there."

John Charles shortly thereafter reached Portland and then Seattle, beginning his park planning in these cities for the first time. (Altogether, he made 12 work-packed trips to

John Charles and Sophia. *Fairsted*

Sophia White Olmsted
(1862–1956)

Sophia lived almost her entire life on one avenue in Brookline, Massachusetts. During her engagement, she resided with her parents in a home with servants at 222 Warren Street, while John Charles' office and home stood just down the same hill, at 99 Warren Street. After marrying in 1899, John Charles and Sophia rented a house farther down the avenue at 16 Warren Street, where they resided for a decade. Soon after Sophia's parents passed away, the couple and their now teen-aged daughters moved back to the White family home at 222 Warren Street.

Though Sophia was homebound with the "babies," John Charles' long letters provided her with details about the outside world afar. On November 11, 1907, for example, she told her husband, "I ought to have a pretty fair idea of what our country is like from your letters which I enjoy reading so much."

the Northwest in 1903 and 1906–11, while his daughters and wife wished he were closer to home.)

After two months in the Pacific Northwest during the first visit in the spring of 1903, he returned to Brookline, which he did each summer to join his family at a summer home in Maine on his days off. He always spent summers back east and insisted that clients grant this concession to family life.

"Felsted"—the summer house at Deer Isle, Maine, overlooking Penobscot Bay—actually had been built for Olmsted Sr., who by then was permanently lodged in institutional care in Massachusetts. At Felsted, John Charles found a welcomed retreat from office and client demands.

"Felsted," Deer Isle, Maine. *Olmsted Family*

Sadly, Olmsted Sr. never was able to see his sons take over the sprawling summer house and nearby "Binnacle" cottage.

In summer, to beat the Boston heat, Sophia Olmsted and the two young daughters retreated to Felsted. John Charles would join his family there on weekends. Olmsted had at first found his wife reluctant to leave the confines (and family familiarity) of Brookline for summer leisure in Maine, but Sophia soon warmed to Maine in summertime. Both parents instilled in their "baby" daughters, Carolyn and Margaret, a lifelong appreciation of fir-clad Deer Isle. Today, Barred Island Preserve is an Olmsted legacy—left by the family—near the Olmsted summer compound.

During John Charles's first Seattle stay, his father's deteriorating health produced several reflective letters to Sophia. "I am glad you felt well enough to go to [the McLean Asylum at] Waverly with Mother. It would be harder for her to go alone," Olmsted wrote on May 12, 1903. "I can appreciate her idea that if possible she ought to have Father at home but I do not think she is strong enough and I should strongly advise against it. It is well that I should hear about him."

Two weeks later, while still in Seattle: "It is a pity you have to see Father in his present condition. It must be depressing. He repeatedly expressed the hope to me that he would die suddenly 'in harness' as he expressed it, but his wish was not gratified." Confined in an institution on a hill in Belmont, surrounded by a landscape he helped design in 1875, Olmsted Sr. continued to slip away.

After returning to Boston that summer, Olmsted wrote Sophia in Maine, keeping her informed about Olmsted Sr.'s condition. The news in late August grew sadder by the day. "I went with Mother & Rick to see Father at the McLean Asylum this afternoon. He was unconscious & breathing heavily…he was sinking and might live only a few hours."[4]

News of the death reached the Deer Isle summer house shortly thereafter. "My father died this morning at 2 o'clock. Rick went back to Waverly last evening & spent the night there. He has made all needed arrangements for the funeral, which will be on Monday & entirely private."[5] The Olmsted Sr. era ended quietly, just as his wife Mary and their sons intended.

"We had an extremely simple funeral this morning at eleven at the chapel…in Mt. Auburn Cemetery…Only a few were present as the funeral was purposely not announced…Mother did not go," John Charles wrote Sophia on August 31.

Thus, one of America's most public of figures in the late 19th-century was quietly put to rest, so that a smooth and uninterrupted transition would allow continuance of the family firm.

For years afterward, however, friends, clients, and colleagues still remembered the man who left such an indelible imprint on the new profession of landscape architecture. As late as 1947, Gifford Pinchot—first head of the U.S. Forest Service early in the century—wrote in his autobiography, *Breaking New Ground*: "Mr. Olmsted was to me one of the men of the century. He was a quiet-spoken little lame man with a most magnificent head and one of the best minds I have ever had the good luck to encounter [at the Biltmore Estate]. His knowledge was far wider than his profession. He knew the territory of the United States as few men knew it, and he was full of stories of early days."

Olmsted Sr. left big shoes to fill, but for many years the shy, self-effacing John Charles had dutifully and very capably filled in at the office and on the road, while his renowned father traveled extensively. Now it was John Charles's time to finally emerge as the most qualified landscape architect of the early 20th century. Furthermore, John Charles was the one best qualified from the firm to travel widely.[6] With the "Olmsted" name having achieved such wide acclaim, John Charles confided to Sophia his awe at carrying on such a reputation.

In the years ahead, brother Rick would continue to carve his own credentials in the adjunct area of city planning. He embellished the landscape architecture profession to encompass broader urban and suburban site plans, while John Charles continued the older tradition of designing specific parks, parkways, and parks systems. The two brothers, through cordial and careful collaboration, carried on their father's dedication to high standards.

Suburban sprawl and the automobile began to change the face of American cities in the decade before World War I. The "Olmsted" era in landscape architecture might have ended with Olmsted Sr.'s death in 1903, but due to the highly capable sons and their adaptability to the changing times, the Olmsted legacy continued for many years. Indeed, it was just getting started in the Far West. This is the story of the one brother who shaped Pacific Northwest greenswards in the Olmsted Sr. image.

"Rick"—Frederick Law Olmsted Jr. *Fairsted*

Archival Collections

Library of Congress

Most of the Olmsted Brothers' vast office correspondence, field notes, reports, and other written materials—along with the extensive papers and documents from the earlier Frederick Law Olmsted Sr. era—are now housed in the Madison Library Annex of the Library of Congress, Washington, D.C.

Librarians note that this large repository of primary materials—for a century of the firm's work until the mid 20th century—is one of the most visited and consulted collections at the National Archives. Today, numerous regional park historians, consultants, and other researchers examine the collection in regard to the thousands of private properties, campuses, parks, boulevards, and other public places that the Olmsted firm designed or provided advice for throughout the United States and in Canada.

Harvard University

John Charles Olmsted's 5,000 private letters, including more than 500 written almost daily from the Pacific Northwest (particularly to his wife Sophia), are housed at Special Collections, Frances Loeb Library, Harvard Graduate School of Design. These original letters were donated to Harvard University by John and Sophia's daughter, Carolyn, in 1977.

"Fairsted," Brookline, Massachusetts

The Olmsted Brothers' drawings—keepsakes of almost a century of work—are still housed at the former Brookline family home and office (both under the same roof), purchased by Olmsted Sr. in the 1880s. The "Fairsted" estate, including its period garden, now is owned and managed by the U.S. National Park Service as the Frederick Law Olmsted National Historic Site. John Charles' keen interest in the new medium of photography shows in his early snapshots, taken from upstairs windows at Fairsted.

Notes

1. For overviews of Frederick Law Olmsted Sr.'s life, see Laura Wood Roper, *FLO: A Biography of Frederick Law Olmsted* (Baltimore, Maryland: Johns Hopkins University Press, 1973), and Frederick Law Olmsted Sr., et al., *Forty Years of Landscape Architecture, Volume 1, Early Years and Experiences*, and *Volume 2, Central Park* (original publisher: Putnam, New York).

2. Letters, Arnold Arboretum archives, reproduced from originals in the Olmsted collection, Library of Congress.

3. See: Catherine Joy Johnson, *Olmsted in the Pacific Northwest: Private Estates and Residential Communities, 1873–1959: An Inventory* (Seattle: Friends of Seattle's Olmsted Parks, 1997); Charles E. Beveridge, *The Master List of Design Projects of the Olmsted Firm, 1857–1950*, known as "The Green Book," (National Association for Olmsted Parks [NOAP]/Massachusetts Association for Olmsted Parks, 1987); and Lucy Lawliss, Caroline Loughlin, and Lauren Meier, eds., *The Master List of Design Projects of the Olmsted Firm, 1857–1979*, 2nd ed. (National Association for Olmsted Parks/Frederick Law Olmsted National Historic Site, 2008). The latter work is a revised "Master List" by the National Association for Olmsted Parks with added essays and insights.

4. Letter, August 27, 1903.

5. Letter, August 28, 1903.

6. Though Rick Olmsted was a bachelor and thus seemingly less tied to domestic life in Brookline, he was considerably younger than John Charles and had less experience in traveling to client jobs. Also, he was absorbed with teaching at Harvard University. Rick did not marry until March 1911, to Sarah Sharples.

Opposite: Bainbridge Island's Restoration Point, as it appeared near the turn of the last century. Note the logged over landscape—most old-growth trees near Puget Sound population centers recently were logged, leaving single conifers to grow robustly, and second growth to fill in. Olmsted ferried to this island west of Seattle for three clients during his decade out West. *Bainbridge Island Historical Society.*

1

First Northwest Impressions

It is the moisture that makes it so perfect.—April 10, 1903

*J*ohn Charles Olmsted arrived in the Pacific Northwest in the second week of April 1903, having promised the Portland organizers of the Lewis and Clark Centennial Exposition (scheduled for 1905) that he would be there by Easter. Rushing through prior commitments— including a visit to Catalina Island off the southern California coast, and resigned to giving up most sight-seeing during the long train journey—the dutiful heir to the Olmsted legacy arrived in Portland just in time.

Nearly four decades had passed since his first visit to the West Coast. In 1864, when only 11 years old, John Charles had rode pack-mules in the High Sierras with his father.[1] On June 25, 1864, the senior Olmsted had written to his

own father back in Hartford, Connecticut: "If California does nothing else for them [referring to the four Olmsted children at the time[2]] it will educate them to be clever observers in geology & botany."

Now entering his 50s, John Charles found himself once again on the West Coast. Indeed, carefully trained to observe even the smallest outdoors detail, John Charles carried the same exceptional talent of his father-mentor, Olmsted Sr., into the new century. Intrigued by the exotic Catalina Island vegetation, and then the Northwest's even more unfamiliar native trees and shrubs, John Charles confided he needed an office plantsman out west rather than— or in addition to—his draftsman.

The western clients helped him absorb his new surroundings. In Portland, park commissioner Lester L. Hawkins in his tally-ho escorted Olmsted from the west hills down to the Willamette River. "I have seen Portland from above today so to speak," Olmsted wrote his wife from the Hotel Portland, the day after he arrived. "I was up on a hill back of the city with one of the Park Commissioners…One of the parks (107 acres) includes a piece of primeval forest, mostly Douglass [sic] fir & a big cedar like our arbor-vitae as to foliage & lots of great fallen trees & rich dense undergrowth and a covering of ferns & bright green moss below. One rarely sees such a deep shady green wooded ravine & such towering trees."[3]

When John Charles moved on to Seattle at the very end of April, park commissioners there gathered daily to show Olmsted the woods, hills, and shorelines of the "Emerald City," with the spring season becoming more advanced in May. By tugboat and skiff, horse-drawn carriage, newly-built trolley cars, and on foot, Olmsted spent his first few weeks in Seattle taking in the open landscapes and horizons, as more bays, lakes, and hills broke into his view practically every day.

City Towers and Distant Mountains

Olmsted's Portland and Seattle hosts, as was the custom then, took him to the tallest towers in town to get a panoramic look at the locality. In Portland, Park Commissioner Ion Lewis—of the Whidden and Lewis architectural firm, and the Portland exposition's official architect—showed Olmsted the view from the *Oregonian* building, the city's first high tower.

Olmsted took special note of two majestic mountains off to the east, as noted in an April 12 letter to his wife: "Mr. Lewis called for me and we went up to the top of the tower of the Oregonian Bldg. & spent some time there talking & looking at the views. I took one snap of the view toward Mt. St. Helens, said to be 100 miles away…and another of Mt. Hood said to be 65 miles away…Both show

7972. Mount Hood Showing Lost Lake, Oregon.

Mt. Hood and other Cascades peaks were commonly depicted in travel postcards of a century ago.

very distinctly & had the sun full upon them. They stand up remarkably high especially as I saw them through my field glass. Both are snow-clad way down from the top. St. Helens is a nearly perfect rounded out cone & the snow is deep and smooth and unbroken upon it. It really seems too smooth to look as rugged as a mountain should."[4]

Olmsted thought Mt. Hood to be scenically most appealing. "Mt. Hood on the other hand has ridges & tremendous ravines breaking its mass and an irregular rocky ridge breaking off to the left—all covered with snow but showing its rocky structure by light and shades & therefore more characteristic and interesting. Mr. Lewis liked Mt. Hood best," Olmsted added.

His host, Ion Lewis, shared another perspective on viewing the peaks. "He…prefers to see them from lower places in the city where the intervening wooded mountains are hidden and the snow covered part of Mt. Hood only shows above buildings. I saw it so later & it certainly did make it seem nearer and in a way more impressive."

On Olmsted's first whirlwind day in Seattle, he arrived by train at 7:30 a.m. on April 30, and within two hours, four park commissioners escorted him on an all-day tour. "A bird's-eye view of the city" was gained from Seattle's courthouse cupola, followed by a visit to the top floor of the Washington Hotel, as Olmsted related in a letter to his wife from the Knickerbocker Hotel that night. (Four days later, Olmsted would view the nearby hills from the tallest point in the city—the Queen Anne Hill water tower).

"I was out with the park commissioners all day. It is an extensive city and it will take me some time to take it all in," Olmsted wrote his wife on April 30. After a second all-day outing across Seattle to Lake Washington with most of the park commissioners, Olmsted viewed "Mt. Rainier for the first time. It is huge."

He arrived in the heyday of the horse and carriage, and after the bicycle had achieved some popularity as a means of transportation. However, eight years later in the autumn of 1911—when Olmsted left the Pacific Northwest for the last time—automobiles had taken over the roadways so carefully planned and graded by the Olmsted firm. However, his first Northwest impressions and the subsequent basis for his planning had been conducted from riding in carriages on rutted paths. One of his last Seattle letters, though, would express acceptance of the changing situation: "It is fine the time the auto saves."[5]

Oregon Mist and Little Summer Rainfall

The slower pace of travel by buggy and on foot during the first decade of the last century provided more time to reflect upon surroundings, including a careful observation of soils, smells, and vegetation. Olmsted often wrote home about these impressions. Like most travelers, he also commented on the local weather, but he probably absorbed more other details than most tourists.

"I went out for a little exercise at 5:30 or so in what they call an 'Oregon mist,' but it was a pretty wet one. I saw Fuchsia today in full bloom," he added.

"The season has advanced greatly in 2 weeks. Dandelions are rampant. The dogwoods on lower & sheltered ground are getting nearly white. The blossoms are pale green or greenish white for about 2 weeks," he commented when signing off to his wife from the Portland Hotel on the night of April 25.

From Seattle a month later: "It has been another cloudy showery day but no heavy rainfall. It is much like England and Ireland as to cloud and rain I should say, only more so in winter and decidedly dry in summer, they say. Lawns have to be watered. Still moss grows abundantly on shingle roofs in the full sunlight and it would be harder to find a drier place than that. Still even then it grows most on the north slopes of roofs. The ferns are huge here."[6]

Island Scenery, West and East

In the years to come, Olmsted's voyages to the San Juan Islands and the British Columbia coast would bring further observations about the Pacific Northwest's varied landscapes. The peaceful voyages, too, were pleasant interludes in his intensively filled Pacific Northwest work schedule.

"The sail here was about 28 miles from Bellingham and was very delightful," Olmsted wrote after journeying to Orcas Island in April 1907 for client Robert Moran. "The islands are very much like Penobscot Bay only they are much larger and much higher and the fir trees are many sizes bigger. There is a beautiful cove here with a nice clean dark gray gravel beach. It is open for miles to S.W.… [Constitution] mountain is 2400 feet high which is a little higher than the mountain of Mt. Desert…The view was somewhat similar but a great many more islands and the snow clad ranges," he wrote, providing his wife with a mental picture to compare to the "Bay" and island views from their own summer house on Deer Isle, Maine.

The vistas and impressions gained from the bluffs of Puget Sound and Lake Washington, too, when visiting Seattle clients, often filled Olmsted's letters home. The snow-clad mountains on the horizons east and west of the cityscape drew his special attention. Maintaining these views became attendant in his landscape assignments in the Northwest.

Negative Park and Garden Reviews

Interspersed with Olmsted's abundant favorable reviews and raptures, however, there were impressions of parks badly planned—Seattle's then-existing Denny Park being one example (see Appendix B).

On May 19, 1910, a Bellingham park also drew special scorn as a blueprint for bad planning. "I went this afternoon to see a little flat park 8 ac. in the N.W. part of the main city which the Supt. I presume designed. The grass is green & he has lots of flowering shrubs and plants but the plantations are too mixed & too much made up of specimen effects. It's like a room that has too many sorts of bricabrac on the shelves, mantel and table, though he has to be sure some extent of simple lawns."

Private gardens, too, came under the sharp end of Olmsted's critical pen when clients were unwilling to appreciate or consider retaining the natural shrubbery so abundant under tall Northwest trees. "Mr. Clark is clearing the dead trees and fallen logs and most of the underbrush with disastrous effects upon the beauty of the woods," Olmsted wrote his wife after a May 28, 1908, visit to The Highlands, a residential development near the northern border of Seattle.

"Of course all the men detest everything wild except the big leaved maple tree and madronas," Olmsted continued. "Bushes are to them merely weeds to be trampled down and destroyed so grass can be sown. It seems especially queer that they cannot appreciate the beautiful evergreen undergrowth they have here—the Oregon grape, the Sallal [sic] and the evergreen huckleberry."

The abundant and often locally derided alder also garnered praise from Olmsted, as did ferns and other natural vegetation. Soon after he arrived in the region, he often encouraged their retention or planting in his plans.

A Walla Walla park commissioner's own private garden drew one of Olmsted's most critical reviews, written as field notes to his office. "I yielded to his repeated request to look at his place although it is planted and practically finished. It is a small place with a frontage of 150 feet or 200 feet on the street that bounds the Whitman College land on the north…His house is…picturesque and [an] ornate one in a

A Spokane park gathering. *Fairsted*

free style…He has filled in thousands of loads of earth…he has raised a great mound…the mound is off center…The whole thing is 'playing to the gallery' as it is intended to be seen by people on the street and probably it is expected that strangers will gasp and exclaim 'The man that did that must have been a successful businessman!'…and as I was only a short time on the place, I concluded to make him, as President of Park Board, no charge."

Interior Northwest Plant-life

Olmsted came to appreciate not only the coast's lush vegetation, but also the dry country plants carpeting the rolling hills of eastern Washington. His East Coast sensibilities rarely prejudiced his evaluation of the terrain and natural vegetation out west. Bunchgrass, sagebrush, and ponderosa pine caught his eye and admiration on Inland Northwest train trips.

"The frost on the sagebrush was very pretty and the atmospheric effects, early, very beautiful," Olmsted wrote to his wife from the Hotel Spokane on January 27, 1908, during one of his first winter visits to the Inland Northwest. When spending his days trudging through deep snow, he noted: "It is decidedly colder here than in Seattle."

The wholesale scraping of thin top soils to plant fashionable eastern plants was disapproved of by this student of nature. Though greatly admiring the City of Seattle's vast sluicing of steep waterfront hills to make way

COLUMBIA RIVER CASCADE MOUNTAINS ON THE SPOKANE, PORTLAND AND SEATTLE RAILWAY. © KISER, 104095

"I took the 10 a.m. train so as to see the Columbia River scenery, which is fine."—October 8, 1911.

for a better downtown district, the disturbance of Kennewick's top soil to rid the landscape of native vegetation displeased Olmsted.

"This afternoon I went out on the land and studied the rough part…They are clearing the sage brush off. I did not get close to the horses but I understand a couple of railroad rails are wired together & then dragged sideways by teams at each end. This smashes & tears up the bushes, the roots being very brittle. The land is left pretty humpy because the wind has blown the sand & dust away from the spaces between the bushes & it piles up among the bushes making lumps." Thus Olmsted wrote to his wife from the Hotel Kennewick, describing his developer client's land-clearing activities near the Columbia River.

Hayden Lake, east of Spokane, where Olmsted designed a resort community. *Fairsted*

Little Firs and the UW Campus

In 1903, during one of Olmsted's first visits to the then untidy University of Washington campus, acting President Thomas F. Kane strolled the dusty paths along with Olmsted, pointing out a half-dozen recently erected buildings, including the boys and girls dormitories.

Olmsted reported on the tour to his office on May 26. "The slope behind the girls' dormitory does not appear to be as steep as I imagined from the contour map. A good deal of it is covered with little fir trees making it difficult to get over it and impossible to see anything when there."

Inside the girls' dorm, "the whole basement is used for dining rooms…and in the wing for the kitchen…the boys and girls dine together promiscuously. The boys' dormitory had bedrooms only." The university trustees "having trouble in the management of the dormitories, are disposed to adopt the policy of having no dormitories but this idea may

change. Dr. Kane said a plan [by Olmsted] should provide for dormitories."

Campus planning in 1903, for Olmsted, included combining social and landscaping skills to bridge the gap between trustee and student expectations. The following spring—and continuing for the next three decades—an annual "Campus Day" clean-up became a lively University of Washington tradition, when boys rode horseback and cleared brush, and girls delivered drinks before serving the main midday meal—outside rather than in the girls' dormitory.

John Charles's "Rainier Vista" days were yet to come, when the University of Washington and the Alaska-Yukon-Pacific Exposition organizers asked him back in 1906 to design an unused portion of the campus below the campus's existing oval. Majestic Mt. Rainier had immediately impressed Olmsted in 1903 during a boat tour on Lake Washington. Three years later, the view become the centerpiece in Olmsted's expanded campus plan.

Campus Day, 1907. *University of Washington Libraries*

These first impressions would remain with Olmsted, influencing his work in the years ahead. Remarking over and again about the lush vegetation west of the Cascades, he had quickly found the reason for it. Writing to his wife from Portland on April 10, 1903: "It is the moisture that makes it so perfect."

Notes

1. Victoria Post Ranney, ed., *The Papers of Frederick Law Olmsted, Vol. V, The California Frontier, 1863–1865* (Baltimore and London: Johns Hopkins University Press, 1990).
2. Frederick Law Olmsted Jr., or "Rick," had not yet been born.
3. Letter, April 10, 1903.
4. The "perfect rounded" profile of Mt. St. Helens was massively altered 77 years later during the May 18, 1980, eruption.
5. Letter, October 5, 1911.
6. Letter, May 27, 1903.

Portland Exposition, Parks, & Clients

*Spent a good deal of time on this Lewis & Clark [Exposition] matter. Still, it is interesting...
to plan such a large affair in the very beginning as Father & Henry Codman did in the case of
the Chicago World's Fair.*—April 15, 1903

At the beginning of the 20th century, world's fairs and expositions were in full bloom across the nation. After the success of the 1893 Chicago World's Fair—with the grounds designed by Frederick Law Olmsted Sr.—other expositions followed in short order. Portland soon proposed its own fair, set to open as the Lewis and Clark Centennial Exposition in 1905. Seattle followed in 1909 with the Alaska-Yukon-Pacific Exposition.

By 1901, two years before the Portland exposition directors summoned him west, John Charles was serving as the first president of the newly-formed American Society of Landscape Architects (ASLA). The new born profession mainly was an East Coast development. The Olmsted firm also had gained recognition for its exposition grounds work, most notably the 1893 World's Columbian Exposition in Chicago. It was logical for exposition and park proponents in Portland or Seattle to look to the Olmsted Brothers to introduce new landscape architecture principles in the West.

John Charles already had advised the selectors of the Buffalo Pan-American Exposition site. Also, when acting on behalf of the ASLA, Olmsted wrote to the St. Louis fair

Oregon Historical Society

president, D.R. Francis, in the spring of 1901 for advisory status on the upcoming Louisiana Purchase International Exposition.[1]

Much was at stake in such major undertakings. With fairs following in rapid succession, many lost money. Cities in the East and Midwest competed against each other. For example, St. Louis had lost out to Chicago for 1893, but later put on its own spectacular Louisiana Purchase International Exposition in 1904. Meanwhile, competition in the Northwest was just beginning, though Portland seemed to have no competitors in 1903.[2] However, beating its rival city—Seattle—would be a pleasure for the Portland organizers.

Lewis and Clark Centennial Exposition

Portland, nevertheless, was in a hurry. Having been initially called on from afar by park board member Thomas L. Eliot, Olmsted arrived on April 9, 1903, and settled into the Hotel Portland until the end of April.[3] Park board members in Portland, and a month later in Seattle, probably hardly realized that the firm's famed leader, Frederick Law Olmsted Sr., lay dying in a Massachusetts institution at the time.

Early during his visit, Olmsted was taken to survey the Guild's Lake area in northwest Portland, which was a finalist on the site selection list for the Lewis and Clark Centennial Exposition. He also was requested to present a site plan for the fair first, before beginning his Portland parks work. Some organizers, however, temporarily held off the final vote for choosing the exposition site, hoping Olmsted would pick a "park" site, rather than Guild's Lake.

John Charles immediately undertook the task earnestly and quickly, when business leaders convinced him to agree to the Guild's Lake location. Though limited to being a "consulting landscape architect" only for the exposition grounds,[4] Olmsted would

Oregon Historical Society

have the luxury of an on-site engineer, Oskar Huber, and an architect, Ion Lewis, who later were willing to carry out most of his ideas through to the finish.

The Portland fair report, so quickly needed, was "quite a piece of work, there are so many points to advise upon," Olmsted wrote in a letter to Sophia on April 15, 1903. Indeed, the previous day he had expressed his worry: "My work I think will please the committee though it is taking more time than anticipated."

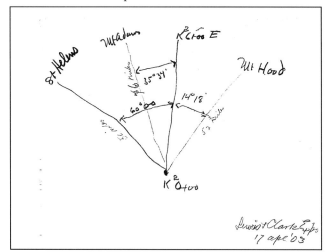

Olmsted's sketch of mountain views from the Lewis and Clark Centennial Exposition site, April 17, 1903. *Library of Congress*

He disliked rushing the report, and especially handing it over prematurely to the *Oregonian* for publication. On April 23, he released the 25-page document—after reading it aloud in his Hotel Portland room to exposition grounds committee members. Olmsted and the "impressed" committee then "adjourned to basement" for drinks. "It seems to be the custom of businessmen & some professional men here," Olmsted wrote home that night.

The fair's location included a plateau and low-lying ground, situated northwest of the city center alongside the Willamette River. The leased property surrounded Guild's Lake—more of a swamp than an actual lake. The lake would be the primary natural feature at the site, but its water level was a concern. Pumps would be needed, Olmsted advised, to keep the lake at a proper level during the late spring flooding, and then again during the dry season in late summer. (Indeed when the Lewis and Clark Centennial Exposition opened in 1905, the "lake" was regulated.)

Knowing of an earlier disagreement among Portlanders over where the fair should be located, Olmsted responded diplomatically. "The site for the exposition chosen by your committee is an admirable one, and all things considered, it is apparently by all odds the best which could have been secured in time if at all."

The approaches to the site "are as good as could be found in a city laid out so strictly on the rectangular plan." He also gave advice regarding the lake, saying it could be "further improved by a few islands." The Portland committee, however, ignored Olmsted's advice that these islands ought to "be relatively near the shore so look natural [with] pebbly beaches all about them." In its final form, the lake did not retain Olmsted's "natural" look.[5]

Little was asked of John Charles regarding planting advice for the fair grounds, although when reading his final report to the committee, one member did ask about Portland's favorite flower—the rose. He replied that roses "could be used in the decorative planting about the buildings."[6]

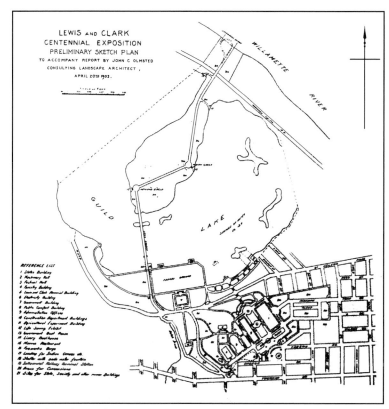

Olmsted Brothers' preliminary plan for the lake, road system, and general layout. The exposition developers ignored advice regarding natural-appearing islets, instead choosing to create one large show-stopping island. *Fairsted*

The rest of Olmsted's time in Portland was consumed in city park planning and private client work. While taking long horse and buggy reconnaissances around the city's ridges and lowlands with park commissioner Lester L.

Oregon Historical Society

Hawkins, he had few moments to look back at his proposals for the fair.

On April 19, one more tramp around the future exposition site did occur. On this occasion, he was joined by Percy R. Jones, the Olmsted firm's newly-arrived staff assistant. Jones was fresh from unfinished Olmsted Brothers business on Santa Catalina Island.

Finds Weeds, Color Images

Olmsted returned 3½ years later—in early December 1906—to view the Lewis and Clark Centennial Exposition grounds, now closed. Initially he was horrified by the site's bleakness. But a week later when writing to his wife, he expressed his pleasure at seeing picture postcards showing how the fair looked at its peak attraction a year earlier.

"I was surprised at them [postcards]. They seemed to make the whole thing so much more ornate and interesting. The crowds of people, the lake being full, the flags flying, the architectural garden decorations, statuary, columns, lamp posts, balustrades, fountains, booths, band stand and a lot of things all of which were gone when I saw the grounds last week, and the flowers and the foliage on the dogwoods and other trees too were gone. And the walks and roads muddy or weedy or almost grown over by grass. The art building was gone, the water tower vine covered from boxes fastened to it, were gone. The railings of the bridge were gone. The gay concession buildings were gone."

In returning again in 1909, Olmsted reluctantly agreed to help the contracting firm of Lewis and Wiley design the hill-hugging Westover Terrace neighborhood above the former exposition site.[7] He wrote his wife: "They have employed me to make a plan for some land they are going to cut down 100 ft. or so at Portland. I hate the idea of such huge gradings (2,000,000 cubic yards) in a residence section of the city."

Principles aside, Olmsted finally accepted the Westover Terrace commission. "I do not like the job, but must earn a living somehow I suppose. It won't be so bad in the end if they will do it with a nice finish."[8]

As the local boosters intended, a building boom indeed began after the conclusion of the exposition.

Tally-Ho Rides with Hawkins

On his last full day spent in Portland during the initial April 1903 visit, John Charles would sum up his scouting of park sites during the three-week stay. "I have enjoyed my park reconnaissance very much as the landscape is fine and the possibilities for parks, so far as land is concerned, are excellent, but I fear the money will be deficient. Besides that the people I have dealt with have treated me very well, so I have only pleasant experiences to recollect. Then, as to creature comforts, the weather has been mild (if rather showery), the food is excellent, I have slept well."[9]

Olmsted's three weeks in Portland in April 1903, much of it spent with park commissioner Lester L. Hawkins, had proved to be valuable time studying the Willamette River locality and the nearby flats and hills. The city proper presented various challenges for creating a new parks system and for further developing its existing parklands, both of which John Charles had charge. With undivided attention from his advocate, commissioner Hawkins—in each Northwest city, Olmsted would meet at least one such champion—Portland's puzzle of landscape pieces finally fit into a whole.

In an April 20 letter, John Charles informed his wife: "Lunched early and at one o'clock went to drive with Mr. Hawkins, the most active of the Park Commissioners. He drove me for 5 hours including a short walk or two. It was interesting because it was on or over the hills back of the city which are high & for the most part very steep, and command extensive views. There are a few patches of the original tall firs left but plenty of smaller sizes. Some of the slopes toward the city are more or less occupied with streets, vacant lots and improved lots with houses but often on fearful grades. It is too bad the fronts of the hills and the ravines could not have been preserved with the woods on them as a natural park and background for the city but the land boomers have played havoc with them and

Colonel Lester L. Hawkins. *William J. Hawkins III*

run values clear above anything reasonable and beyond the power of the city to purchase them. It is to be hoped that some steep slopes can be taken by the city and preserved. Mr. Hawkins wants to do something along this line and I shall look into it and report in some shape favorably and I hope my report may help."

Two days later, Olmsted was again following Hawkins' horses. "I went out with Mr. Hawkins this morning at 9 and he drove me over the south half of the part of the city east of the river. Got back at 1:30 p.m., 4½ hours drive—good horses—bad roads, generally, and plenty of mud, some rain, a little sun and a few chances for small parks and one fairly large on Mt. Tabor."

Then the next day, Olmsted further noted: "I was driven by Mr. Hawkins over the north and northeast sections of the city—the bluff along the river and the views from it were the most interesting features. We drove about 7 miles down the river as well as to places near by along the way & then circuited and zigzagged back going far out on the east borders of the city. I saw what small parks there are in that section of the city and which are unimproved. The land speculators have been at work everywhere and with rather pitiful results,"

On April 25, Olmsted summed up his relationship with the commissioner. "I have had a pleasant time with Mr. Hawkins. While he has opinions he is not opinionated & he is very fond of nature and good to children so I have had no friction and he has been very helpful. He is a retired banker and rich 'they say' but very modest and simple. He belongs to the Mazamas [mountaineering club] of whom I have read in the Geographical Magazine. They correspond to the Appalachian Club of Boston."

Had Hawkins lived long enough to receive Olmsted on future Portland visits during the rest of the decade—and had he been able to influence succeeding mayors and park commissioners as he did in 1903—Portland's park program might have moved along at a quicker pace and with more thorough results.

After John Charles' relatively short time spent touring Portland in Hawkins' tally-ho, his 1903 park report would be months in coming—the typed, 123-page park blueprint was not submitted until December. "I can't seem to get more than 2 hours to concentrate on my Portland report," Olmsted wrote from Chicago in October 1903. "One needs big blocks of time to get 'going.'"

In contrast, his Seattle parks report in this same time period was written and polished in June 1903, months before completing the Portland report. In the autumn of 1903, during business travels to cities in the East, he mentioned several times how he was "bothered" for not getting to his Portland report.

Whereas only a couple of weeks in April 1903 were portioned out to study park sites in the Portland area, in Seattle he had the entire month of May. The Seattle report proved easier to produce. With fewer overall landscape planning principles needing to be discussed, Olmsted's Seattle report came off relatively easily.[10]

His park planning not only paid special attention to specific conditions, natural features, and climate, but also to political realities. Olmsted was particularly adept at grasping each city's potentialities and fitting recommendations to local priorities and governmental concerns. Some park principles held true for all far western cities. His Portland parks report, however, covered wider issues, and did so more extensively, than most of his other park reports.

First Portland Parks Report, December 31, 1903

The first one-third of Olmsted's original 123-page report to the Portland Park Commission presented a land-use sermon and roadmap for park planning and holdings that garnered great acclaim a century ago and remains of value today. (The second portion of the report presented highly-detailed and site-specific recommendations regarding parks, land acquisitions, boulevards, parkways, and reservations in the Portland area.) In coming years, Portland officials reprinted these findings, sending them off, at outsider request, to dozens of park and city offices around the country. The long document appeared in print as an Appendix, pp. 13–75, in Portland's *Report of the Park Board*. With the profession yet in its early stages, John Charles' guiding document became much more than just a Portland landscape study.[11]

Several years later, on July 15, 1907, Portland park commissioner Ion Lewis would write to Olmsted in this regard. "This report was printed and the supply soon exhausted, so that we were obliged to reprint the report the succeeding

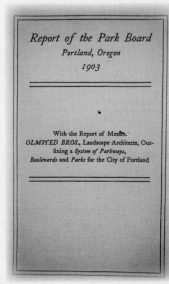

Portland Parks Report Preamble

In the December 31, 1903, report, John Charles identified 18 principles or benchmarks that municipalities should consider in planning for future park needs. (See Appendix A for extended excerpts from his discussion of these principles.)

1—Importance of Municipal Parks...
2—Duty of Citizens Toward Parks...
3—Parks and Park Purposes Should Be Defined in Advance—Park Units...
4—The Parks of a City Should Be Parts of a System...
5—Parks Systems Should Be Comprehensive...
6—Park Systems Should Be Well Balanced...
7—Parks Should Have Individuality...
8—Parks Should Be Connected and Approached by Boulevards and Parkways...
9—Parks and Parkways Should Be Located and Improved to Take Advantage of Beautiful Natural Scenery and to Secure Sanitary Conditions...
10—Park Systems Should Be in Proportion to Opportunities...
11—Parks and Parkways Should Be Acquired Betimes...
12—The Land for Park Systems Should Be Paid for by Long Term Loans...
13—Park Systems Should Be Improved by Means of Loans, Special Assessments and Annual Taxation...
14—Park Systems Should Be Improved Both Occasionally and Continuously...
15—Park Systems Should Be Improved According to a Well Studied and Comprehensive General Plan...
16—Park Systems Should Be Governed by Qualified Officials...
17—Park Systems Should Be Improved and Maintained by Specially Trained Men...
18—Park Systems Should Be Managed Independently of City Governments...

year. The calls for copies have been many, not only from all parts of the United States, but also from abroad."

The report's stunning success had astonished Portland officials, who nevertheless struggled to pay off the Olmsted Brothers' fees. The park commissioners, however, readily agreed to bring John Charles back in 1907 for further detailed park planning despite the high cost. Voters had since approved bonds to buy parklands, and there was added urgency because of rapidly rising land prices in the years after the 1905 exposition.

Portland wanted more of Olmsted's advice. "The writer has been requested by members of the Park Board to communicate with you in relation to formulating a more definite plan," Commissioner Lewis wrote on behalf of the park people.[12]

Olmsted agreed to combine the trip for Portland work, once again, with Seattle duties, thus saving both cities from paying additional traveling expenses. In October 1906, his site planning for Seattle's 1909 Alaska-Yukon-Pacific Exposition had begun in earnest. The new AYPE contract called for twice-a-year visits from Boston. Thus, this assignment would allow for extended stays in the Northwest with simultaneous visits to Seattle, Portland, the Willamette Valley, British Columbia, and the Inland Northwest. In all, Olmsted visited Oregon on 11 separate trips for park and boulevard planning, designing college campuses, and in pursuing private client work. Twice, Olmsted would spend Thanksgiving in Portland, 3,000 miles from his family.

During his autumn 1907 stay in Portland, Olmsted reviewed his 1903 park recommendations and honed suggestions that matched local political and government practicalities. The comprehensive 1903 plan called for a decades-long view into the future, recommending land acquisitions, good park governance and administration, and well-designed parks, boulevards, and parkways. Much of this eventually was fulfilled, though parts of the plan were not adopted or suffered from the public's desire to provide only limited funds. Some neglect occurred, too, because of the city's intense focus on the 1905 exposition and subsequent land development, and also due to the untimely death of Olmsted's influential champion, Lester L. Hawkins.

Second Portland Parks Report, 1907

On December 5, 1907, Olmsted submitted a new report to the Portland park commissioners with recommended budget proposals to fit the recently approved $1 million in public funds. He had some regretful findings: "We have been disappointed to find that owing to the great rise in value of lands in and about the city since our examination and report upon a system of parks made in 1903, the present loan will probably not accomplish half of the system of parks then contemplated."

His December 1907 recommendations revealed the regrettable reality for Portland. "Our first effort was to lay out a system of parks and parkways embracing most of the close in features of our recommendations of 1903. After cutting these down in detail as much as seemed reasonable…we discovered that the total amounted to about twice what could be safely allowed for land purchase."

Olmsted had to contend with a Willamette River divide—property owners of the more open east side of the river generally wanted even more parks, whereas landowners on the west side near the expanding downtown and dense residential districts were remaining silent or even resisted the sale of potentially high value properties for parks.

Olmsted's carefully written report tried to appease both groups. "In both the west and the east sides we have included the most important and precious landscape features adapted for park purposes." More than half of the available money was intended for west-side property acquisitions, whereas more than half of the total land acquired would be located east of the river.

A bluff parkway (Forest Park) on the west side overlooking Portland would prove to be the most expensive of all. "Although this is a very costly park, both for land and construction, relatively to its breadth, yet its relation to the physical growth of the city is such that if not taken now the needed land will soon be impossible of acquirement." Olmsted added: "Other portions of the parkway system recommended in 1903 can, we are confident, be postponed for a few years with far less danger."

On the east side of the river, Olmsted ruled out parkways as too expensive or unwanted. Instead, one large park—at Mt. Tabor—and a number of smaller parks or squares were more desirable for the residents there. Rather rarely, Olmsted allowed his awareness of political undercurrents to become fully obvious, but in this instance he publicly noted: "We are satisfied that there will be no just ground, after the suggested parks shall have been acquired,

Olmsted Brothers, Oregon (projects started, 1903–20s). Job numbers (#) and names of files opened by the Olmsted firm. Compiled from Charles E. Beveridge, *The Master List of Design Projects of the Olmsted Firm, 1857–1950* (1987), and Lucy Lawliss et al., *The Master List of Design Projects of the Olmsted Firm, 1857–1979* (2008), with additions from Catherine Joy Johnson, *Olmsted in the Pacific Northwest: Private Estates and Residential Communities, 1873–1959: An Inventory* (1997).

College campuses
#3383—Oregon, University of, Eugene
#3411—McMinnville [Linfield] College, McMinnville
#3595—Pacific University, Forest Grove
#3699—Oregon Agricultural College, Corvallis
#5340—Reed College, Portland

Country clubs
#2689—Portland Country Club
#5510—Waverly Golf Country Club

Exposition
#2399—Lewis & Clark Exposition
#5174—Lewis & Wiley Exposition Tract

Monument design/cemetery
#3797—Portland Cemetery

Parks/parkways/park systems
#2640—Portland Parks
#2641—Hillside Parkway
#2642—Terwilliger Boulevard
#8234—Mt. Hood Park

Private residential clients (Portland locality)
#0453—Cary, Charles*
#1050—Brewster, William L.
#2627—Brewster, W.L.
#2632—Ayer, W.B.
#3125—Ladd, Mrs. W.
#3218—Corbett, Mrs. Henry S.
#3219—Failing, Miss Henrietta
#3220—Hewitt, Henry Jr.
#3221—Lewis, Miss Frances
#3224—Ladd, C.E.
#3226—Ladd, William M., "Hazel Fern Farm"
#3412—Failing, Mrs. J.F.
#3414—Willis, P.L.

#3418—Ainsworth, J.C.
#3439—Ainsworth, Misses Maud & Bell
#3542—Page*
#3593—Hamblet*
#3594—Lombard, B.M.*
#3633—Mills, A.L.
#3634—Adkins, Miss Ora L.*
#3719—Corbett, Harry L.
#3720—Spanton Co., Multnomah County*
#3722—Kerr, Peter, "Elk Rock"
#3747—Gilbert, Wells
#3756—Giesy, A.J.*
#3915—Kerr, Thomas
#3916—Voorhies, Gordon
#3919—Kerr, Peter, "Waverly Heights"
#3991—Hogue, Harry Wildey*
#3992—Biddle, Mrs. William S.*
#4015—Lewis, C. Hunt
#4057—Lewis, C. Hunt
#5090—Simpson*
#5515—Lewis, R.W.
#5653—Lewis, David C.
#8073—Autzen, Thomas
#8074—Squires, Cameron
#8090—Corbett, Hamilton

Private clients (other localities)
#3642—Page, J.F., Clatsop Beach
#3721—Palmer, George, La Grande
#5090—Simpson, L.J., North Bend
#7504—Dorrance, E.M., Radnor

Subdivisions/suburban communities
#3413—Portland Heights
#3417—Hazel Fern Farm
#3740—Lewis & Wiley Land Subd., "Westover Terrace"
#5527—Irving Park Association

---

* Catherine Joy Johnson's inventory in *Olmsted in the Pacific Northwest* indicates private clients making "inquiry only" in these job files.

for the slight undercurrent of dissatisfaction which we have been told has occasionally made itself manifest, based on the idea that the East Side has been somewhat neglected in park development."

John Charles also urged Portland to place a professional parks man in their city (in Seattle, Park Superintendent J.W. Thompson played this role for the Olmsted Brothers). By the spring of 1908, a onetime Olmsted employee, Emanuel Tillman "Emil" Mische, filled the professional park superintendent's job in Portland. Mische left a new position as park superintendent at Madison, Wisconsin, to come west. He would carry the Olmsted parks banner in Portland for a number of years.

Oregonian

From the beginning, the *Oregonian* heralded Olmsted's presence in Portland with headlines and stories designed to promote his city parks work. The headlines featured Olmsted's celebrity status, enabling park proponents in Portland (as in Seattle) to summon and impress local financiers and politicians. Private clients and college presidents, too, soon took note and lined up to seek advice from the most noted practitioner of the day.

"Expert gardener Olmsted is due to arrive in Portland Monday to look over the public parks and examine the 1905 Fair site," the newspaper announced on April 4, 1903. "Two members of the Board will show him over the parks and secure his advice as to beautifying them as soon as he is able to undertake the work."

Two weeks later—on April 18—the *Oregonian* headlines provided a progress report: "Landscape Architect Likes Location of Fair Grounds." In regard to city parks: "John C. Olmsted Says Their Proximity to the City Makes Them Especially Valuable."

Extensive coverage of Olmsted's Portland work continued in later years. Publicity—wanted or unwanted—came with his duties as he settled into either the Arlington Club or Hotel Portland during visits.

On November 25, 1907, for example: "Should Buy Parks—Leading Landscape Architect Says Portland Should Extend System of Playgrounds to Give People Fresh Air." This was followed by the lead paragraph: "Parks are a public necessity…said John C. Olmsted, of Brookline, Mass., at the Arlington Club yesterday. Mr. Olmsted is one of the leading landscape architects of the world." And, on December 3, 1907: "Expert Outlines System of Parks."

On June 16, 1909, two weeks after the opening of Seattle's fair, Olmsted's presence back in Portland was the news of the day. "Park Expert Here…Olmsted Wants City to Buy Park Sites Now…Inspects Present Tracts…Landscape Artist Praises Natural Advantages Here and Is Pleased with Acquisition of Land for Scenic Driveway." This announcement was included in one headline and three subheads, taking as many column inches as the brief story itself.

In 1908, the arrival of Olmsted's hand-picked park superintendent, Emil Mische, was also heralded in the *Oregonian*. But with this news came a dispute and publicity that Mische and Olmsted could have done without.

"No Funds to Pay Park Supervisor," a bold headline above the fold announced on January 28, 1908. "Council at Outs over Park Expert," read another bold faced headline on January 30.

By February 24, Portland's park commissioners publicly entered the fray with a letter to the newspaper proclaiming: "Even if bonds for carrying out the Olmsted system should not become available for several years, the city is still not without means of making progress in the working out of this system." Architect Ion Lewis was writing on behalf of his fellow park board members in support of the former Olmsted employee.

"All this calls, in the estimation of the Board, for skilled superintendence, for a superintendent not only of thorough preparatory training in the various subjects required for his office, but of a wide experience in park work, supplemented by actual observation of the great parks and park systems of this country and of Europe, for a man having, withal, if not a real genius for parks, at least a strong feeling for park improvement and park development.

"Such a man, sooner or later, Portland must have if the park system is to keep pace with the city's growth in other respects, if that system is to be a worthy expression of the city's taste and liberality and of this generation's forethought for the next. The Park Board thinks that the time for such a man is already here, and for this reason has asked the Council to make the necessary appropriation for his compensation."

Emil Mische was successfully retained, but other disputes followed.

"Fairsted"—the Olmsted home and office in Brookline, Massachusetts, preserved today as the Frederick Law Olmsted National Historic Site.

Portrait of JCO as a youngster.
Harvard GSD

Olmsted home sleeping porch, with office wing to the right.

An illustrator created a rather exaggerated depiction of the bridge and Guild's Lake in this postcard view of the Lewis and Clark Exposition. *Oregon Historical Society*

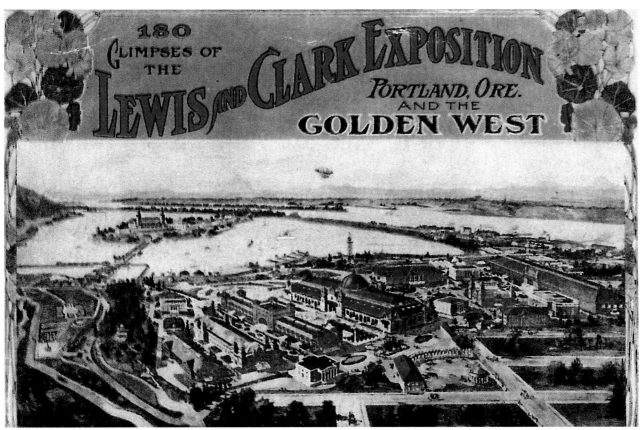

Bird's-eye view of the Lewis and Clark Centennial Exposition, as it would come off the drawing board. The United States government building occupied the prime spot on the "island" created for the exposition out of the river bottom. *Washington State University Libraries*

Portland's Rose Festival was proposed to the public during the Lewis and Clark Centennial Exposition and first held in 1907. *Oregon Historical Society*

Aerial view of the Oregon Ag campus as expansion kept coming—with changes as fast as artists could render—during the years following Olmsted's original June 1909 campus visit. *Oregon State University*

A modern-day view of Pioneer Hall at Linfield College. Constructed in 1882, Pioneer Hall stood almost alone on the McMinnville campus when Olmsted arrived to give President Riley advice on campus design.

Mische Didn't Plant the Roses

On January 8, 1910, "MISCHE IS EXONERATED" shouted an all-caps *Morning Oregonian* headline in reporting on a squabble that perhaps thankfully was buried on page 18. Further headlines that day announced: "Park Board Takes Blame for Transplanting Roses. Sunshiny Places Best for Flowers."

The problem? Mische's fired predecessor apparently had planted roses—the city's floral symbol—in the shady parts of South Park two years earlier. "Superintendent Mische, of the Park Department, was fully exonerated by the Board yesterday morning in relation to the planting of roses in the park blocks February 22, 1908."

The January 1910 article continued: "Charges of incapability and general incompetence as to rose-planting were made against Mr. Mische. It was developed that the roses referred to were not planted by him, but by A.D. Montieth, who was discharged by the board, and that Mr. Mische was not employed until one month after the episode." Members of the board "all of whom have many rose bushes" then voted to transplant the offending roses into the "sunshine," removing them from under the canopy of park trees.

Mische had given up the park superintendency of Madison, Wisconsin, to take the Portland job at Olmsted's request. Realizing the often delicate circumstances of Mische's new Portland position, Olmsted tried to keep his spirits up on each brief visit. "Mr. Mische talked with me for a long time, over two hours I think," Olmsted wrote after seeing Mische installed in his new position in 1908. "I let him use up my time because I want to help him all I can, having gotten him out here. His main complaint is that the commission is so slow to authorize anything to be done."

A year later in Portland, an Olmsted Brothers reunion of sorts ensued, far from home base. John Charles, Emil Mische, and James Frederick "Fred" Dawson, Olmsted's able assistant who was finishing up the Seattle exposition work, gathered for a half day in Portland between trains, assignments, and grueling work schedules.

"Mr. Mische was anxious to have me call at the park office to talk over a matter so I went over and have been with him all day till after six which did not accord with my contemplated use of the day for writing records. I hadn't been there an hour before Mr. Dawson telephoned Mr. Mische, & soon he came to the office and has been with us all day. He is on his way from Los Angeles to Seattle & was 12 hours late so he had to stop over…So he had time for quite a long conference with me as to various matters & Mr. Mische advised as to certain kinds of plants—whether they did well or not in this climate, &c."[13]

Dawson took the night train to Seattle. Olmsted, meanwhile, stayed the evening because the old train timetable in his pocket did not indicate the proper time for boarding to Kennewick in eastern Washington.

In 1908 and later, Olmsted continued to meet the new park director for meals and counsel. "Mr. Mische took me off to supper at his house…I was delayed there until 10:45…I hated to add to work by going there but they would feel hurt to have me refuse…but tomorrow is Sunday & I may be able to sleep an hour later."[14]

After one of Olmsted's last visits with protégé Mische, he wrote Sophia from the Hotel Portland on May 28, 1910: "I had Mr. Mische to lunch with me, and he insisted upon having me come to dinner this evening. I did not want to but did not see how to refuse without hurting his feelings…He says the Mayor's policy is economy. Economy is all right in its place but to stop acquiring land for parks when the city is bound to have parks some time is poor economy because the land is rising in value rapidly…Boston would have saved millions by buying parks when it was the size Portland is now."

Playgrounds

It was playground planning—and the time it took away from land acquisition and pure park design—that in 1910 began to encroach on John Charles' carefully crafted ideals and timetables for public places.

The *Morning Oregonian* of September 10, 1910, indicated the changing times when reporting about the first season's success in "amusing" the youths in Portland. "The public playgrounds, maintained by the city at the instance of the Park Commission, were closed for the season yesterday and the equipment for amusing the youngsters will be stored until next June. The public playground is strictly a vacation devise for the oversight and amusement of children during the interim between the closing of the schools in June and the reopening in September. The scheme is new in this city. Its initial season has proved satisfactory to its promoters and to parents and a source of delight to hundreds of children."

In Seattle, too, playground issues would increasingly appear in park reporting, much to Olmsted's annoyance. He continually advised on putting a primary emphasis on acquiring land, then the careful planning of park layouts, and, finally, to establish budgets and plans for play apparatus. Public opinion, however, leaned toward rapidly setting up playground equipment, no matter how it fit into a park system's overall design.

Private Clients

Landscape architect Emil Mische, well trained under Olmsted, helped plant and design private as well as public spaces in Portland. Mische stayed on as park superintendent only until the First World War; afterward, he was free to practice his craft with private clients, who in many

instances first had been in contact with John Charles. The gardens at the Peter Kerr mansion in southwest Portland, today now known as Bishop's Close at Elk Rock, is a prime example of Mische's and the Olmsted Brother's involvement in continuing private projects over the years.

The Elk Rock design originally was a John Charles plan and remains today as one of the Olmsted Brothers' best and lasting garden creations in Portland. It was designed for, and with help from, the owner and expert gardener, Peter Kerr, who was a Portland grain business magnate. Originally debating whether to build a new home on his current Elk Rock residential property on the west side of the Willamette, or at a new site east across the river at the Waverley Golf Club, Peter Kerr asked for John Charles's advice on which place to choose, and what should be done once this was decided.[15]

Olmsted spent a chilly day in December 1909 above the Willamette, studying both sites, as reported in a letter

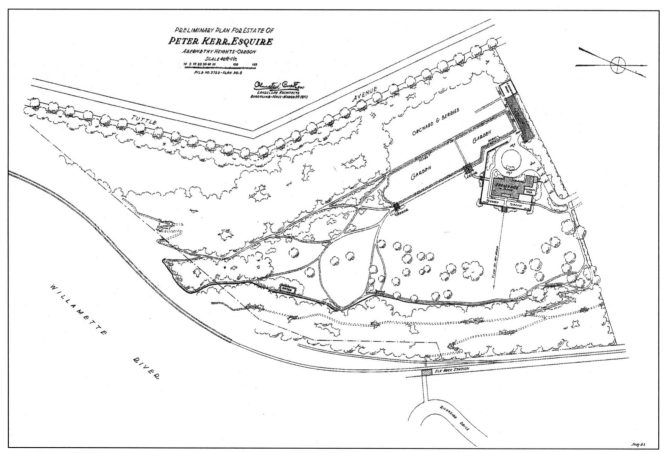

Fairsted

written that night. "This morning I took the 8:50 train (gasolene) [sic] to Elk Rock (up the river—next stop beyond Rivera) & was met by Mr. Peter Kerr. He showed me his place with Mrs. Kerr and I gave him some advice."

Olmsted's recommendations regarding the Elk Rock property included keeping the mountain scenery paramount in the planning. To Olmsted's surprise, Kerr was less interested in always retaining Mt. Hood in view. Olmsted reported in disbelief to his office: "We then discussed site for new house…my other idea was to set the house further west and turn it so as to front toward Mt. Hood, which I said was to my mind a far more important feature than his lawn or any attractive architectural formal layout. He did not care so much for Mt. Hood as he had got so used to it he did not feel the need of facing the windows directly toward it."

In a 10-page letter to Kerr on January 1, 1910 (Olmsted often worked holidays when out west), he emphasized the importance of the Mt. Hood view. "If I were you I should build on the Abernethy Heights place [at Elk Rock]. My preference is based mainly upon its superior landscape advantages. It is larger, higher, bolder and more picturesque than the other [property at the golf club across the river]…The views of Mount Hood and of the river from this place are not only extremely attractive and valuable in themselves, but they will be an unceasing source of gratification both to yourself whenever you are there and to visitors."

A modern view of Bishop's Close at Elk Rock Garden.

Setting the house back from the west river bluff was another Olmsted idea presented in his January 1st letter. (This recommendation was later followed when Peter and Laurie Kerr started building their new house at Elk Rock in 1914 and remains key to the property's character today.) "With respect to the new house site, my feeling was that in spite of the manifest advantages of a site close to the bluff, the distant view would be more agreeable from a house site further back from the bluff, because in that case you could provide a picturesque foreground on your own place and

could so manage the plantations as to conceal the sordid little houses of the town of Milwaukee across the river, while still retaining a full view of the wooded hills beyond and the magnificent view of Mount Hood. It is true that from a site further back from the bluff you would lose a good deal of the view of the river, but by setting the house with the first floor some feet above the present surface of the ground, you would have glimpses of the river toward the south or southeast which could be improved at will by thinning out more of the fir trees at the south end of the lawn."

The garden itself was, in Olmsted's view, already a fine one, but Scotsman Peter Kerr disagreed. "Thought his garden good, but he is dissatisfied…there is a group of native oaks and a fir at the brow of the bluff which may be in the way of the Mt. Hood view…but he did not seem averse to cutting or topping them; in fact, he seems to greatly prefer exotic trees and shrubs."

Olmsted advised that an existing straight path of "poor design" on the bluff should fork and curve around the wilder south grounds, close to but above the wide river views. An existing "low rustic wooden bridge" should, it was further advised, remain, which client Kerr "thought of doing away with by filling," Olmsted added in his field notes.

Across the Willamette, Same Day

After Olmsted investigated the Elk Rock property, he crossed to the east side of the river to meet with Peter Kerr's brother and business associate, Thomas Kerr,[16] as well as Kerr's golf club neighbor, Gordon Voorhies.[17] When at Waverley Heights, Olmsted provided site-specific advice that afternoon, recognizing that Gordon Voorhies might build sooner than either of the Kerr brothers.

"Mr. Voorhies appears to be the only one visited that is going to build at once. Also he seems to have more capacity for making up his mind as to his residence project than the others," Olmsted confided in his office notes. John Charles fully described that day's interaction with his Waverly Heights clients.

"About 11:30 we [left Elk Rock and] started for the Golf Club. We had to borrow a skiff and row across the river as the man could not make his gasolene launch go. Then we walked to the club & had lunch about 1:30—It seems strange that 2 hours were consumed in getting to lunch. After lunch they turned me over to his brother Tom Kerr & Mr. G. Vorhees [Voorhies] and his architect Mr. Whitehouse. We walked first to lot of latter and Mrs. Vorhees arrived & I had to go over a good deal of it again with her. Then we went to Tom Kerr's lot nearby and Mrs. Kerr was there waiting. She had some ideas and I tried to do the best I could with them and gave her & him other advice. Then I had to go back to the Vorhees lot to advice about a tennis court. Then Mrs. Vorhees sister, Mrs. Biddle asked me too to her lot. But I begged off saying it was going to be dark pretty soon & suggested about 1st of April for the visit. The fact is I was getting chilled & thought I had done enough for one day & might not have valuable thoughts if I did go to her place. I thought I was going to walk to the electric cars and go get warm but they insisted upon taking me with the rest to Sellwood, so I got colder yet in the automobile in the keen wind. There I had a little walk with Mr. Whitehouse to the car. He came with me to the [Hotel] Portland and I stood treat: I thought I was cold enough to warrant…taking a cocktail. When I got upstairs I found Mr. Mische who took me off to supper at his house…I got pretty chilled at their house too as the water heater had gone out."

When Voorhies had brought along his architect, Morris Whitehouse, to the Waverly Heights meeting, this convergence of client, architect, and landscape architect made it easier for Olmsted to exert his influence. Despite the cordiality of sharing a spontaneous cocktail (a rarity for Olmsted) with Whitehouse that evening at the Hotel Portland, or perhaps because of it, Olmsted stuck to his design principles when writing to client Voorhies on January 1, 1910.

"The idea of your architect to have stairs descending from the middle of the terrace did not strike me favorably. The bluff there, although not excessively high, is steep and close at hand…As to the garage, I do not approve of your architects idea of having the horses on the ground floor and the automobiles in the story above."

He continued: "I think it would be better to keep the stable low and have the garage and horses on the same floor, using the second story for rooms for the men servants and for the storage of hay. I showed your architect how the yard in front of the stable could be shaped so as to afford room for the switchback turning of the automobile."

Olmsted prepared an 8-page letter—also on January 1, 1910—for Thomas Kerr, though still suspecting that Thomas might wait a time before building. "Standing where I supposed the south front of the house would be there was no distant view whatever and the site seemed so uninteresting that I moved on further south searching for a place where Mt. Hood might be seen or a glimpse of the river. It seemed to me the house should be near the brow of the hill…Mt. Hood would be in view." Thus, for Thomas Kerr at Waverley Heights, Olmsted suggested a house site on the brow of the hill, whereas for Peter Kerr, on the opposite shore, Olmsted insisted on a house set back from the bluff.

John Charles had quickly detected Thomas Kerr's concern about costs. "In deference to Mr. Kerr's feelings, finding that anything that was suggestive of expense was like waving a red flag to a wild bull, I suggested this long forecourt could be framed in by hedges."[18]

The Olmsted Brothers high fee schedule, in fact, intimidated a number of potential clients in Portland. Of 38 private client inquiries, 16 actually resulted in full commissions for the Olmsted firm over the years.[19]

Westover Terrace Design

After John Charles completed private work for the Westover Terrace residential development from 1909 to 1911, contractors Lewis and Wiley continued with Olmsted's recommendations through the decade. Years later, on December 7, 1920, partner William H. Lewis of the firm would inform the Olmsted Brothers in Boston about the neighborhood's fate, located above the old exposition grounds.

"You will be interested to know that Westover Terraces [sic] in Portland has finally come into its own. It absolutely bankrupted the Lewis-Wiley Hydraulic Company, since we were forced to hold on to it so long, paying interest, street assessments, taxes and other maintenance charges when there was no market for it. We finally sold it four years

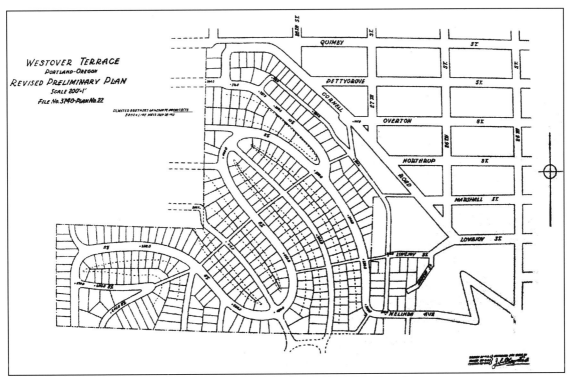

The 22nd sketch in a series for clients Lewis and Wiley prepared at the Brookline office. *Fairsted*

ago." But Lewis also added: "We understand the syndicate that purchased it has done very well this year and that many beautiful houses have been built there."[20]

Though Olmsted had complained about the excessive sluicing done to reduce the Westover Terrace hillside, the end result was a finely-tuned neighborhood that almost lived up to Olmsted's standards. By the early 1920s, Portland projects put on hold during World War I were picking up (though John Charles' death on February 24, 1920, signaled another turning point for the Olmsted Brothers' western work. By then, however, hand-picked associates had been carrying the greater load of work).

During one of Olmsted's last train stops at Portland, in 1911, he had observed the city's new Rose Festival in full swing. He commented to his wife on June 5: "The Rose Festival has begun. Ladies give a rose to each passenger— even those who don't stop." As his failing vigor and health would restrict John Charles from ever visiting Portland after 1911, his closing words to his wife were unwittingly predictive: "Mine soon wilted so I discarded it."

University of Washington Stadium

Lewis and Wiley each prospered after their sale of Westover Terrace in Portland. William H. Lewis, with the Puget Sound Dredging Company, wrote a December 7, 1920, letter to the Olmsted Brothers regarding his firm's work on the new Husky Stadium for the 1919 Dartmouth-Washington opening day game. "We consider the Stadium our most remarkable achievement, and its completion within six months was only made possible by the same use of sheerboard construction by which we built Westover Terraces in Portland with which you are familiar."

Contractor Lewis also sent a November 28, 1919, *Post-Intelligencer* article about the stadium's opening day game with Dartmouth. The excavated earth stadium was intended to later be extended upward "with a steel and concrete superstructure, which will eventually give a seating capacity of sixty thousand, whereas the present capacity is only 28,000." As intended, Husky Stadium today is partially enclosed, but it also is clear of the "Rainier Vista" that Olmsted intended to preserve on campus.

Notes

1. Olmsted job #2889, Louisiana Purchase International Exposition; Library of Congress.
2. John E. Findling and Kimberly D. Pelle, eds., *Historical Dictionary of World's Fairs and Expositions, 1851–1988* (New York: Greenwood Press, 1990).
3. When John Charles arrived in Portland, the untimely death of the exposition president, Henry W. Corbett (serving 1/21/1902 to 3/31/1903), filled newspaper headlines. Corbett family members later became private clients of the Olmsted Brothers into the 1920s.
4. For Seattle's Alaska-Yukon-Pacific Exposition in 1909, John Charles would serve as the "principal" landscape architect.
5. Like Frederick Law Olmsted Sr.'s vision for natural, or at least unadorned, islands at the Chicago World's Fair, John Charles was bound for disappointment with the Portland exhibition's lake.
6. Field notes to the Brookline office, Olmsted job #2399, Lewis and Clark Centennial Exposition; Library of Congress. Field notes, which often were more detailed than the official reports, today are enclosed in each Olmsted Brothers job file archived at the Library of Congress.
7. Olmsted job #3740, Lewis and Wiley Land Subdivision; Library of Congress.
8. Letter from Seattle, November 27, 1909. John Charles's daily letters to Sophia are now housed at Harvard University.
9. Letter, April 29, 1903.
10. Olmsted's Spokane parks report also was completed quickly enough in 1908, but remained under wraps for years while the city quietly conducted property purchases to complete the park plan. John Charles' Walla Walla report came out even more quickly, almost the same day that he completed a survey in December 1906.
11. Olmsted job #2640, Portland Park System; Library of Congress.
12. John Charles Olmsted Papers, Special Collections, Harvard Graduate School of Design.
13. Letter, February 2, 1909.
14. Letter, December 18, 1909.
15. Olmsted jobs #3722 and #3919, Peter Kerr, Abernethy Heights; Library of Congress.
16. Olmsted job #3915, Thomas Kerr; Library of Congress.
17. Olmsted job #3916, Gordon Voorhies; Library of Congress.
18. Field notes to the Brookline office, December 18, 1909.
19. Catherine Joy Johnson, *Olmsted in the Pacific Northwest: Private Estates and Residential Communities, 1873–1959: An Inventory* (Seattle: Friends of Seattle's Olmsted Parks, 1997).
20. William H. Lewis sent the December 7, 1920, letter to the Olmsted firm eight months after John Charles' death. Lewis provided an account of the building of Husky Stadium in Seattle as well as Westover Terrace in Portland. The letter had been requested by Seattle parks proponent Charles Saunders.

3

Oregon College Campuses

I got in a wheat field where it was muddy in places. I got my foot out of one of my rubbers, but fished it out and got it on while standing on the other leg. Later I had to stand in the edge of a puddle & wash the accumulated mud off my rubbers.—November 26, 1907

Over the decades, with more than 300 school and college consultations to the Olmsted Brothers' credit—almost 100 of these before John Charles' death in 1920—the firm became the leading landscape advisor to college presidents in America. Accumulated with each campus project in the East, this expertise easily transferred to the West when college presidents sought advice on campus size and configuration, and the planning challenges that lay ahead.

Other particular insights regarding western institutions grew with each campus survey in the Northwest—the first being John Charles' consultation with the University of Washington in 1903. This was followed in 1906 by a visit (and report) for Whitman College in Walla Walla, and soon after for the University of Idaho, before Olmsted advised his first Oregon college president in late 1907.

Within three years, Olmsted would write reports and make sketches for two Oregon schools (McMinnville College and the Oregon Agricultural College), and give verbal advice to a third (Pacific University). Initially, an artistic campus design probably was far removed from the agendas of most trustee boards, but the three Oregon college presidents saw a need to step forward and invite Olmsted to provide a vision for the future. Unlike the 1905 Portland exposition, which was planned in haste and remained intact only for a short time, good portions of these college plans—principles included—would endure despite a century of campus change, expansion, and building booms.

Olmsted's campus reports provided descriptions of why buildings ought to sit oriented north or west, why the paths ought to follow curved or straight lines, why buildings ought to have dignified front and back entries, why and

where each building ought to expand, and a host of other observations. In addition, he presented planning advice focusing on student needs and the encouragement of scholarship. With each additional campus visit, he quickly judged spatial and academic needs, and then explained to the presidents how other colleges and universities worked out similar challenges.

McMinnville College

"Mayor Lane tells me that you are soon to be in Portland, so I address you here," McMinnville's newly appointed president, Leonard W. Riley, wrote Olmsted on October 29, 1907, beginning a cordial relationship between the two men. "McMinnville College has a Campus consisting of 30 acres which we are desirous of having properly laid out before we proceed with the new buildings which we are hoping to erect in the not distant future."

"When and where can I see you?" Riley inquired in the letter. (This refrain would be repeated again during the next few years, both before and after Olmsted's McMinnville report was presented to the college's trustees.) Riley would wait another three weeks before Olmsted arrived from work he was completing in Dayton, Ohio.

Failing to find John Charles at the Arlington Club in Portland, but, instead, just twice missing the young associate, Fred Dawson, who had preceded Olmsted west, Riley quickly hired Portland surveyors Elliott and Scroggin to plot the campus grounds in anticipation of Olmsted's November visit.

Of the three college presidents that John Charles dealt with in Oregon, Riley proved most likely in offering to meet away from campus, and to travel a greater distance to do so. Olmsted, however, rarely accepted such visits, since Northwest clients would be billed hourly (and at rates perceived to be inflated Eastern prices). Clients might object to even bigger bills than those already coming for site visits. President Riley also was the pluckiest, and won Olmsted's admiration, which emerges in their correspondence.

Riley's persistence and ability were, some historians say, the reason why the McMinnville institution (renamed Linfield College in 1922) survived a bleak era early in the century. In 1922, Riley's key role was later noted in the campus yearbook, *Oak Leaves*. "In 1906 when the outlook was particularly black and no one else could be found to take the position, Leonard W. Riley, at that time General Missionary for Oregon, was led to accept the presidency of the school. He was to keep it from going to the wall 'if he could.' The history of the past 16 years shows that he did."

His dramatic assumption of the presidency is interestingly told in a campus history.[1] The trustees were looking for a new president and were unable to find a candidate for the position. They had practically given up in despair when the unexpected happened. One day the Reverend James Whitcomb Brougher, pastor of the First Baptist Church of Portland, and the Reverend Leonard W. Riley, general missionary of the Oregon Baptist Convention, met on a street in Portland. Both were members of the committee to find a president for the college. The following conversation ensued.

Brougher: "Do you know, Riley, what the Portland bunch of trustees are going to do at the January meeting?"

Riley: "No, what?"

Brougher: "They are going to move that the college be closed and the income from the endowment be devoted to the payment of debts."

Riley: "Not much! We must have a college in the Northwest. Before I'll see that done I'll take it [the presidency] myself."

Brougher (laying his hand on his companion's shoulder): "Old man, you are elected."

Whether a fanciful or accurate conversation, the trustees agreed on January 10, 1906, to elevate Riley to the presi-

Most Linfield College historians agree that without President Leonard W. Riley's timely persistence, McMinnville might have closed during lean years in the early 20th century. Riley was the first Oregon college president to call on Olmsted for advice. *Linfield Oak Leaves*

dency rather than close McMinnville's doors. The trustees "elected Riley as president and told him to get the college out of the hole, if he could."

Olmsted would later confirm, in field notes sent back to his office, the dire situation of the campus (and its grounds) that Riley set out to reverse. Leaving nothing to chance, Riley informed Olmsted about traveling by train between Portland and McMinnville in the fall of 1907, even hinting that the two might meet on the same train if schedules allowed. "McMinnville is thirty-nine miles south of Portland on the Yamhill Division of the Southern Pacific and fifty miles on the West Side Division," he wrote Olmsted in October. Then, on November 22, Riley further elaborated: "You will note by the enclosed time card that you can leave on the Yamhill Division forty minutes later, travel eleven miles less and reach McMinnville but ten minutes later than by the West Side Division. This train starts from the foot of Jefferson Street."

One determined college man was about to meet one observant visitor from Massachusetts, whose description of the journey from Portland and campus visit was penned on the night of November 25, 1907, from the Hotel Elberton.

"My Dear Wife; Here I am in a little country town, the county seat of Yamhill County and I dare say the largest in population in the county.

"It claims a population of 2500 but hardly looks it… plenty of stores though for it supplies a large district of pretty thriving farms and villages. It is I think 40 miles from Portland and the train takes 2h 15m.

"Coming from Portland the railroad follows the river to Oswego, 7m. Most of that distance the river scenery is picturesque. At one place are high rocky cliffs & rocky islands. From Oswego it turns away from the river & follows lakes and streams over this way. This is a valley tributary to the Willamette. It is the Yamhill River. S[outh] of here is Yamhill Mountain. I don't know why they have both hill and mountain in the name but perhaps it is an Indian name and didn't mean Yam nor hill in English. Mr. Riley says English walnuts are going to be planted very extensively. There are already 1000 acres of them in the county. He is very fond of them to eat himself."

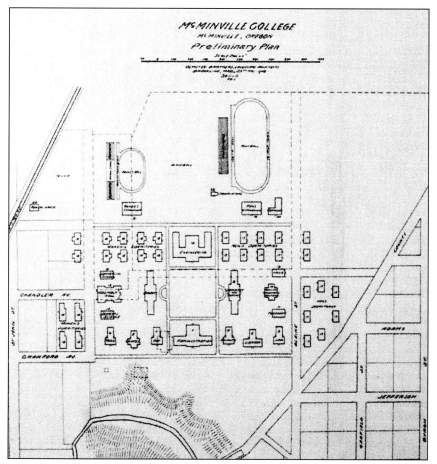

Olmsted Brothers' sketch of McMinnville College, May 29, 1908, which included President Riley's campus expansion plans. In addition to precisely locating future structures, it bolstered the trustees' confidence in the institution's future. John Charles' written advice accompanying the sketch called for saving open space in front of Pioneer Hall, and erecting future buildings around formal quads. These principles held through the early years of campus growth. *Fairsted*

based on these precise first field notes, such as in the following from McMinnville on November 25–26, 1907.

"At present they are much crowded in the present building. This building [Pioneer Hall] is a common brick 4-story building, with trim in jigsaw style of the [1860s and early 1870s]…very ugly. The basement is of stone and almost wholly out of ground, making the four stories. The gymnasium is the cheapest possible barn construction. The observatory is of wood and very cheap, but the telescope is said to be one of the largest, if not the largest, in the Pacific Northwest. The students use the Baptist Church for services and also certain social functions."

Of a wooden structure across the road, which the school hoped to purchase for a music building, Olmsted wrote: "I should think it too flimsy. Ought to be solid and sound-proof, as nearly as possible." The campus site's extensive oak woods and stream-fed ravines, however, came in for favorable comment, as did a view of the surrounding landscape seen from the top of the college's lone stone building.

He also noted to Sophia that President Riley "employs us because he thinks a good plan will help him to get money out of the well-to-do baptists. He wants me to meet some of them tomorrow evening in Portland and explain my plan."

His field notes reveal that President Riley, Dean Northrup, and Olmsted repaired to a hotel dinning room for long conversation about land purchases and college goals, which John Charles reported in detail. He further confided to his wife and office that "this is now the only" Baptist college in the Northwest.

When scouting out the college's land, he became mired in a muddy field. "I spent the morning walking about and pacing some distances," He wrote Sophia on the 26th. "I got in a wheat field where it was muddy in places. I got my foot out of one of my rubbers, but fished it out and got it

Turning to the campus: "The college is a Baptist institution. It had run down financially, was soon to be closed as have been four others in Oregon and Washington, Idaho and Montana. He has taken hold and in twenty months has made income balance expenses and has collected enough to cancel 1/3rd of the debt. They have now only one bldg. and a wooden gym and a wooden observatory… Ever your loving husband"

Trained by his father to observe and then write down each day's landscape observations before his memory dimmed, Olmsted sent field notes to Brookline, outlining for office draftsmen the situation on the ground. Typically, when an official report reached clients months later, it was on while standing on the other leg. Later I had to stand in the edge of a puddle & wash the accumulated mud off my rubbers. That was about the only 'adventure' I had."

Earlier that day, the pacing of lots had brought out at least one suspicious neighbor living adjacent to the college, requiring Olmsted to hide his and President Riley's intentions. "In pacing off some properties back of the campus I took pains to conceal what I was doing from an interested man who watched me from in front of one house. I paced on the opposite side of street & stopped at trees and stared at them while making notes so he would think I was only pacing the college land & locating trees. If the owners got the idea the college was after their land they would no doubt ask a higher price thinking the college must have their land." Later that same day, Riley and Olmsted journeyed back to Portland together on the 3:37 train.

The following May, when President Riley learned that Olmsted was again near—this time at the Savoy Hotel in Seattle—he asked him to prepare a written report for the trustees meeting in June. Within a week, John Charles submitted from Seattle a typed 31-page preliminary campus report to the trustees.[2]

"McMinnville College will on no account permit itself to become a university," he acknowledged at the outset, thus recognizing the trustees' intent for a smaller size campus. The preparatory school, on site, should eventually be phased out, he advised, adding "our plan shall make no provision for a building for the preparatory department." (In the early 20th century, incoming students at both private and state colleges often were academically insufficient to immediately begin "collegiate" classes. Consequently, "preparatory" instruction gave them the final prerequisites and skills so that they could enter freshman classes. After new "credited" high schools expanded to most Northwest communities by the 1910s, turning out better prepared high school graduates, preparatory departments usually were not needed on college campuses.)

For any future McMinnville buildings, first and foremost was a caution to keep buildings low and fireproof. But realities were reflected in the report: "As few, if any of the buildings can be made fireproof, owing to the expense, and as land is cheap, it is clearly advisable as a means of lessening fire risk that the buildings should be of moderate size and isolated to a reasonable extent from each other."

Olmsted then gave guidance on the campus's overall architectural approach for the future. "As the buildings will be erected one or two at a time over a period of many years, it is altogether likely that different architects will be employed and it is probable that the buildings will not be in very marked harmony with each other. Hence they will look better, as a group, if they are somewhat openly spaced."

He next turned to fitting new buildings to existing land forms on the McMinnville site. "We have no hesitation in advising a formal general plan with as much symmetry in the location and design of buildings as possible…although there is a fine large ravine or small valley, well wooded, there is no space for grouping college buildings in connection with it."

Olmsted listed 23 needed buildings, with administration and library structures as top priorities in the future. He recommended three quadrangles, around which either "stately" or "working" buildings would stand.

Dormitories for women and men received separate treatment. Large windows should face east and west to allow the best sunlight into the rooms. Thus he advised: "No architect should be permitted to plan rooms with only north exposure."

A large assembly hall and its substantial siting requirements then came in for review. "The classical school architects usually attempt some stately plan for the interior of such an auditorium but the best plan seems to be that usual in a theatre…to seat at the least cost the largest possible audience where all can see and hear to the best advantage." He further noted: "The acoustics of most theatres seem on the whole to be more uniformly good or fairly good than in churches and halls in which architects have broken away from the typical theatre plan."

An art building was another large structure recommended by Olmsted. Near the end of the report, he revealed a lifelong inclination to draw parallels between a student's immediate surroundings and their lessons learned. Although preaching to the choir, he let the trustees know part of his philosophy about campus life.

"Art should receive much more attention in our colleges than has usually been the case. It is assigned to an important site in the front row because it should be a particularly good looking building and with the idea that more women students than men students will feel that they can afford the time for some study of art. It is of great importance that all civil engineering students should have a good grounding in art in order that they may have a fair appreciation of its importance in the many conspicuous works which they may subsequently be called upon to design or at any rate in order that they will not so thoroughly despise art as most civil engineers appear to do. The Art School ought to be one of the most important departments of the college, for an appreciation of beauty can best be cultivated at the student age and will do much to make life enjoyable even if the ability to create beauty be deficient. It is as uncertain and undesirable to leave the appreciation of beauty or good taste to be picked up after life as it is to leave religion or efficient business habits to be picked up casually in after life."

Even his gymnasium recommendations revealed an "everyman" philosophy. "We feel convinced of the importance of careful physical development for the majority of the students…It is a pity that the traditional idea still prevails to some degree that the gymnasium is a place containing trapezes and other apparatus for performing difficult show feats which only a small minority of students would try to learn, and that it is a building presided over by an ex-prize fighter or a retired professional athlete and implies more or less sporty inclinations on the part of students who voluntarily patronize it. But a gymnasium should be a scientific school of physical culture in which the students should learn their physical deficiencies and how to cure or minimize them; in which they should exercise in certain definite ways for certain definite purposes and mainly to the end that they may become or keep healthy by proper exercise and diet."

As he also later advised at the Oregon Agriculture College, there should be a uniformity of materials and trim color on campus, even if "common" red brick was the only choice. Temporary buildings, Olmsted suggested, might be of wooden materials and easily removed later to make way for permanent "dignified" structures. This recommendation was immediately seized upon by President Riley.

The report finished with advice on the greensward (actually more brownsward, with oak tree duff on the ground in autumn and winter). "As the college develops architecturally, the woods should be somewhat thinned and particular views should be opened across them to provide pleasing glimpses…we propose to leave all the land at present owned by the college north of the main row of college

buildings as a sort of park or large front door yard." (Today oaks remain—part of the early tree-dotted landscape Olmsted first viewed.)

In the early summer of 1908, Riley called at the Hotel Savoy in Seattle soon after the report was received. Olmsted had completed the report when staying at the Savoy, but he already had departed for the East, stopping in Spokane for clients there. He never allowed work to intrude upon his summer weekends spent with his family in Maine. Consequently, his visits out west occurred in spring or fall, or even winter, when he could stay for weeks or months at a time.

The McMinnville trustees selected a committee to oversee the recommendations and appointed overworked President Riley to see it through, just at a time when funds were particularly low. Not until 1910, after Riley related heartbreaking stories about long overdue faculty salaries, did the college finally settle accounts with the Olmsted Brothers, and gradually started following John Charles' 1908 advice. President Riley continued to consult with Olmsted long after the submission of the campus report.

Physical reminders of Olmsted's advice and planning remain visible on the campus today. The open, informal woods in front of Pioneer Hall, and the formal quads directly behind the Pioneer and Riley buildings reveal two concepts important to him—using informal elements where appropriate, and adopting formality near inner campus groupings.

Pacific University

A year after the McMinnville work began, Milton W. Smith of the Pacific University board of trustees contacted Olmsted, asking him to consider a site visit to the Forest Grove campus. Portland Park Board member Ion Lewis—a partner in the architectural firm that designed Marsh Hall on the campus—had recommended Olmsted to the university.

Architect Ion Lewis.
Oregon Historical Society

Trustee Smith, also the attorney for the school, had written to Olmsted at the Hotel Portland on December 1, 1908. "Pacific University which is situated at Forest Grove, Oregon, about twenty-five miles west of Portland, would like to know

Pacific University, 1906—the scruffy grounds, overly-worn paths, rutted vehicle delivery tracks, and un-kept Garry oaks were unchanged when Olmsted arrived in late 1908. *Pacific University*

whether you would be willing to undertake to formulate a plan for the location of its buildings and the laying out of its grounds. It has about thirty acres of campus. It is a very beautiful location, and it is thought that there may be some additions made to this campus if necessary. If you are willing to undertake to do this matter for the University, I shall be very glad to either call on you or have you come to my office and we will talk the matter over."

A week later, on December 7, the trustee visited Olmsted at the hotel and drew a crude sketch of the campus—recognizable even today by the indicated swale, cutting across the southeast corner of the rectangular acreage.[3] Milton Smith "called about 2:15 and stayed till 3:20," Olmsted reported in his field notes. "Arranged to have me make a preliminary visit without report for $100 and traveling expenses." He had given the trustee an alternate suggestion for a campus visit (which would include a full written report and sketching), but for now, only the site visit was approved.[4]

Four days later, Olmsted boarded the train on a dark winter morning. "I went out to Forest Grove by the 7:20 train. It was so dark [in Portland] at 7:05, as the electric lights had just been turned off, that I could not read the

street signs more than 2 yards away. It was cloudy and slightly foggy so I did not get any mountain views, but as we climbed the hill I could see across the river. The R.R. is very steep. I should think it climbed over 500 ft maybe 700 feet in 4 miles. Then it gets on a rolling plateau & runs easily 20 miles more to Forest Grove."[5]

Busy watching the scenery and depending on Smith's advice about the length of the trip, Olmsted missed the station for Forest Grove. "It wasn't near the time Mr. Smith said train was due. Fortunately I caught a return train at the next station," He confided to his wife that night. This would not be the only thing in which Smith let Olmsted down. In his field notes: "I had supposed Mr. Smith was going with me, but he did not turn up."

Another mile-and-a-half connection by electric car from the station brought Olmsted to Pacific University and a meeting with President William N. Ferrin, who escorted him around campus that day. "Pleasant people, as most college people are," John Charles wrote his wife that night.

During lunch, he observed students poorly dressed (his clothing standards were high) "but fresh & in earnest." The campus "has two brick buildings & 3 small wooden ones. Fine oaks. Said to be fine views."

At Ferrin's office, "I discussed various matters of detail with him and then gave him my general ideas as to the proper relation of college buildings...As I was to make no written report, he made a few notes of what I said and said he would make more that evening. I felt that he would fail to remember most of it, however," Olmsted critically explained in his field notes sent to Brookline.

In the president's office, Olmsted noted with interest a campus "plan, neatly drawn and colored in the German style framed and hanging on wall...It was by M. Scheydecker. The area is staked at 28.5 acres. On each margin is a profile to scale. Roads and walks are all on curves and not very logical I thought for shortcutting and cutting the grounds up too much. Existing buildings are shown and sites for new ones, but these... are not placed on axes nor symmetrically, but are all oriented parallel with boundaries. I could see no system as to facing of buildings and no consistent rule as to drives to front or rear doors."

Trustee Smith had informed Olmsted that Scheydecker once served as gardener to the prominent Ladd family in Portland. President Ferrin added that Scheydecker apparently supervised improvements at the Riverview Cemetery. However, "the President said they had done nothing toward following Scheydecker's plan" for the Pacific campus.

Continuing (and lamenting) in the field notes: "It was clear to me that the college is very poor and will be wholly unable to execute any far seeing plan and must therefore pursue the usual higgle de piggledy way of putting each building as it comes in the next best site. Donors are hardly likely to consent to have their building put away off in a distant and lower site."

With the knowledge that the previous plan survived only as a sketch on the president's wall, Olmsted gave advice to Ferrin, recorded in the four pages of field notes sent back to the Brookline office. Purchase the southeast corner, save the center space for important working buildings, keep the dormitories farther away, replace wooden boardwalks with more dignified materials, urge supply deliveries to the back of buildings rather than across rutted lawns nearby, and place the library near a corner of the campus for possible combined city funding. Completing his work for the long day, Olmsted rushed back to Portland for a dinner date at the home of a Portland park commissioner.

In the following February, the Pacific University board appointed a committee to study Olmsted's suggestions. In addition, soon after the college trustees met in early February, Smith again wrote Olmsted asking for a second site visit and alluding to a "misunderstanding" in the previous December when Smith did not accompany Olmsted to campus. Smith's tone was disapproving and unpleasant, drawing a dignified written reply from Olmsted on March 10, in which he suggested a complete campus report be done, rather than just another advisory trip.

President William J. Ferrin of Pacific University was less willing than Riley to follow up after Olmsted's campus consultation in December 1908. Ferrin left details to a Portland trustee who soon was ousted, leaving Olmsted in the wings. *Pacific University*

Before other correspondence occurred between the two, Smith in the months ahead was quietly asked to resign from the board and give up his legal advisory status. "Members of the Board of Trustees of Pacific University think you ought to tender your resignation, both as member of the Board and as attorney for the corporation," President Harvey Whitefield Scott of the trustees wrote Smith. "Your name, in connection with the affairs of the Pacific University is a hindrance, not a help." Scott, the first Pacific University graduate (1863) and now the influential *Oregonian* editor, wrote the December 24, 1909, letter on his newspaper's letterhead.

President Ferrin—"never popular with the trustees"[6]—would meet the same fate in 1913. Along with Smith's earlier departure, this left no proponent to fully carry on Olmsted's ideas or plans at Forest Grove, unlike in his association with McMinnville College, the University of Washington, Whitman College, the University of Idaho, and later the Oregon Agriculture College, where enthusiastic sponsors carried through the proposals. The then meager Pacific University campus in 1908–9 was in a phase of its development where no one person was positioned or willing to fully take hold of Olmsted's vision for the future. The unfortunate timing was not conducive for continuing consultation.

Marsh Hall (1895) at Pacific University, designed by Portland architects Whidden and Lewis. *Pacific University*

Nevertheless, at the university today, the direct, straight path leading from the campus's west entry toward Marsh Hall is a remnant of his advice. Also, a long curved low brick wall at the west entry is a variation on his recommendation to avoid stand-alone gates unattached to fences or adjacent walls. Also, campus growth has shifted slightly to the north, as Olmsted intended. However, he did not anticipate satellite campuses, in addition to land acquired on the east side of the university. Buildings south of Marsh Hall, however, are closer to the boundary line, as Olmsted advised, especially the library placement nearer the town.

Oregon Agricultural College

On June 9, 1909, soon after the Alaska-Yukon-Pacific Exposition opened in Seattle, a telegram from the Oregon Agricultural College president arrived at the AYPE office. "Would like you to visit College earliest convenience for investigations and preliminary report. Wire. W.J. Kerr."

Olmsted replied immediately: "Telegram received expect me Thursday fifteenth one thirty pm."

President William Jasper Kerr had only recently come from Salt Lake City. Like Riley at McMinnville, newly installed Kerr in Corvallis sought bold strokes early in his tenure. In the future, along with newly arrived Professor Arthur Lee Peck, he would provide the continuity allowing Olmsted's campus vision to be carried out during a decade of rapid growth. As with the continued support of President Thomas F. Kane and Professor Edmond S. Meany at the University of Washington, the Oregon Agricultural College was able to tap public funds, which neither McMinnville nor Pacific had access to.

On the night of June 15, John Charles wrote his wife from the Hotel Corvallis. "I came along up here in a slow train changing cars at Albany and waiting there quite a while 3/4ths of an hour at least. Upon arriving here I came first to this hotel & secured a room and then walked most a mile I should think to the college which I had seen from the train. They have gradually got the grounds planted and walks laid out and lawns are mowed & some flower beds

President Kerr had just arrived at the Oregon Agriculture College to begin a long tenure when he summoned Olmsted from Seattle's AYPE office. Two weeks after the Seattle exposition opened, Olmsted took a train to Corvallis to meet President Kerr. *Oregon State University*

planted so it looks quite civilized. Two of the buildings are of stone but not large enough and three are of brick, one of the three the oldest plastered over and the rest are of wood. They have had a very sudden growth since 1903 or 4, graduating then 50 or 60 and now 122. As usual their buildings and teaching force are entirely inadequate. I happened here at commencement time & so cannot get much of President Kerr's time. Still he briefly told me the problems he had in mind and drove me around some and one of the professors drove me some more when Pres't. Kerr was called off."

Olmsted was invited to the alumni dinner that night, when he formed further impressions of the people and the place. "I sat between Pres't. Bryan of the Washington Agricultural College [Pullman] with the wife of one of the Regents on my other side. I got on fairly well in the matter of conversation more particularly with Mr. Bryan."

The following day, Olmsted missed his train connection to Portland. "Had to hire a buggy at an expense of $2.50 to drive 11 miles over to this town [Albany] which is on the main line—I was conferring with Pres't Kerr, and the sun was so high that I did not think to look at my watch until 6:01 and the train left at 6 & it would have taken me 8 minutes or so to get to the station. However it is a pretty country & it was a very pleasant ride. 11:30 p.m. I have now arrived at Hotel Portland."

Olmsted's 60-page typed report to President Kerr followed on October 1, 1909. With an even better grasp of western campus requirements than on earlier trips and with more money on hand and two men at the college willing to carry through his recommendations, Olmsted filled his report with exacting details.[7]

Kerr immediately responded: "I have carefully examined your report on the Oregon Agricultural College and am very much pleased with it. The recommendations you make will be very helpful in planning future improvements." Kerr was especially supportive of having a panel of "disinterested experts" to advise on overall architecture and siting, on making sure delivery roads were separate from paved walkways, and on purchasing land immediately to widen the campus footprint.

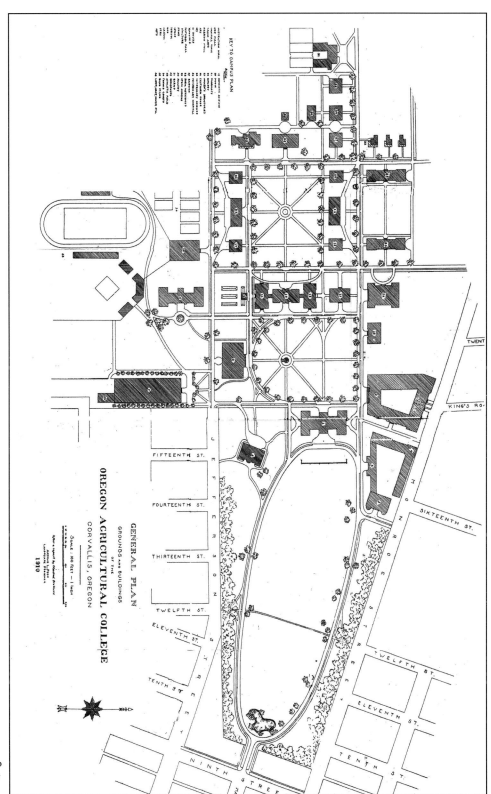

This sketch, "after a report by Olmsted Brothers," was produced by Professor Peck following Olmsted's second visit to the Oregon Agriculture College in early 1910. *Oregon State University*

That winter, when Olmsted was in Seattle on business, Kerr tracked him down at the Hotel Washington Annex to ask for a second campus visit. Olmsted rarely agreed to more than one visit, but Professor Peck had offered to sketch out Olmsted's advice on an existing map. Though traveling without draftsman, he reluctantly agreed to the plan.

On January 31, 1910, he returned to Corvallis. "I left for the college at 8:30 [a.m.] and was there until 5:40," John Charles wrote his wife that night after supper at the Hotel Revere in Albany, while waiting for his train. "Professor Peck is drawing my ideas out and I criticized his plan & made him & Dr. Kerr various suggestions. Both seemed to be gratified by my ideas. The President of the Board of Regents was there in afternoon and I explained my ideas to him. He treated me very respectfully."

To the office, Olmsted relayed four pages of field notes covering his trip to the campus and recording details of the day's discussions. "President Kerr said the main thing was that there was to be an important reunion of Alumni and he wanted to get as many of the walks and drives done as possible before then and the land cleaned and smoothed and seeded. The President of the Board of Regents came from Albany in the afternoon and heard what was proposed. It appeared that we were not to be employed to make plans but to be consulted as to plans made by Professor Peck. He had a plan drawn out in pencil on tracing paper, following pretty nearly the suggestions made in my report…President Kerr had instructed Professor Peck to make his plan with drives and walks combined, for economy and simplicity, but I objected strongly to it and I gathered that he was disposed to yield."

In 1914, Kerr asked for another round of advice. "You will recall having done some work for the College during the year 1909. Since you were here we have completed a number of comparatively large buildings," Kerr boasted, while enclosing a birds-eye view of the campus. The college obviously was thriving.

By this time, however, Olmsted had given over his western work to junior partner Fred Dawson, "who did much of the most attractive work on the Alaska-Yukon Exposi-

tion Grounds," Olmsted wrote Kerr on February 17, 1914. Kerr and Peck decided to rely on Olmsted's earlier plan, which became the standard for decision-making regarding the campus design until 1926.

Arthur Peck became a full professor at the college in 1912 and is credited with introducing formal education in landscape architecture to the Pacific Coast. His association with Olmsted was certainly a life lesson for the young scholar, who had only recently attended Massachusetts Agriculture College. Peck remained at Corvallis for 38 years, and Kerr stayed on as president until 1932. Though Olmsted had the most cordial relationship with McMinnville's Riley, his interactions with Kerr also were very good, and they kept up correspondence longer, with Olmsted providing further advice long after his two visits to Corvallis.

At Oregon State University today, more of Olmsted's direct imprint remains than on the other Oregon campus sites. Two large impressive quads of the inner campus, and matching materials on buildings (brick with light trim), are reminders of his repeated advice to harmonize and beautify. The campus's open eastern vista—plus land purchases between the early quads and the railroad tracks—are due to Olmsted's urging that landscape features are as important to a campus as the buildings and structures.[8]

Notes

1. Kenneth L. Holmes, ed., *Linfield's Hundred Years: A Centennial History* (Portland: Binfords and Mort, 1956).
2. Olmsted job #3411, McMinnville College; Library of Congress.
3. Smith's rough sketch of the campus is preserved in the Library of Congress files.
4. Olmsted job #3595, Pacific University; Library of Congress.
5. Letter, December 11, 1908.
6. Gary Miranda and Rick Read, *Splendid Audacity: The Story of Pacific University* (Seattle: Documentary Book Publishers, 2000).
7. Olmsted job #3699, Oregon Agricultural College; Library of Congress.
8. For another published version describing John Charles' work at Oregon colleges, see Joan Hockaday, "John Charles Olmsted and Campus Design in Oregon," *Oregon Historical Quarterly* 108 (2007), no. 2: 84–99.

4

Seattle Parks & Boulevards

I saw Mt. Rainier very distinctly...It is tremendous and being covered with snow looks at first like a cloud on a clear day...It certainly is a grand site.—October 21, 1906

Olmsted's month long stay in Seattle beginning on April 30, 1903, was his most celebrated and best remembered visit, due to the parks and survey reports resulting from that period. His second visit in the fall of 1906—to start planning for the Alaska-Yukon-Pacific Exposition (AYPE) on the University of Washington campus—turned out to be his second most successful benchmark. But in all, the results of his subsequent 10 visits would prove equally enduring for Seattle parks, the University of Washington, and private clients alike.

Olmsted's overnight stays in Seattle totaled more than his visits to Portland and Spokane combined. During these years, he wrote over 300 letters to Sophia from Seattle. His letters reveal a commitment to public projects above all else, even when increasing (and lucrative) private client work also began in 1906. His dedication to solving challenges and satisfying client demands out west meant his own family and Brookline office duties often suffered from his absences. He was dedicated to keeping western work coming in—especially in Seattle. He continued this pattern into 1911; afterward, his declining health and demanding eastern work largely restricted him to the Olmsted office and duties there.

Olmsted had two "babies" back home when he first set foot in Seattle—daughters Margaret and Carolyn, both under five years of age. They grew accustomed to his long absences, and receiving engaging letters from a father far

Margaret, Carolyn, and Sophia Olmsted. *Harvard GSD*

away. The affection and sage advice included in the letters written to his wife and daughters are compelling. According to family members today, this fondness and devotion was fully returned in kind by the two daughters.[1]

Across the country in the first years of the 20th century, the park work done by the Olmsted Brothers was evident in many cities. Celebrated New York and Brooklyn parks, of course, had made Frederick Law Olmsted Sr. a leader in landscape planning. Projects had followed in Buffalo, Baltimore, Boston, Washington, D.C., Atlanta, Chicago, Louisville, and Lexington, to name some of the park systems already on or just off the drawing boards at the growing Olmsted Brothers office in Brookline. Park planning across America peaked in the years before World War I. (By the 1920s, however, extensive park designs began taking a back seat to emerging city planning.)

Seattle's park system became as extensive as in cities back east. In all, John Charles would open more than 35 separate files for the Seattle park system. After his initial 1903 report, Olmsted wrote more than a dozen other reports for the Seattle Board of Park Commissioners, which included a noting of progress (or sometimes, lack thereof) in park development. City parks people out west sometimes needed even more ardent convincing and encouragement than John Charles' growing number of private clients in the Northwest beginning in 1906.

His sketched park designs were prized accomplishments of his Seattle visits. Remarkable remnants of the parks system plan can be seen today, including Volunteer Park, around Green Lake, the boulevard following a brook in Washington Park, and greenscapes beside Lake Washington and stretches of the boulevard south of Madison Park to Seward Park. Also, Cowen, Frink, and Schmitz parks are named for three men Olmsted associated and dined with during his frequent visits out west. These latter properties not only exhibit the Olmsted firm's capable handiwork, but these parcels also were much-needed donated land, which helped influence the shape of Seattle's park system to come.

After Olmsted's initial 1903 city parks report was accepted, however, he often struggled to convince park commissioners—when he was in Seattle or in far off Brookline—that each individual park needed a precise sketch and master plan. These drawn plans over the decade—for Volunteer Park, Woodland Park, Cowen Park, and others in the early days; for Seward Park and West Seattle (Hiawatha) Playground among those in later years—all show his very capable design and landscape skills, and their lasting advantage to the city.

In October 1906, while on an eastern working swing, Olmsted was summoned from Chicago. He quickly changed his schedule, arriving in Seattle—without winter clothes or enough cigars—to begin planning the AYPE at the University of Washington site. This vast project also provided the opportunity to produce a grand plan for the university's much neglected campus.

May fete at the Hiawatha Playfield in West Seattle, 1914. *Don Sherwood Collection #29274, Seattle Municipal Archives*

With this personal and professional backdrop, John Charles Olmsted's three hundred days in Seattle unfolded in 1903 and 1906, and continued until 1911.

Initial Contacts

Concern over Woodland Park—and an electric car line that ran through the pristine property southwest of Green Lake—provided the reason for Seattle's first contact with the Olmsted firm. In March 1902, J.S. Blackwell, a Seattle Electric Company engineer, wrote to Olmsted assistant Percy R. Jones saying the city's parks "were in danger of being butchered by persons unskilled in park work."[2] Also, word of the Olmsted Brothers' pending work with Portland's park commissioners and the Lewis and Clark Centennial Exposition organizers soon drew even more interest in Seattle.

The city was flush with prosperity due to new railroads, spectacular population and urban growth, vigorous economic revival following the Panic of 1893, wealth from the Alaska/Yukon gold rush, and the opening of new Pacific markets following U.S. acquisition of Hawaii and the Philippines. Community leaders were searching for a facelift from a rough and tumble frontier town to a well planned civilized community.

On December 16, 1902, park board secretary Charles W. Saunders wrote to Frederick Law Olmsted Jr.: "We feel sure that the problem of the improvements of the parks of our city will prove a very interesting one for you, for it possesses not only a peculiar and varied contour, but is also rich in natural scenery of mountains, lakes and Sound, and the opportunities offered for a Park System are certainly far beyond the average of other cities throughout the United States."

Charles W. Saunders. *Secretary of State, Olympia*

The Olmsteds huddled and replied on December 23, 1902. "Mr. F.L. Olmsted, Jr., is employed by Harvard University to deliver lectures and otherwise direct the course on Landscape Architecture...Mr. John C. Olmsted, our senior member, has the designing of parks and numerous other works on hand but can arrange to visit Seattle at almost any time within a week or two after receiving notification that your Commission is ready for him."

To assure park board secretary Saunders, the Olmsteds presented John Charles' qualifications. "Mr. John C. Olmsted has been practicing the profession steadily from 1875 when he graduated from Yale University, and from that time until the retirement of Mr. Frederick Law Olmsted he was most closely connected with him in all of his professional practice."

In the following spring when preparing for travel out west, John Charles visited Washington, D.C., meeting with Captain John F. Pratt of the U.S. Coast and Geodetic Survey, who was well informed about Seattle. Olmsted realized that developing an efficient connecting boulevard system was as important in Seattle as plans for any existing or future parks. Olmsted recorded in his March 19 field notes: "What the park commission hopes is that a plan can be adopted by the city for parkways so that all private and public land subdivisions hereafter adopted shall be made to conform to the parkway plan."

John Charles reviewed Pratt's increasingly out-of-date survey maps, which had been specially authorized by the Seattle park commissioners. He realized the intricacies that would be involved in designing parks and connecting boulevards in a quickly expanding city landscape with numerous hills, bluffs, and deep ravines. At this meeting, Olmsted also "inferred that the main effort at present would be to get parkways as these would, some of them, benefit real estate schemes" in the rapidly growing city. Captain Pratt would reappear two months later in Seattle, accompanying Olmsted and four park commissioners on a tugboat tour beneath Magnolia Bluff, around the West Point Lighthouse, and into Salmon Bay.

The new Seattle park commissioners—seizing the chance to shape the entire parks and parkway system while real estate prices remained low enough to allow city purchases—had quickly agreed to invite John Charles west. Also, he would arrive at a time when the city's old established bicycle paths were just then going "out of fashion" and some even "neglected."[3]

Lake Washington Boulevard bicycle path, 1900. Bicycle routes often became the basis for paved paths and boulevards. *Don Sherwood Collection #29568, Seattle Municipal Archives*

As in Portland, the special drive and determination of key park commissioners would assure initial success for Olmsted and his park plans. Commissioner Charles W. Saunders—the architect for two of the few new buildings then standing on the relocated University of Washington campus—kept Olmsted informed of the park board's intentions leading up to his arrival in Seattle on April 30, 1903.

Without Saunders' persistent correspondence and effort (first as secretary, and then as president, of the park board), Olmsted's 1903 visit and report might have been less advantageous for park and boulevard planning. The two—architect and landscape architect—became working colleagues and lifetime friends, with lasting satisfactory results for the city parks design. Saunders moved projects along when city inertia took hold, and proved a most able friend of the firm—and the new profession of landscape architecture—in the Pacific Northwest.[4]

Park board president Elbert F. Blaine also urged prospects along. In Olmsted's view, he was the second moving force behind a park plan for Seattle. A prominent lawyer and president of the Denny-Blaine Land Company, Blaine proved to be "the broadest minded," as John Charles later noted to his wife.[5] After Olmsted arrived in Seattle, Blaine loaned a friend's boat launch for shoreline exploration, treated Olmsted and park board members to lunch and dinner at his Denny-Blaine Park lakeside house, and handed out cigars to curious (and often concerned) waterfront property owners when Olmsted and his surveyors worked on the boulevard routes.[6]

E.F. Blaine served on the Seattle park board from 1902 to 1908; in the latter year, he was honored as the "Father of the Seattle Park System." Loyal to the end, he and John Charles differed on only a few proposals (one of these being

Elbert F. Blaine, the Father of the Seattle Park System, and "the best man for the job" in Olmsted's opinion. *Curtis Collection, Rainier Club*

the Washington Park Boulevard boundary in relation to an adjoining golf club). Blaine's obvious influence translated into assured success for Olmsted in 1903 and in following years.

John Charles' initial visit, and this first set of park commissioners, provided the main impetus for major park planning and expansion in Seattle. Olmsted's 1903 report especially provided the park commissioners with fine arguments to present to the citizenry in upcoming elections for funding land purchases. As the decade progressed, however, park board members came and went, sometimes to Olmsted's advantage or disadvantage. During his final visit to the city in 1911, for example, he met yet another set of commissioners, some unknown to him. Yet, with another handshake, and another new park commissioner engaged, Olmsted effectively worked through the potential political and practical pitfalls during his western park planning days.

Arrival in Seattle

After coming from Portland on April 30, 1903, along with assistant Percy Jones, Olmsted's first days in Seattle involved a flurry of investigative field trips by buggy, trolley, boat, and on

foot. At the time, Seattle possessed only five major parks— Denny, Kinnear Volunteer, Washington, and Woodland— though there also were a number of significant privately owned parks. At the end of each day, he sat down at a writing desk in his hotel to inform Sophia about his activities. The boat rides on Puget Sound and Lake Washington— around the West Point Lighthouse, to Bailey Peninsula (Seward Park), and along the Washington Park shoreline— all received full attention.

When receiving a letter from Boston, he replied about family matters, as well as his Seattle work. On days he did not receive word from home, his letters were filled with even more details about his Seattle work. Four or six-page letters were the norm; rarely did he write just two pages in the early days. The exuberance that appeared in Olmsted's private letters only rarely spilled over into his meticulous field notes, which were written and filed after each property visit. His private letters, then, present a more intimate assessment of park work and the people he encountered.

Nevertheless, his frequent appraisals sent to the Brookline office and in daily field reports included astonishing note-keeping detail. For example, on his fifth day in Seattle, May 4, he recorded the following: "Some of the Park Commission called for us about 10 but we waited for Mr. Blaine. All but Mr. Fowler were of the party and also Mr. Walters, Supt. of Streets and Parks who had his own

A May 1903 Olmsted photo of future Queen Anne Boulevard and Queen Anne Hill Parkway, from corner of 10th and Lee. *Don Sherwood Collection #30030, Seattle Municipal Archives*

buggy. We had two carriages and drove first to Denny Park (this is marked Seattle Park on Chapman's Pocket guide map). It occupies two blocks on a hillside sloping rapidly down to E[ast]. Walks and planting designed by Swagel [E.O. Schwagerl, Seattle park superintendent, 1893–95]. We then drove to the water tower on Queen Anne Hill and climbed it. Elev. of ground by coast survey 450 ft., by city datum according to a local resident 462 ft. We then drove to Kinnear Park and walked the length of it and part way back.

"We then drove through a rough half wild district to a suburb named Interbay, and across a trestle over Great Northern R.R. yards to a little cabin of rough boards where the bicycle path comes first to the face of a bluff and commands a view over Smith Cove. Then at 2 P.M. we lunched.

"At 2:35 we walked on the bicycle path through the woods to Fort Lawton where we arrived at 4:35 P.M. The carriages met us there and we drove thence to Interbay by the road which is on the slope overlooking Salmon Bay. We then drove by Grand Boulevard (a wild pasture) over a divide and down into Ross, a poor quarter near proposed [Lake Washington] ship canal, and then to Fremont. We then turned partway up the hill to S. and followed an old country road on a bluff overlooking Lake Union, past sand pits to the regular city streets. We then went past the new baseball grounds or Athletic Park and looked at some open blocks of land between Republican and Mercer Streets and 3rd and 4th Avenues. Nob Hill Street could be discontinued. We then drove to the Knickerbocker [Hotel] where we arrived about 6.45 P.M."

Olmsted's powers of observation and constant note taking were legendary, and his discipline in recording it all down at the end of each day was quite extraordinary. (His Olmsted Brothers associates rarely achieved the same level of concentration or detail when on the road day after day, as is clearly evident in the documentation left by them in the same decade or in later years.) Consequently, historians today are left with a vast archive due to John Charles' precise and valuable observations in a variety of letters, reports,

The Queen Anne Hill water tower.
Seattle Municipal Archives

site plans, etc. Trained in keen observation and plain expression by his famous stepfather, John Charles wrote with ease and alacrity.

The forests of Ravenna Park, then privately owned, amazed Olmsted on his first viewing. The height and girth of the native trees elicited these remarks to Sophia on May 5, 1903. "The biggest tree seems to be 8 or 9 feet through at 8 ft. above the ground where a logger would cut it but is about 15 ft. in diameter at the ground. The big trees have mostly been left at the time the surrounding country was first 'logged' because of the difficulty of building a logging road in a ravine, where it is more or less wet and muddy and where there are a great many fallen logs to cut out of the way & too soggy to burn."

Parks and landscapes in Seattle inevitably come in for a comparison with Portland parks just seen. "Although not as deep and steep sided a ravine as Macleay Park at Portland it [Ravenna] has a larger brook and more variety of surface and some nearly level land so it is better adapted for a park. The electric cars go right to the gate."

Located just north of the new university campus, Ravenna Park was owned and operated by the Beck family at the time of Olmsted's initial visit. Olmsted soon placed it on his "must purchase" list for public holding (with success only finally assured years later). In addition to assessing Ravenna Park, Olmsted scouted sites on Queen Anne hill (he advised purchasing land near the water tower), Magnolia Bluff (he recommended buying its entire length while the price was still low), and Fort Lawton along the "beautiful bicycle woods" (he saw great potential here). He also recommended additions to Washington Park's western boundary and along Lake Washington south to the Bailey Peninsula (now Seward Park), located well beyond the city limits at the time.

Closer to downtown, Olmsted paid special attention to Lincoln Park (today, Cal Anderson Park) alongside the city reservoir on Capitol Hill. The park commissioners were eager to improve the site, giving Olmsted one of his first special assignments.

To the south side of Seattle, he hiked the Cedar River pipeline road and commented on a park set-aside site,

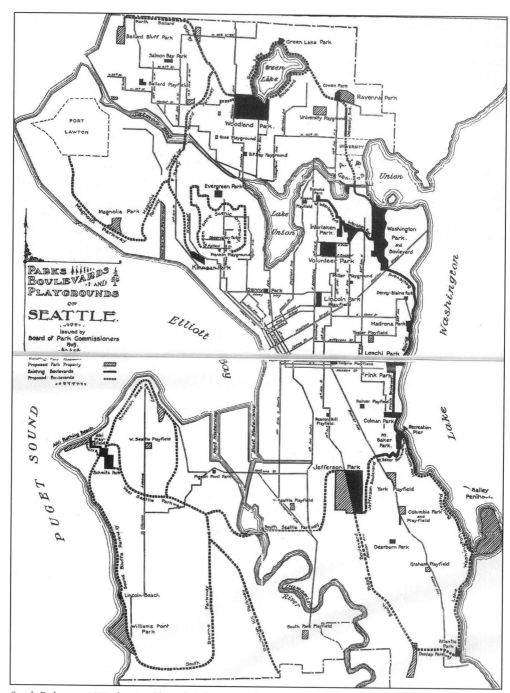

Seattle Parks map, 1909, showing Olmsted's influence and designs. In 1903, city water reservoirs on "Volunteer Hill" and in Lincoln Park off Madison Street needed transformation, and the old bike paths required modernizing. The boulevard system, laid out by Olmsted, soon threaded its way along Lake Washington and between Ravenna and Green Lake, with recently donated parks also receiving the Olmsted design touch. Cowen and Frink parks were two early donations, along with Schmitz Park after the 1907 annexation of Ballard and West Seattle into the city boundaries. The remote Bailey Peninsula was an Olmsted favorite for purchase, which the city eventually brought into its planning sphere. *Seattle Municipal Archives*

along with a racecourse location on the Duwamish River favored by one of the park commissioners. Olmsted always paid particular attention to the concerns of individual park board members.

Olmsted's Lake Union ramblings and scouting sessions—and comments made by his traveling associate Percy Jones—showed just how close the city was coming to losing valuable potential park land during Seattle's greatest land boom. Having previously promised to stay for two weeks, Olmsted extended his time for hiking in the hills and ravines to a month. On May 24, he wrote his wife: "I am much exasperated at having to stay here so long as I want to get back to you and home very much."

1903 Seattle Parks Report

As Olmsted completed a month of field work, the park commission wanted him to write a full report "here & now," but he deferred as he busily finished up in Seattle and returned east. However, in the days ahead he quickly wrote and polished a report, rushing it to a stenographer while many of the exacting details were fresh in mind. Completed by the end of June and sent to the park board, it was published in the commission's annual report for 1903.

Despite more than a dozen subsequent reports, sketches, and drawings completed for the city between 1903 and 1911,[7] John Charles' 1903 report remained Seattle's main blueprint for planning parks and parkways in a continuing professional manner.[8] Park board secretary Saunders replied in August 1903: "We fully appreciate its completeness and…it will be a great assistance to us as an argument in convincing the people of the necessity of adopting the plan you have so ably presented."

The comprehensive plan included a greenway boulevard system eventually linking, north to south, Washington Park, Frink Park, Colman Park, and Seward Park along Lake Washington's shoreline and bluffs. Another boulevard plan included Ravenna Park. Over the years, his other proposed boulevard extensions connecting Fort Lawton, Magnolia Bluff, Interbay, Ballard, and the summit of Queen Anne Hill would only be partially created in the planned 20 mile system linking greenways, parks, playfields, lakes, and shorelines. The report recommended specific land acquisitions, including several privately owned parks. Volunteer Park, the lowering of Green Lake,

and a redesigned Woodland Park also received Olmsted's special attention.

In his later Seattle reports, Olmsted elaborated on further landscape guidelines, as the city annexed more land and asked for additional professional advice. Succeeding Seattle park boards hired Olmsted again and again, to scout out more playgrounds and parks and to meticulously design some of the individual parks already selected.

His November 1906 follow-up parks report was realistic in its priorities, given the limited funding on hand. Olmsted urged the immediate purchase of boulevard property leading to the University of Washington area and to Green Lake. He also presented a stern warning that property in the Lake Washington Boulevard vicinity near the Mt. Baker Park residential district would escalate in value, as would land on the then remote Bailey Peninsula. Because the latter two localities were east and south of the densest part of the city (and the electric car tracks), Olmsted advised acquiring these acres quickly while they still were available, and before rising land values outstripped the park commission's means.

Independent Park Board

John Charles' completion of the 1903 parks report—thoroughly reviewing prospects for each of the present and future parks and boulevards—might have ended the Olmsted's firm's association with Seattle. However, the park commissioners, particularly Charles Saunders, held Olmsted's expertise in the highest regard and soon asked for other advice after the parks report went to press.

In a letter on December 11, 1903, Olmsted advised: "It seems to us that the most important step to be taken now in park matters is to secure a modification of the city charter by which the whole park business can be put in charge of a park commission working independently of the Common Council as completely as is customary in most of the larger cities of this country." At the time, the parks committee reported to the Seattle city council, an arrangement not to the liking of the park commissioners.

When the Seattle city council snubbed the park commissioners' effort to break away and form an independent entity, Saunders and his park allies collected 3,000 signatures and won independence in an election held on March 8, 1904.

Only the day before, the outcome hardly seemed secure. "The city election takes place tomorrow and by Wednesday we shall know the fate of the proposed Park Amendment to the Charter," Saunders wrote Olmsted on March 7. "The fight against it has been covertly waged by some of the councilmen and their friends, and more particularly by the members of the Board of Public Works…the City Engineer…and the Superintendent of Parks," Saunders reported.

"The result of the election is very much in doubt. We are hoping our friends will be stronger than the politicians. I will send you papers, giving statement of election returns."

Four days later, the news went out to Brookline: "We have great pleasure in notifying you of the success of the Park Amendment, and although it carried by a bare majority of 140 votes in face of the bitter opposition of the politicians and their friends, it is none the less gratifying to us," Saunders wrote on behalf of the Seattle park board.

Barely looking back after an exhausting campaign, the park board then asked Olmsted, 3,000 miles away in Brookline, for advice on a new park superintendent. "At an informal meeting held yesterday we decided to take up the matter of the employment of a Park Superintendent… will you kindly let us know…so that we may know how to proceed…on information requested from you, we will promptly take up the matter."

The new park commissioners wanted help in finding an able superintendent for Seattle, working under an Olmsted contract at first, so that city rules could be temporarily bypassed. With so many of the city's officials and employees having worked against the park independence vote, the commissioners thus saw a way clear to hire their own man.

The Olmsted firm provided the names of three experienced and capable parks people from the East. The commissioners chose John W. Thompson from Watertown, New York, to carry out the Olmsted proposals. Thompson's two competitors for the position also had experience carrying out the firm's plans—G.A. Parker, the Keney Park superintendent at Hartford, Connecticut, and young Allen Hope, who was George W. Vanderbilt's gardener at New Dorp, Staten Island, New York.

When Thompson got the job, he asked for and received a house alongside Woodland Park. He would remain as the Olmsted firm's man on the ground for the next 17 years. Work on Washington Park Boulevard began in earnest

soon after Thompson arrived from upstate New York in the spring of 1904, and it occupied much of his attention until the time AYPE overseers invited Olmsted out west again in 1906. With the assignment to implement the Olmsted plan, but with limited funds to carry out the entire design even in its first phase, Thompson supervised teams of horses and men scraping soil for new Washington Park Boulevard along the brook in the ravine.

In 1904, under contract to follow up on the park recommendations of 1903, John Charles asked a young associate, James Frederick Dawson, to come west and report on the progress of their own park superintendent, Thompson, and other park plans.[9] Fred Dawson proved an able right-hand man not only on this reconnaissance, but several years later as the Olmsted Brothers' plantsman on the AYPE grounds, during the design and planting months of 1908 and 1909.

Volunteer Park

Located on the crest of Capitol Hill, Volunteer Park remains as a crown jewel of Olmsted's Seattle designs. It was one of Seattle's existing parks when viewed by John Charles in company with park commissioners—a largely forlorn property with a wide, open, city reservoir, and standing next to a large cemetery. Over the years, Volunteer Park would remain a constant source of design work for the Olmsted firm. Not just content with seeking John Charles' advice on boundaries and the park's eventual use, the city eventually turned to the Olmsted Brothers for ever more specific planning—including the placement of a water tower (1906) and the conservatory (1912).

"Rather a novel name for a park," John Charles had written to Sophia on May 20, 1903, after learning it honored Spanish-American War soldiers. His first design for Volunteer Park recommended purchasing land just west of its boundary to preserve a park vista. This is an example, however, of an Olmsted recommendation that failed to be implemented. Instead, in the years ahead, new mansions would line Federal Avenue along the western park boundary. Olmsted insisted that public parks and the landscaping for private homes should not approach close to each other—negative nuisances, he believed, would develop between the two. His rigid warning had to be ignored, however, because the city had insufficient funds to purchase this already high-priced Capitol Hill real estate.

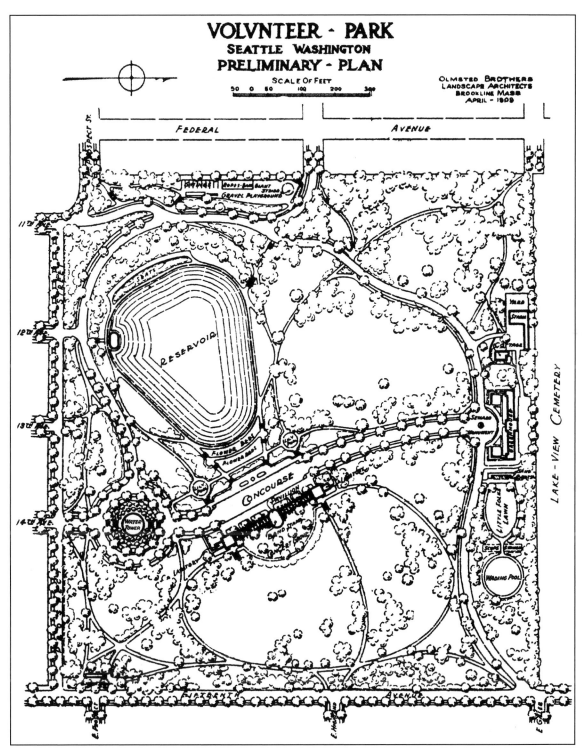

Volunteer Park, as designed by the Olmsted firm and completed before World War I. The reservoir, left beyond the two lily ponds, was the only planned feature before Olmsted first viewed the site with park commissioners in 1903. An art museum later replaced the trellis at right, against Olmsted's advice. *Fairsted*

A view over Volunteer Park from the water tower, with reservoir at the left.

the landscape value of this park by consenting to the placing of such a building in it."

On this occasion, his views helped cancel the plan. (Years later, however, a new Seattle Art Museum would be built in the park; the Art Moderne structure dates from 1931–33.)

Earlier, in 1905, the new Volunteer Park water tower—not included in the original 1903 report—also kept Olmsted busy in advising the city regarding its setting on a prominence in the southern part of the park. From a Chicago hotel room, Olmsted wrote detailed

Each city request for advice on the park, however, added to a cohesive design, grandly accomplished in 1912. Olmsted had many details to work through, and he won in regard to most of the principled points he wished to implement. He also recommended against unnecessary intrusions, particularly regarding a proposed art museum.

"We beg to report on the question referred to us…as to whether or not we advise your Board to grant a building site in Volunteer Park to the Washington State Art Association for a large museum building," Olmsted began in an October 11, 1910, reply to the city.

"Volunteer Park is obviously a landscape park—not an ornamental public square nor primarily a public playground. The conclusion is evident that the proposed art museum is not suggested as a means for the public to enjoy the landscape of the park."

The park commissioners were giving Olmsted little time to reflect on the matter. Within 60 days of the request for John Charles' advice, the art association wished to start work on the building.

"Owing to its size and style of architecture the art museum is in no way to be subordinate to the park landscape, but on the contrary the museum would completely dominate a large part if not the whole of the park." Olmsted continued: "In our opinion, there is no emergency which would justify the Park Board in destroying much of

The Volunteer Park water tower in early 1900s, left, and present day, showing mature landscaping. *Seattle Municipal Archives (left)*

instructions to the city regarding the siting of the handsome brick tower. (Today, this landmark houses an Olmsted exhibit for those hardy enough to walk up the many steps to the top and the observation deck.)

The original conservatory, a ramshackle glasshouse as noted in John Charles' field report to the Boston office, was later replaced as he recommended. This included a sleek, upgraded design and selected placement within the park. Olmsted—anxious to locate larger structures at the edge of the park—had the conservatory placed next to the northern border, adjacent to Lake View Cemetery. Such a locality also was Olmsted's recommendation for an alternate site for the art museum, had it been built at that time.

The lily ponds adjacent to the reservoir were part of the earliest design, but later came in for review after children climbed and fell off the pond edges. Olmsted associate Fred Dawson advised, in January 1911, a strong mesh wire just beneath the surface—which kept the children at bay.

At Volunteer Park, the city and the Olmsted Brothers maintained a constant vision from start to finish during the site's early years. The park remains today as one of Seattle's best examples of early 20th century professional landscape planning and design.

Woodland Park

Olmsted's long letters to draftsmen back in the Brookline office—especially his 21-page Woodland Park report to Percy Jones on January 21, 1910—illustrate his attention to detail and a willingness to write it all down. With its magnificent forest as the centerpiece, Woodland Park presented an entirely different planning proposition than Volunteer Park.

Woodland Park was near the northern boundary of the city confines in 1903, when Olmsted was called in to advise on design and land use. Gradually developing an overall plan from the southwest corner, he exerted influence on an entire park design when Green Lake, near the northeast corner, came up for review. With exotic animals increasing at the Woodland Park Zoo—especially after park commissioners brought back prized "catches" on foreign holidays—Olmsted included zoo requirements in later designs. Here, the electric railway line runs through the center of the park, as it appeared when Olmsted first arrived in 1903. *JCO Photo Album, Fairsted*

Before Olmsted's May 1903 visit, the Woodland property had been purchased in 1899 for $100,000, a great expense causing considerable grumbling from sectors of the city. The park originated from the private estate of millionaire lumberman and real estate developer Guy Phinney, who had passed away in 1893. In 1903, the property was situated beyond most settled neighborhoods, but it would need much work and alteration to prepare it for the future, when the growing population in the northern quarter of the city would need public gathering places.

Essentially three different park elements would be combined—a high, level, upper park on the west, which was Phinney's former fine estate; a north-south center strip with splendid woods; and low land at the eastern base, bordering Green Lake marshland at the time. Olmsted retained all three elements as distinct parts of the whole Woodland Park plan.

After taking a long winter walk upon learning of his beloved father-in-law's death back in Boston, Olmsted wrote to his mourning wife on January 20, 1910: "The woods are so beautiful." John Charles found special solace here during this sorrowful time.

In his later report on road-building through the park, he reminded city officials: "These woods are so rare in a city, where grubbing is the norm."

Road construction along the shorelines and slicing through Seattle parks, Woodland in particular, drew him into city politics. He would have preferred avoiding such confrontations. At the peak of neighborhood protest over a "commercial route" in Woodland Park, Olmsted confided his frustration at trying to please both sides in the controversy.

To John Charles, however, credit is given for helping deflect a proposed second road through the park. The city's Stone Avenue Extension was on the drawing board when neighbors and park commissioners sought his advice on its placement, extending to undeveloped lands north of Woodland Park. His field notes and letters show how much convincing he needed to exert on city engineers during tense negotiations.

Noting that the city electric car line, which already sliced through the park, was only on lease until the 1930s and probably would (and did) become a major automobile route, he temporarily beat back a second macadamized route through Woodland Park.

Advice against avoidable or overly intrusive new roadways in the parks was a theme in Olmsted's writing. Another proposed route through Ravenna Park gave Olmsted another chance to stand up and argue against unacceptable intrusions. Also, when John Charles submitted a Fort Lawton plan in 1910, his relief was palpable when reminding military officials that the fort's park plan required no through roads. Because of the fort's rather remote location on a peninsula, it was spared from encroachment by Seattle's expanding main-traffic grid system.

Washington Park

Washington Park Boulevard, meandering today alongside a brook through Washington Park, also came off Olmsted's drawing board. Located just south of Union Bay, Washington Park had been donated by the Puget Mill Company. When first hiking its length in 1903, Olmsted encountered newly logged-off land full of stumps and downed trees. In his planning, Olmsted delineated the roadway along the western part of the park. He also encouraged property expansion to the north and northwest, taking in platted lots to prevent residential encroachment on the watershed and the views that Olmsted so desired to preserve.

He urged the city to broaden the boulevard's right-of-way, so new homes would sit well above, rather than on, the meandering Washington Park roadway that connected with Madison Park to the east and the new university campus to the north. His office submitted a detailed planting plan along the curves, matching the gentle slope of the terrain. Today, Washington Park Boulevard remains as the major thoroughfare through the park.

Olmsted's request to submit a full Washington Park plan in its entirety, however, fell on deaf ears in the early part of the century. However, the situation changed years later, in the 1930s, when associate Fred Dawson was called upon to plan the upper arboretum portion of Washington Park. Funds from the Seattle Garden Club assured this second-phase park plan along with approval secured from city and University of Washington administrators.

Magnolia Bluff

Handsome Magnolia Bluff and remote Fort Lawton on the city's then northwest boundary with Puget Sound delighted Olmsted during his first visits (by boat and then on foot). Olmsted's planned boulevard west and along the Magnolia Bluff was, in those days, far afield from downtown Seattle. It would be years, however, before either would come under the scope and protection of a precise design.

Visiting Magnolia Bluff again in January 1908, he regretted the lack of neighborhood resolve to save the bluffs and to support a broad boulevard concept. "This morning I went on an excursion with 4 park commissioners and 4 other gentlemen friends of theirs to see Magnolia Bluffs. We went out in the electric car to Ft. Lawton. Then we walked back along the bicycle path…I was sorry to see clearings and street grading encroaching considerably on our park area for that district. The parkway will have to be scrimped and the area of woods much lessened. The park commission hasn't heretofore paid attention to that district. The people there haven't brought pressure enough to bear."

Olmsted had seen possibilities for these places in his 1903 report, and ultimately plans would be realized years later.

Changing Park Commissioners

Park commissioners had their own areas of personal interest, but few championed Magnolia Bluff, although park board president E.C. Cheasty pushed for a nearby Fort Lawton plan late in the decade (as well as music shells and concerts in city parks). When Cheasty lost his parks position in 1910 over political differences with an incoming elected official, Olmsted absorbed the blow of one fewer

The entrance to Cowen Park, as envisioned by the property's donor. Charles Cowen hired Olmsted Brothers to design this park entrance on gently sloping land just north of the new University of Washington campus. *FSOP*

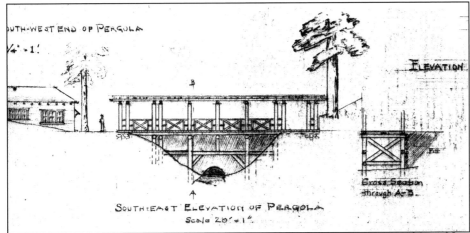

Details of an Olmsted-designed entry that Ferdinand Schmitz commissioned for his donated park land. *Seattle Municipal Archives*

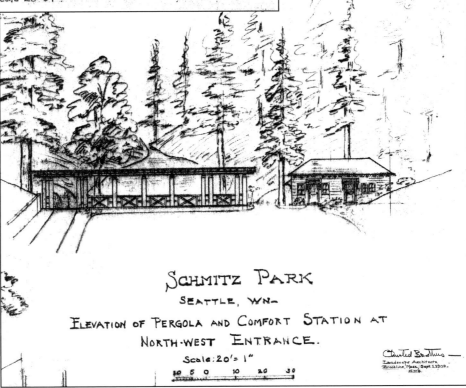

SCHMITZ PARK
SEATTLE, WN.
ELEVATION OF PERGOLA AND COMFORT STATION AT
NORTH-WEST ENTRANCE.
Scale: 20'= 1"

friend with influence in Seattle. When Olmsted worked in his Brookline office, friends in far away Seattle were essential.

After Charles Saunders, and also E.F. Blaine (1908), left the board, two other commissioners would greatly influence Olmsted's course in Seattle. Beginning in 1908, park board member Ferdinand Schmitz urged Olmsted to fold Schmitz's personally donated West Seattle park property into the system. Olmsted admired Schmitz, a prominent banker and realtor, for his determination and gardening skills.

John M. Frink, on the opposite city shore, also donated land to the city and asked the Olmsted firm to design his private garden at his own property on the hillside above Lake Washington. As was common for park board members, Frink was a prominent Seattleite, having founded the Washington Iron Works.

In addition, two of the parks were finished with entrances designed by the Olmsted firm, paid for by individual park board members—these included Charles Cowen's rustic "Cowen Park" arbor north of the university and adjacent to Ravenna Park, and Ferdinand Schmitz'

automobile turn-around that led into the woods of Schmitz Park in West Seattle.

Downtown and Lake Union

Finding space for waterfront parks in the core downtown area proved most difficult. Practically every foot of the Elliott Bay shoreline was filled up with wharves, as well as sewer and storm outfalls from Seattle's thriving business

Olmsted Brothers, Western Washington (projects started, 1903–30s). Job numbers (#) and names of files opened by the Olmsted firm. Compiled from Beveridge, *Master List* (1987), and Lawliss et al., *Master List,* 2nd ed. (2008), with additions from Johnson, *Olmsted in the Pacific Northwest* (1997).

Arboretum/garden
#2699—Seattle Arboretum, "Washington Park"

City planning/improvement
#08/2—Tacoma Land Co.
#2712—City of Seattle
#3735—Everett Improvement Co.
#3743—Aberdeen Improvement Association

Country clubs
#3353—Seattle Golf & Country Club, "Highlands"
#8065—Nile Temple Country Club
#8207—Bainbridge Island Country Club

Exposition
#2739—Alaska-Yukon-Pacific Exposition
 (listed under Parks in NAOP listing)

Monument design/cemeteries
#5784—King County Crematorium
#6773—Evergreen Cemetery Co., Seattle
#9566—Bonnell, J.J. Cemetery lot

Parks/parkways/recreation (Seattle locality)
#2690—Seattle Park System
#2691—Lincoln Park [Capitol Hill]
#2692—Kinnear Park
#2693—Ravenna Park
#2694—Woodland Park
#2695—Volunteer Park
#2696—Queen Anne Hill Parkway
#2697—Magnolia Bluff
#2698—Seattle Playgrounds
#2700—Leschi Park
#2701—City Park
#2702—Madrona Park
#2703—Madison Park
#2704—Denny Park
#2705—Admiral Phelps Park
#2706—Lake Washington
#2707—Cowen Park
#2708—Frink Park
#2709—Pendleton Miller Playground

#2710—Park in Hill Tract
#2711—Washington Park Addition
#2713—Interlaken Boulevard
#2714—Green Lake Boulevard
#2715—West Seattle Play/Hiawatha Park
#2716—Alki Point Bathing Beach
#2717—Delmar Park
#2718—Lake Washington Boulevard
#2719—Schmitz Park
#2720—Fort Lawton
#2721—Coleman Park
#2722—Montlake Boulevard
#2723—West Seattle Parkway
#2724—Seward Park
#2725—Jefferson Park
#2726—Columbia Park
#2727—McGraw Monument
#2728—West Seattle Park

Parks/parkways (outside Seattle locality)
#3213—Fairhaven Park, Bellingham
#3579—Everett Parks, Everett
#5790—Sedro-Woolley Park, Sedro Woolley

Private residential clients (Seattle & environs)
#3168—Black, C.H.
#3204—Baker, F.W.
#3205—Hill, Samuel
#3206—Jones, W.G.
#3207—Leary, Mrs. John
#3208—Sheffield, W.M.
#3210—Upper, H.S.
#3324—Burke, Thomas
#3355—Trimble, W.P., "Blake Island"
#3425—Farrell, J.D.
#3446—Spooner, Charles P.*
#3447—Struve, F.K.*
#3490—Clark, C.H.
#3491—Stimson, C.D.
#3499—Heineman, M.C.
#3589—Smith, C.J.
#3590—Stimson, F.S.
#3592—Clise, J.W.
#3709—Stewart, A.B.

#3717—Backus, M.F.
#3718—Edwards, J.H.
#3723—Anderson, A.H.
#3724—Kerry, A.S.
#3870—Hoge, James D.
#3871—Baker, B.W.
#3872—Hamm, David
#3873—Hughes, E.C.
#3875—Farnsworth, Clare
#3877—Balsom (Bolcom), W.
#3878—Merrill, R.D.
#3956—Beaton, Alfred (Wilfred)
#4053—Peterson, Peter
#4070—Hyde, Samuel
#4081—Donahue, M.
#4082—Conner, Herbert S.
#4083—Frink, J.M.
#5095—Force, Ridgley
#5278—White, C.F./Bullitt, A.S.
#5676—Wight, M.F.
#5787—Heffernan, J.T.
#5788—Frederick, D.E.
#5859—Bolcom, Harry S.
#5877—Boeing, W.E.
#5888—Hambach. A.*
#5911—Lewis, L.D.
#5971—Arnold, N.A.
#6002—Merrill, R.D.
#6056—Phillips, W.R.*
#6075—Agen, Mrs. John B.
#6089—Moss, D.H.
#6110—Colvin, O.D.*
#6171—Dunn, Arthur G.
#6217—Jones, Ray W.
#6364—Whitcomb, David
#6619—Ostrander, H.F.
#6692—Ballinger, J.H.
#6712—Foster, Newton*
#6798—Bogle, Mrs. Lawrence
#7315—Frost, A.C.
#8068—Goodwin, E.S.
#8075—Krauss, Mrs. Arthur J.
#8091—Douglas, J.F.
#8092—Douglas, W.T.

#8208—Garrett, Mrs. Edward
#8217—Baillargeon, Cebert
#8221—Milburn, Mrs. Anna
#8242—Paine, Alex B.
#8245—Beck, B.C.*
#9552—Garrett, Edward I.

Private clients (other localities)
#3273—Moran, Robert, Orcas Island
#3416—Blattner, F.S., Tacoma
#3421—Donworth, George, Port Orchard
#3422—Rust, William R., Tacoma
#3494—Thorne, Chester, Tacoma
#3725—Griggs, E.G., Tacoma
#3874—Wilkinson, Mrs. Samuel, Tacoma
#5448—Jones, Frank E., Aberdeen
#6635—Gordon, E.M., Bellevue
#7014—Weyerhaeuser, S.P., Tacoma
#9281—Bonnell, J.J., Renton

Public buildings/grounds
#3212—Seattle Public Library
#5350—Washington State Capitol, Olympia

Residential institutions
#3390—Soldier's Home, Port Orchard
#3678—Sedro-Woolley Insane Institution
#3727—Washington State Reformatory, Monroe
#3912—Antituberculosis Hospital, Seattle
#3914—King County Consumptives Hospital

Subdivisions/suburban communities
#3209—Mt. Baker Park Subdivision
#3347—Licton Mineral Springs Co.
#3348—Golden Gardens
#3876—Ainsworth & Blaine [Highlands]
#6454—Baker, John S., subdivision, Tacoma
#7367—Frost, A.C., Magnolia Bluff
#7399—Frost, R.C./Jefferson Park Tract
#8243—The Highlands

University campus
#0346—"Washington, State Univ. of"

---

*Catherine Joy Johnson's inventory in *Olmsted in the Pacific Northwest* indicates private clients making "inquiry only" in these job files.

City of Seattle regrade work along 4th Avenue, 1908. *A. Curtis #11442, University of Washington Libraries*

and hotel district. Playground possibilities here (and elsewhere in the city) proved elusive in 1903. On later trips, however, Olmsted succeeded in scouting more nearby districts for available land and devoted a separate report entirely to playgrounds.

Just north of the downtown business area, Denny Park sat almost alone in a quickly expanding neighborhood that greatly needed open space. Denny Park received a negative review from Olmsted in his first viewing.

Also in 1903, Olmsted, with office assistant Percy Jones, first hiked around the perimeter of nearby Lake Union. "I went with Jones this afternoon to visit possible sites for small local parks on the shores of Lake Union which is north of the heart of the city. It has the shape of the letter 'Y'" Olmsted wrote Sophia from the Hotel Knickerbocker on the evening of May 28. "We walked along the foot, or south end, all the east side and around the northeast corner and southwest down into the point of the Y and up to the other prong, which took us 2½ hours. The latter part we walked rapidly in half an hour. I took off my coat yet got pretty warm."

He preferred this ramble on foot to his subsequent rough automobile ride in January 1909. "Most of the way the streets have been graded and left rough earth & now with rain they are pretty deep mud…It was most uncomfortable."

Months later, Olmsted again took a pleasure walk to Lake Union and wrote his wife about it. "At 5:15, I started for my stroll [Olmsted often took long exploratory walks at the end of each working day]…I went to the shore of Lake Union and I want to get a little shore park there if it can be afforded. It will have to be away out in the water as it is planned to fill in for a wide avenue and some railroad tracks and then a row of manufacturing and commercial warehouses. There are hills not far to fill with where lots have been left 10 or 20 feet above the streets recently regraded."[10]

In regard to the busy commercial waterfront, the dense business district, and the fast growing Lake Union locality, Olmsted had fewer opportunities to develop park plans for the inner city.

Lake Washington Boulevard and Steep Parks

Designing a boulevard route along Lake Washington took up much of Olmsted's roadway planning time during his May 1903 visitation. He made specific notations about existing pockets of privately owned parkland (such as Madison Park) and recommendations for land acquisitions.

By 1907, John Charles began worrying, in written communiqués with the board, that park funds would dry up for his newly built Lake Washington Boulevard parkway, and for developing additional shoreline property and steep park lands sloping down to Lake Washington. Citing newly donated Frink Park on the hillside above the lake, Olmsted pointed out that private lots intervened between the park and the boulevard running along the shoreline. He urged the sporadic purchase of steep lots to preserve the park-like setting along the lake. (Today—directly along and above Lake Washington—steep city parks donated by the Colman estate, John Frink, and the Mt. Baker Park developers preserve a green backdrop along picturesque portions of the shoreline roadway.)

At the base of the slope on Lake Washington, Olmsted took into account the old city pumping station in his planning. He also prepared separate parkway plans between the then-remote Bailey Peninsula (now Seward Park), north to Washington Park Boulevard, and on to the 1909 AYPE site on the Montlake campus—an almost 5-mile stretch of roadway that needed a constant watch.

After the city rushed to finish boulevards before the 1909 exposition, Olmsted provided, at park board request, his professional opinions on the completed boulevards. The

Olmsted intentionally made views of Mt. Rainier central in a number of Seattle and Tacoma locality commissions. *FSOP*

An early Lake Washington Boulevard postcard, showing the finished roadway after the city's ambitious AYPE preparations hurried construction along. *FSOP*

During his first week in Seattle, Olmsted and park commissioners took a launch from Madison Park pier for scouting the Lake Washington shoreline. Madison Park, north of this scene, was mostly in private ownership when Olmsted arrived to survey waterfront possibilities. His boulevard later skirted the neighborhood entirely. *FSOP*

Olmsted stayed at the Knickerbocker Hotel during his early Seattle parks work in May and early June 1903. Later, in fall 1906, and again in spring 1907, he roomed at the Rainier Club when planning the AYPE grounds. *FSOP*

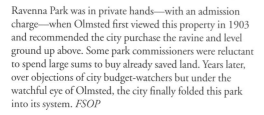

Ravenna Park was in private hands—with an admission charge—when Olmsted first viewed this property in 1903 and recommended the city purchase the ravine and level ground up above. Some park commissioners were reluctant to spend large sums to buy already saved land. Years later, over objections of city budget-watchers but under the watchful eye of Olmsted, the city finally folded this park into its system. *FSOP*

FSOP

Early postcards of Volunteer Park.

Seattle Municipal Archives

Modern-day view of the Volunteer Park conservatory, placed by the Olmsted Brothers (1912). The siting of this glasshouse was intended to screen off Lake View Cemetery just to the north, where Robert Moran and other Olmsted clients are buried today.

A contemplative path through Woodland Park, so admired by Olmsted. *FSOP*

FSOP

Schmitz Park pathway. West Seattle, recently annexed into the city, benefited from resident gardener and park commissioner Ferdinand Schmitz's donations of land (and time) to the city park system. Olmsted visited the Schmitz garden and accompanied him on field trips to scout park locations in the newly-annexed neighborhood after 1907. *Southwest Seattle Historical Society*

Entry to Schmitz Park in West Seattle. *Southwest Seattle Historical Society*

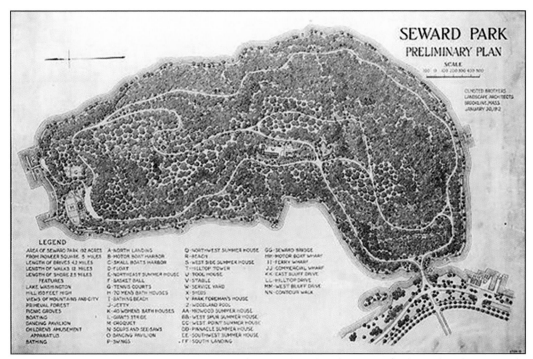

LEGEND

AREA OF SEWARD PARK 192 ACRES	A-NORTH LANDING	O-NORTHWEST SUMMER HOUSE	GG-SEWARD BRIDGE
FROM PIONEER SQUARE, 5 MILES	B-MOTOR BOAT HARBOR	R-BEACH	HH-MOTOR BOAT WHARF
LENGTH OF DRIVES 4.2 MILES	C-SMALL BOATS HARBOR	S-WEST SIDE SUMMER HOUSE	II-FERRY WHARF
LENGTH OF WALKS 12 MILES	D-FLOAT	T-HILLTOP TOWER	JJ-COMMERCIAL WHARF
LENGTH OF SHORE 2.5 MILES	E-NORTHEAST SUMMER HOUSE	U-POOL HOUSE	KK-EAST BLUFF DRIVE
FEATURES	F-BASKET BALL	V-STABLE	LL-HILLTOP DRIVE
LAKE WASHINGTON	G-TENNIS COURTS	W-SERVICE YARD	MM-WEST BLUFF DRIVE
HILL 150 FEET HIGH	H-70 MENS BATH HOUSES	X-SHEDS	NN-CONTOUR WALK
VIEWS OF MOUNTAINS AND CITY	I-BATHING BEACH	Y-PARK FOREMAN'S HOUSE	
PRIMEVAL FOREST	J-JETTY	Z-WOODLAND POOL	
PICNIC GROVES	K-40 WOMENS BATH HOUSES	AA-MIDWOOD SUMMER HOUSE	
BOATING	L-GIANTS STRIDE	BB-WEST SPUR SUMMER HOUSE	
DANCING PAVILION	M-CROQUET	CC-WEST POINT SUMMER HOUSE	
CHILDRENS AMUSEMENT	N-SCUPS AND SEE-SAWS	DD-PINNACLE SUMMER HOUSE	
APPARATUS	O-DANCING PAVILION	EE-SOUTHWEST SUMMER HOUSE	
BATHING	P-SWINGS	FF-SOUTH LANDING	

The Seward Park plan for the Bailey Peninsula was one of the last Olmsted Brothers designs for the Seattle park system. Early on, Olmsted recommended guarding the entire peninsula from residential development, making sure the city purchased the whole property. The park's name commemorates Secretary of State William H. Seward of 1867 Alaska Purchase fame. *Fairsted*

A later view of Lake Washington and Mt. Rainier from the Seward Park locality, surrounded by sketched scenes of Elliott Bay and downtown's new Smith Tower and King Street Station. *FSOP*

Olmsted hiked around the "Y" of Lake Union in 2½ hours and wrote Sophia about the excursion after scouting for potential park sites. Today, the modern Gas Works Park on the north shore and a new South Lake Union Park are popular destinations. *FSOP*

Baseball games here were not necessarily a "hit" with surrounding neighbors, mainly due to noisy crowds and broken windows. Lincoln Playground is renovated today. *FSOP*

FSOP

Early views of Seattle showing the red alder groves, fir trees, and other ever-present natural vegetation that Olmsted preferred above all else. *FSOP*

Path along Lake Washington. *FSOP*

A former officer's residence at Fort Lawton (Discovery Park).

The 500 horses at Fort Lawton outnumbered soldiers when Olmsted arrived to advise officers on future land use. *Peter S. Hockaday*

In 1903, the views from West Point and Fort Lawton impressed Olmsted regarding future park development in this locality.

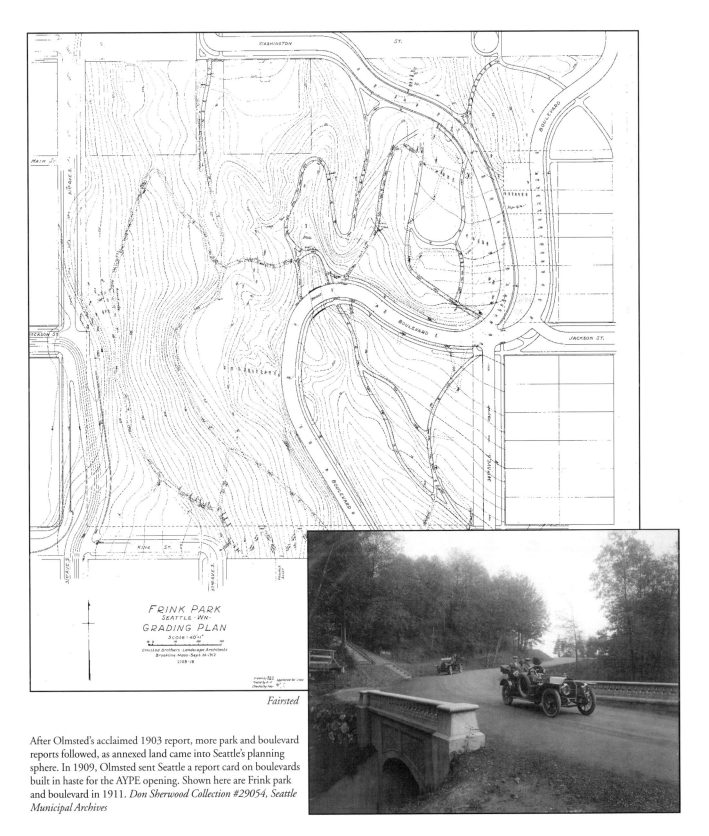

FRINK PARK
SEATTLE · WN ·
GRADING PLAN
Scale: 40'=1"

Olmsted Brothers · Landscape Architects
Brookline · Mass · Sept. 26 · 1912
2708-18

Fairsted

After Olmsted's acclaimed 1903 report, more park and boulevard reports followed, as annexed land came into Seattle's planning sphere. In 1909, Olmsted sent Seattle a report card on boulevards built in haste for the AYPE opening. Shown here are Frink park and boulevard in 1911. *Don Sherwood Collection #29054, Seattle Municipal Archives*

parkway assessment presented a mixed report card for city fathers.

In his 10-page typed report of June 14, 1909, to Park Board President Edward C. Cheasty, Olmsted wrote: "There has been what seems to me a most undesirable omission of a walk paralleling nearly all of these drives." As always, he championed the often forgotten pedestrian during city road-building projects.

"My experience in parks elsewhere leaves me without the slightest doubt that it is essential for the pleasure and convenience both of drivers and of pedestrians that such a walk should be provided everywhere along these drives."

Straight, steep flights of steps also should be avoided, he advised. "Particular pains should be taken to design these on curves or broken lines and to avoid long straight flights of a stiff and formal appearance."

The color and materials used on steps and park bridges ought to blend in better with the landscape, too. "All cement concrete work, whether in walks, steps or retaining walls should be made much darker than the natural color by the introduction of non-fading mineral mortar colors." He added: "The surface of all such concrete work which has already been done is unfortunately light and glaring in color, excessively smooth, and altogether too citified to harmonize with the character of the surroundings."

He then wrote about Seattle's new roadway curves. "I regretted to see that the lines of the drives were in many cases conspicuously stiff and formal, consisting of a succession of simple radial curves and straight lines, as is customary in railroads, instead of gracefully varying curves as is customary in the best parks…It is not too late as yet to complete the construction of the drives with more regard for gracefulness in curvature and grade, and I earnestly hope this will be done. There is altogether too much stiffness, formality and monotonousness in the slopes along the drives both in cut and in fill…It is absolutely essential in park work of a naturalistic character…that the cuts and fills… should be varied even at considerable additional expense."

Olmsted turned to Seattle's own special landscape features. "So much of the local landscape effect along the greater part of these drives is due to natural wild growths that the greatest care should be taken in whatever planting is to be done to harmonize the new planting with the existing growths. I regretted to see that in some instances this has not been done, trees having been planted in regular rows and of uniform sorts, and shrubs of recognized garden varieties having been planted and the surface of the ground having been covered with grass instead of with wild creepers and low bushes."

Lake Washington Boulevard near Seward Park, June 1913. *Don Sherwood Collection #29524, Seattle Municipal Archives*

Essential artificial elements, he conceded, must be introduced sparingly along the parkways. "The drive and its accompanying walk must of course be distinctly artificial in order to be durable and convenient in use, and where there is a parking strip between the drive and walk it may very properly be covered with grass; but there should be trees and shrubs planted irregularly in these strips and they should be of wild sorts except in cases where the surroundings are more completely formal than is usually the case."

John Charles used every power of persuasion with his pen to bring his broad schemes into reality. Mailing his park boulevard report from the Hotel Portland just two weeks after attending the opening AYPE day ceremonies in Seattle, Olmsted set out for a new venture the following day. In keeping with his ever quickening western pace, for the first time he met the new Oregon Agriculture College president and advised him on an open Corvallis campus design.

Fort Lawton

Late in Olmsted's park planning years in Seattle, park board president E.C. Cheasty asked him to prepare a report on the U.S. Army's sprawling Fort Lawton (opened in 1900),

By 1909, with the opening of the AYPE, Olmsted's reputation grew while park commissioners changed again from the park board he first met in 1903. E.C. Cheasty asked Olmsted to report on music concerts and a Fort Lawton design—two of the main agenda items during his presidency. Cheasty also kept Brookline up to date on social news during Olmsted's absences. Note also portraits of Frink and Schmitz, two other park commissioners who impressed John Charles with their generous land donations. *Seattle Municipal Archives*

While congressional delegates debated the need for maintaining a military base here or whether to develop it into a beautiful Puget Sound park, Army officials maintained a wary watch in protecting their operations. In particular, Major Hiram M. Chittenden of the U.S. Army Corps of Engineers (and a Western historian of significant note) advanced an argument for the military's continued presence. On May 20, 1908, writing to the Army adjutant general in Washington, D.C., Chittenden said he had become alarmed during recent sewer negotiations with the city, having "overheard…the reservation would have to be, or ought to be abandoned."

Chittenden's "decided opinion" was for retaining Fort Lawton's "ultimate value" to the U.S. Army. "In the first place, I assume that there must be upon the shores of Puget Sound a military establishment of the first rank and importance; and that not only should such establishment be a large one as regards its military garrison, but that, connected therewith, there should be a depot of military supplies for the use of the various local posts and for shipment to the Philippines, Alaska, Hawaii and other points. I assume also that the nearer such military post is to some great industrial center the more convenient it will be and the less expensive will be the operations of the government connected therewith…Based on the above assumptions, I am of the opinion that the present military reservation of Fort Lawton…satisfies the necessary conditions… better than any other place that it is possible to select. Its relation to the City of Seattle is such as to give it all the advantages of proximity to a great city, while at the same time, it is far enough away from the business center (about 5 miles) so that it is not likely to be inconveniently crowded by the development of the city."

Major Hiram M. Chittenden. Land use at Fort Lawton was of special interest to park board president E.C. Cheasty, who urged Olmsted to issue a report and design for the government-owned property adjacent to Magnolia Bluff. Olmsted consulted Chittenden before filing his fort report. *Washington State Historical Society*

located along the city's western shore. Here, more than 600 bucolic acres of potential park land, with a splendid view of the Olympic Mountains, covered the tip of the peninsula extending west between Shilshole Bay to the north and Elliott Bay on the south.

The city fathers kept close watch on federal priorities here, hoping that this land could be developed into a Seattle park. Cheasty was the prime park board advocate for the acquisition of fort property in 1908–9. Should an outright transfer fail, however, sharing park space with the federal government was high on Cheasty's agenda and acceptable.

Between these formidable contending forces—Chittenden and Cheasty—Olmsted was tossed in the middle. He reported to the Brookline office on November 26, 1909: "Mr. Cheasty…took me to lunch at the Rainier Club. His principal topic was Fort Lawton. He said if the Reservation was to be abandoned…he should be in favor of it…given to the city for a public park."

Cheasty, however, had doubts whether the Army was willing to abandon the fort and suggested a backup plan. "He wants to agitate for a good large appropriation for improvements, especially such as would be of benefit to the public. He wanted to know what I would charge for a report and sketch plan on the subject which could be used to educate and stimulate public opinion to back up Senator [Samuel H.] Piles in his application to the Committee of Congress for an appropriation for further improvement of the reservation…he did not know whether the Park Commission would feel justified in incurring this expense, but, if not, he said he would get friends of the project to subscribe the necessary amount. He said he would be glad to go with me any time to look over the ground."

A week later, after dinner together at the Rainier Club to work out their strategy, both Cheasty and Olmsted called on Major Chittenden at his house. "We had a long conversation on various topics before coming to the Fort Lawton matter," Olmsted reported to his office on December 2.

In their conversation, Olmsted and Chittenden acknowledged their similar East Coast upbringings (Chittenden's upper New York state boyhood, West Point days on the scenic Hudson River, and familiarity with the Olmsted firm's work) along with a shared enthusiasm for Yellowstone National Park. Chittenden had engineered the road system in the park during his tenure there. John Charles had made an elongated journey to Yellowstone in just the previous year (June 1908). The two men also shared a love of photography, which enriched their field and finished reports. Chittenden had by then written several substantial scholarly works, which today remain as essential contributions to the history of the early Western fur trade, Jesuit missionaries, Missouri River steam-boating, and Yellowstone National Park.[11] When posted at St. Louis, and during other Corps of Engineers assignments out west, he had gathered and researched a vast amount of primary historical materials for writing these books.

Park employees were as important to the Olmsted Brothers mission as the park commissioners. Olmsted's man, John Thompson, still served as park superintendent in 1911 but now with more supporting cast members advising the city on park design. Sam Lancaster, the renowned builder of the Columbia River Highway, was a consultant for Seattle parks (as well as the private Highlands residential development), working side by side with Olmsted. More engineers and playground staff would soon come on board to complement, or complicate, planning in Seattle. *Seattle Municipal Archives*

Olmsted informed his office: "Major Chittenden can do no active work, as he has creeping paralysis. He expects to retire in the spring…He said he thought the idea of an appropriation by Congress would meet with much more favor if it was shown to be for…a definite and far-seeing plan." Basically, Chittenden was amendable to a parks design. On this joint military-city arrangement, the three agreed. On military firing ranges and off-limits areas, however, the two city park advocates parted ways with the distinguished Army officer.

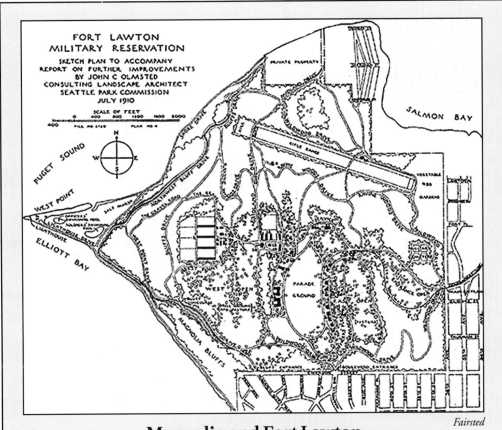

Magnolia and Fort Lawton

Fairsted

Located on the western tip of Seattle's Magnolia neighborhood, Fort Lawton and the Magnolia area together are, in the words of modern Seattle historian Paul Dorpat in *Magnolia Memories and Milestones*, "shaped like a fluffed-up and satisfied jay bird with its beak at West Point, crown feathers in Lawton Wood, powerfully curved back along West Commodore Way [by the ship canal] and its feet sitting in Smith Cove" on bluffs overlooking the downtown skyline.

Chittenden suggested a three-member panel—with Olmsted representing the city, and two career military officers rounding out the review board—as the way forward. "He said it would go easier if the plan were to be prepared by army engineer officers assigned by the Secretary of War through the General in Charge of Quartermaster's Depart.," Olmsted reported to his office.

To Sophia the next night, however, Olmsted confided that he suspected this might be a delaying tactic. "My Ft. Lawton job is postponed. Maj'r Chittenden said last night that it would be better if I work as a member of a

government commission to be appointed by the Sec'y of War to prepare a plan. The Park Board can pay me. The other members being army officers require no extra pay. A Seattle man, Mr. [John H.] McGraw, former [Washington] governor, goes every winter to Washington to watch legislation…and Mr. Cheasty will ask him to urge the matter upon the Secy. of War."

The following spring, with startling news that Cheasty was unexpectedly ousted from the park board and with the park plan on hold, Olmsted pressed the issue. He paid a courtesy call to the sidelined Cheasty on May 20, reviewing again their next move, although obviously Cheasty now was less able to exert influence either in Washington, D.C., Olympia, or Seattle.

The Army's Vancouver headquarters had chosen not to put a civilian on their review board but instead appointed three military overseers. The changing of commanders at Fort Lawton, too, prompted Olmsted to move quickly. Also, when learning that the term of sympathetic Senator Piles in Washington, D.C., ended soon, Olmsted asked the park board to approve a quick report to be produced that summer of 1910 to meet congressional budget deadlines.

Olmsted then embarked on two delicate missions to the fort in May 1910, which were covered in six pages of detailed field notes sent back to the office. He saw sea changes in the attitudes of each passing commander—the current officer in charge, Lt. Col. S.W. Miller, "came some two weeks ago and will go in a month or two to Ft. Wright at Spokane, to be succeeded here by Col. Evans, who will it is expected be reasonably permanent…Major Penrose was in command of Fort Lawton for a good while…Maj. Kutz [of the Corps of Engineers] explained that it was a little unfortunate that this matter could not have been considered by Major Penrose who was in full sympathy with the idea of beautifying this reservation."

Timing—for military and congressional approval—was key to Olmsted's hope to beautify the fort, but finding the right men in the right mood proved difficult. Even Major Chittenden's supportive 1908 report failed to impress the new temporary commander. "He [Lt. Col. Miller]… attacked the plan for rifle ranges…the reservation for being too close to population for target practice and because people overran the reservation and because it was so isolated… apparently [Miller] was disgruntled at having been assigned to such a minor command, and looked forward with pleasure to getting the larger one at Spokane."

Lt. Col. Miller also "particularly and repeatedly" condemned the city "for not giving the reservation an adequate water supply. The main originally adequate is now so drawn upon by people living nearer the city that the pressure is so reduced that he cannot fill the tank nor get water for irrigating the trees and flowers not to mention the lawns and parade grounds."

Olmsted rarely spent an entire day with just one client, particularly with such an unhappy one as Lt. Col. Miller. As if to seal the bad luck during the May 24 visit to Fort

Lawton, rain began falling just after lunch at Miller's residence. When they set out on a field trip, "we took a covered wagon as it was raining quite hard. We drove around the loop again to the corrals where there is stabling for about 500 horses (bound for the Philippines)," Olmsted informed his office.

"We made one tour through the woods…and had to push through dense undergrowth and climb over big logs. But the growths are very pretty," Olmsted wrote his wife a week later. Heavy rain or the bumpy ride failed to dampen Olmsted's enthusiasm for a final acceptable design for the Army.

Due to the large number of horses at Fort Lawton, Olmsted needed to plan for manure piles, proper corrals, and pastures in addition to firing ranges and views of the Olympics. His greatest hope was for a planned extension of the Magnolia Bluff Parkway. This pleasure drive was then on the drawing board at the Seattle park department, thanks to Olmsted's 1903 recommendations.

The military command, however, resisted a through drive. (Today, pathways and paved roads stop just short of the most historic military houses sitting above the bluff. Ironically, this twist of fate probably would have later pleased Olmsted, knowing that a quiet contemplative stroll above the old parade grounds in full view of the Olympic Mountains had been maintained.)

Olmsted also anticipated the intrusion of the automobile, as indicated in his 28-page Fort Lawton report of July 5, 1910. "There should unquestionably be a broad, hard gravel or macadam walk along the outer side of Bluffs Drive [through the fort]…As a general rule, however, the convenience of drivers and automobilists, as well as the safety and enjoyment of pedestrians, require that all drives be accompanied by walks. This has always been a requirement of design in public parks, but now that automobiles have largely superseded carriages for pleasure it has become more urgent because of the greatly increased speed of automobiles."

Largely because of Olmsted's design,[12] Fort Lawton's rolling lawns and pastures, forests, and grand vistas are preserved today. Discovery Park, which now engulfs the oldest parts of the fort, is an early 20th century landscape frozen in time, when traveling was by horse, bicycle, or on foot, and automobiles were few.

Notes

1. Interview with the Stephen P. Gill, grandson of Rick Olmsted, March 18, 2006.
2. Correspondence, Olmsted job #2690, Seattle Park System, 1902–3; Library of Congress.
3. Letter, May 4, 1903.
4. With Saunders encouragement, the Olmsted firm also designed the state capitol grounds in Olympia during the late 1920s. This project overlapped Saunders' term as a state representative from Seattle. In the 1930s, Saunders likewise was instrumental in securing for the Olmsted Brothers the Seattle Arboretum work within Washington Park, which John Charles had advocated three decades earlier.
5. Letter, May 16, 1903.
6. Later, Blaine also assisted a grateful Olmsted in dealing directly with the University of Washington regents in collaborating on city park and university campus plans.
7. Olmsted produced a Park Priority Report in November 1906, an Annexation Report in January 1908, an Engineering Overview in January 1909, a critical Parkway and Boulevard Review in June 1909, a revised Playgrounds Report in October 1910, and other documents.
8. Olmsted's 1903 Portland parks report, on the other hand, was much further delayed, not being submitted until December 1903. However, the Portland report presented more extensive description of the landscape principles and objectives professionally adhered to by John Charles, and thus it received greater national and international acclaim.
9. Correspondence, Olmsted job #2690, folder 2, Seattle Park System, 1904; Library of Congress.
10. Letter, June 3, 1910.
11. Noted historical works by Hiram M. Chittenden include *The American Fur Trade of the Far West* (1902), *History of Early Steamboat Navigation on the Missouri River* (1903), *Life, Letters, and Travels of Father Pierre-Jean De Smet, S.J., 1801–1873* (1905), and *The Yellowstone National Park* (1895).
12. Olmsted job #2720, Fort Lawton; Library of Congress.

Rose Lodge summer resort, south of Alki Point in West Seattle. *Fairsted*

5

Seattle Private Clients

I saw Mr. Moran today. He is the gentleman on Orcas Island I am to visit as soon as I can get there. He is enthusiastic about it…I wish he had called me in before he located and started his house. He has an extinct volcano…on his land.—April 4, 1907

John Charles' return in 1906 signaled the beginning of his private client work in Seattle, which continued throughout the rest of the decade and into the 1910s. During Olmsted's first visit in 1903, park planning had so completely consumed his days that little time was left to socialize with Seattle's men of private means and influence. This changed with Olmsted's stay at the Rainier Club in October and November 1906, when he established close relations with the people then shaping the fast-growing modern city.

Seattle's elite preferred scenic ridgeline or hilltop locations for their new homes, as in this view overlooking Elliott Bay. This Olmsted photo dates from May 1903 during the Queen Anne Hill Parkway planning. *Don Sherwood Collection #30029, Seattle Municipal Archives*

Olmsted for advice, even though the narrow planting strip in front of their building would soon be swallowed by the city's massive downtown re-grading project.

For their new homes, prominent citizens of the Seattle area sought prized hilltop lots. Some wanted to tame the local natural vegetation on their new properties. Olmsted tried repeatedly to convince clients to retain as much of the original vegetation as possible and at least some of the existing tall trees that he so admired.

In addition to monetary and professional gains, his immersion in private client demands had another special value for the future. Olmsted quickly learned western ways and wishes. These were important to know not only in private work, but also before setting out to design a university campus sitting on a hillside location and more than a half-dozen lakeside parks.

Within weeks of his return to Seattle, Olmsted was summoned by private clients in quick succession and with little advanced notice. These included several clients on "Volunteer Hill," two commanding the best sites at each end of higher Queen Anne Hill, and a Washington Park area hilltop owner. The Seattle Library trustees also asked

Olmsted soon learned that his suggested deep verandas would cast unwanted shade. Also, light, brightness, and openness mattered more to a number of home owners than a canopy of towering trees. The locations for grass tennis courts superceded mountain views for several clients.

In regard to these raw, undeveloped landscapes, clients that autumn asked Olmsted's advice on house styles, orientation, and—almost as an afterthought—planting particulars. Naturally occurring madrona trees (*Arbutus menziesii*) were common in Seattle's wooded environments at the time. Madrona, however, frequently stood in the way of construction projects on hilltop lots, yet clients questioned Olmsted about how best to preserve or move these beautiful, chocolate-barked trees with thick shiny leaves and red berries.

W.G. Jones owned a fine hilltop location—near today's UW president's house—above Madison Park.[1] Olmsted responded to the client's request about "the matter of saving the existing madronas" in his final report. "I know that it is a common belief that they cannot be transplanted successfully. I am told by the superintendent of parks that this is not strictly true; if they are removed with a sufficient ball of earth and very few of the roots are cut off, they will move in damp weather with comparatively little danger. The trouble no doubt usually is that people will not go to the necessary trouble and expense of doing the work properly."

The Rainier Club has long been one of the leading gathering places for Seattle's influential men (and today, for women as well). Olmsted stayed here in October and November 1906, and again for two months in the spring of 1907, while planning the Alaska-Yukon-Pacific Exposition grounds. *Rainier Club*

Jones formerly served as a minister in Jamaica Plain, Massachusetts, and knew of the Olmsteds' park work in the East. Like so many in Seattle hailing from the East or Midwest, he needed professional advice regarding the native vegetation. An unusual type of western tree, the madrona's peeling bark and graceful spreading branches especially caught the eye of newcomers. There were few comparable native trees in the forests back east.

This was reflected in work for another client, too. "He…wants to save all Madrona trees," Olmsted wrote his office after a November 10, 1906, visit to the C.H. Black estate, which covered an entire block on the southwest crest of Queen Anne Hill. "He also wants to save an irregular clump of small fir trees in N.E. corner of lot…[which] serve to partially screen the big school." (The school building, since converted to condominiums, today is still screened from the Black house and gardens, although fewer madronas remain on the site.)

Rainier Club

"I am now established at this club…it is designed more like a suburban club than like a city club although it is close to the business quarter…I should think the members got a good deal for their money…the city is evidently growing in wealth," Olmsted wrote Sophia on October 15, 1906.

An old acquaintance from Olmsted's 1903 park planning visit arranged for this accommodation. C.J. Smith—a banking executive, previous park commissioner, and now head of the buildings and grounds committee for the upcoming Seattle exposition—put Olmsted up at the Rainier Club instead of in a downtown hotel. Olmsted had stayed at the Knickerbocker Hotel in 1903, before the handsome new Rainier Club had opened on its new site at Fourth and Marion in 1904 (this was the third and final location for the club, which had been established in 1888).

Olmsted was traveling alone, rather than with office draftsman Percy Jones as in 1903. He now had more time to absorb and reflect upon his surroundings, much of it gleaned from the opinions and through the eyes of Seattle's economic elite. For two months, he immersed himself in the very heart of Seattle's business and social community.

Olmsted's long views of Seattle would emerge during his Rainier Club stay as he interacted with members engaged in business and the legal profession. Mr. C.J. Smith—the Rainier Club president in 1901 and later a garden client of the Olmsted firm—sponsored Olmsted's accommodation from October through Thanksgiving in 1906, and for another two months in the spring of 1907. "I've never stopped so long in one place before," Olmsted wrote his wife from the Rainier Club on Thanksgiving Day, 1906.

C.J. Smith, followed by other club members, took Olmsted by horse carriage and automobile to far-flung timbered properties in and around Seattle. His published—and unpublished—reports and plans for these private properties reveal his garden principles, which often enough departed from his public park advice. Olmsted's appreciation of Northwest native vegetation sometimes conflicted with views held by clients—this remained a constant thread throughout the private reports.

Congenial Rainier Club members would stop by Olmsted's dinner table or approach during smoking breaks to ask favors on the spot. Some even contacted the renowned landscape architect as he was entering the clubhouse after a day's work.

Sam Hill "stopped me as I came into the club this evening," Olmsted wrote his wife on November 4. He "wants me to advise as to the grouping of three houses [of clients] on adjoining plots. So there is another job to attend to here!" Olmsted knew the ebullient and influential Sam Hill—a lawyer, railroad executive, and businessman—from previous Stockbridge, Massachusetts, work that the Olmsted firm performed for the Hill family.

A week and a half earlier, Hill had invited John Charles to luncheon at the club and proved, in Olmsted's view, "a kind host as well as a sprightly and voluminous talker." After lunch, "I met some other leading citizens who are some of the Public Library Trustees," Olmsted added.[2] "There was little for me to advise upon there being a strip in front of the [Carnegie library] building 31 feet wide and at the ends only 17½ feet wide, but there were walks and steps to advise upon & walls & difficulties as to grade."

The pleasant but increasing interruptions to exposition planning work continued, resulting in Olmsted finally postponing his date to return east. He wrote to Sophia on November 13: "I telegraphed our office today that I expected to be here a week longer. Clearly I cannot get through all the reports by Sunday as I had hoped to. I am too much interrupted. In fact I doubt if I can get off by Tuesday of next week."

Details about the Rainier Club often filled his letters at the end of long working days, giving his wife a clear picture of his base out west, and of the Seattle club's social scene at the turn of the century: "The fire which was smouldering for hours has started up and makes a big heat. They use 4 ft. fir logs, I don't know but 5 ft. They are big anyway and burn from end of end all at once. The fireplace in the smoking room is very much larger. I think I told you. It is like a room and one can walk in even a 6'4" man, without bending & look up the chimney and see the sky. I wondered such a big fireplace doesn't smoke but it doesn't seem to—I do not use that room though, but spend my evenings in this library which is usually very quiet with perhaps 3 or 4 men reading or writing…There is a separate entrance and a separate dining room for the ladies, who are seldom seen in the rest of the club—only in case of a dinner or lunch party with men & Sunday evenings when ladies accompanied by men are permitted to dine in the large dining room."[3]

He was one of a handful of people staying in the overnight rooms upstairs. "The regular patronage of the club is for business men at lunch time and occasional dinner parties of men or club meetings or receptions. There are about 10 or 15 staying here like myself & usually a dozen or so in the card room evenings. Not much drinking," Olmsted added.

Kirtland Cutter and other Architects

On a later trip to Seattle—on a bitter cold day in March 1907—John Charles had a pleasant talk with Kirtland Kelsey Cutter, the architect who designed the Rainier Club. Although Olmsted rarely found time to initiate social engagements after hours, he would write his wife when a friendship, so far from home, added to his traveling enjoyment. "During the afternoon I met [Kirtland] Cutter & sat in the big chimney nook by the wood fire and got thoroughly warm…I had a pleasant talk with Cutter and was very glad of it as I did not feel like writing or even reading."

Though from Spokane, Kirtland Cutter remained a non-resident member of the club. He had designed the Rainier Club to resemble an English manor home, which Olmsted could readily agree was a country architectural model in the city.

In reporting on Cutter's fireside friendship, Olmsted revealed his keen interest regarding architects and their involvement with western clients. With the upcoming Seattle exposition, architects appeared in town in increasing numbers for design work. These boom years for the AYPE planning—between 1906 and 1909—produced mutually satisfactory results for Olmsted and the young architects. (After the close of the exposition in the autumn of 1909, though, Cutter largely retreated to his Spokane base.)

With British-born architect Charles H. Bebb, Olmsted worked in conjunction on Rainier Club client C.H. Black's Queen Anne property. With architect Charles Saunders, he helped design a state hospital site in Sedro Woolley. And with John Galen Howard, campus architect at the University of California, Berkeley, he would jointly design the Alaska-Yukon-Pacific Exposition at the University of Washington site. These associations grew stronger as time went by.

Appreciating a common civility with design professionals, Olmsted frequently attended Seattle theater productions with these companions. "It is pleasant to be associated with them," Olmsted remarked to Sophia on May 21, 1907. AYPE architect John Galen Howard and his associate, in particular, were Olmsted's welcomed partners during these entertainment outings.

At the time, however, few architects belonged to the Rainier Club; they had joined the University Club instead, or lunched at the Rathskeller where Olmsted encountered them socially. Kirtland Cutter was rather an exception among the architects, going to the Rainier Club in Seattle when "away" from his Spokane base.

Architects played a significant role in bringing landscape commissions to Olmsted's drawing table, and indeed, in Seattle, Portland, and Spokane, they proved to be among his closest and friendliest companions.

Bankers, Lawyers, and Business Executives

In addition to clients owning new in-town home properties, others possessing lots on remote Bainbridge Island and north of Seattle at The Highlands development stopped by Olmsted's table and initiated landscape discussions. At the time, only a "little clubhouse" and a working farm with a few "cottages" stood on the older Bainbridge country club property. The steep and rough Highlands residential development, on the other hand, had no houses or improvements when Olmsted's advice and planning were sought in the spring of 1907.

Former Seattle Mayor Robert Moran (center) and family pose with furniture made for his new home. He "retired" to Orcas Island after his Seattle boat-building business produced a fortune. He asked for advice on his new island mansion and grounds, now part of the Rosario Resort. Olmsted advised his client to keep the natural vegetation in place. *MOHAI*

Rainier Club members soon asked Olmsted to visit island properties regarding landscape possibilities, with clients on Bainbridge and Orcas being two examples. This preserved "little clubhouse" on Restoration Point was where John Charles attended a picnic with local country-club members, who sought advice for their properties overlooking Puget Sound and Seattle to the east. *Peter S. Hockaday*

This pattern of contacts would hold true into 1911, as word spread when Olmsted had arrived again. Consequently, his workload increased, meeting the requests of prominent Seattleites engaged in the timber industry, salmon packing, real estate, railroading, and other businesses, plus the legal profession.

Robert Moran, a Rainier Club member, shipbuilder, and former Seattle mayor, pestered Olmsted to make a field trip to Orcas Island in the spring of 1907. Moran, then retiring from business and political obligations, was seeking advice regarding his grand property located on a picturesque cove in the San Juan Islands. Olmsted visited the magnificent site several times during his working years in the Northwest.[4]

Seattle hardware executive and club member C.H. Black had asked for just one site visit—which soon multiplied—to his new house atop west Queen Anne Hill. C.H. Black and Olmsted's association lingered through revisions for retaining wall designs, and plans for manure heaps, tennis courts, and a laundry yard. (In later years when no longer making trips to the Northwest, Olmsted enlisted architect Charles Bebb—then in partnership with Louis Mendel—to help with such client questions.)

Alaska-Yukon-Pacific Exposition executives, too, called on Olmsted in his rare off-hours to help with their private projects. It was William Sheffield, the fair's secretary, who asked for advice regarding his South Beach home near the "country club" on south Bainbridge Island. Olmsted's overnight trip there was an early excursion away from his Seattle work.

Olmsted's prestige especially peaked during the AYPE planning years, which helped launch his career ever farther afield. British Columbia clients asked for—and received—several visits from John Charles, resulting in thorough revisions for The Uplands subdivision in Oak Bay, northeast of Victoria. Spokane clients called on Olmsted, too, mostly in tandem with architect Kirtland Cutter's projects, or with the help of local businessman Aubrey White's boosterism. Olmsted stopped for these Inland Northwest clients when traveling to or from Seattle and Portland.

All client requests were handled with equal respect and concern, no matter how large or small the task. His reports—either sent to the

Landscaping and stone wall bounding the lawn of the Leary property on Volunteer Hill as it appears today, overlooking a fine view.

Brookline office or delivered to clients—often generated a dozen or more typed pages of detailed advice along with sketches.

"Volunteer Hill" Clients

The best hilltop locations captured the interest of Seattle's affluent, who were moving out of downtown neighborhoods and building grand homes on these new lots. Consequently, Olmsted's designs frequently had to take into account adjoining deep ravines and drop-offs on these hill-brow hugging properties.

Several eager Capitol Hill clients urged Olmsted to pause in his city park-making work and give timely advice on their new lots clinging to west-facing bluffs beneath Volunteer Park. The new "Volunteer Hill" neighborhood, as Olmsted referred to it, was the in-town choice of those wanting magnificent views of Lake Union and Queen Anne Hill, with the Olympic Mountains beyond.

Sam Hill, the recently-arrived son-in-law of Great Northern Railway magnate J.J. Hill of St. Paul, insisted that Olmsted look at his extensive property, while two established Seattle residents—Mrs. John Leary (the former Eliza Ferry), and her brother, lawyer P.P. Ferry—shared a more cramped family compound to the north of Hill's bluff top site. Banker C.J. Smith, chairman of the AYPE building and grounds committee, also later asked the Olmsted firm for a detailed garden plan at his new home on Harvard Avenue, southwest of Hill's. (Each house remains today, survivors of a century of neighborhood changes but still reflecting Olmsted's design efforts.)

Eliza Leary and her brother needed advice on their individual house sites, situated side by side on the hillside. Already in the planning and construction stage when Olmsted was called upon in the fall of 1906, the property was narrow but deep, leaving both houses close

Samuel Hill

Handsome in midlife, and very rich, Sam Hill had settled out west after leaving St. Paul in 1901. John Charles twice worked on Sam Hill commissions—in 1905 for a summer home in the leafy Berkshires of Massachusetts, and the following year, 1906, at Hill's new "Volunteer Hill" mansion site with a view of Lake Union and the Olympics. These projects tested Olmsted's understanding of both eastern and western requirements in landscape design—and challenged his patience with this colorful and confident client. To his associates, Hill bragged of easy access to the famous landscape architect.

Olmsted's personal correspondence and office reports reveal an effusive overachiever in Sam Hill—"a sprightly and a voluminous talker" John Charles had written after a Rainier Club luncheon. Anxious to know those in power out west and becoming involved in numerous entrepreneurial ventures, Sam Hill is best remembered today for building the scene-stealing Maryhill mansion (today, the Maryhill Museum of Art), standing high above the Columbia River in the starkly beautiful country east of The Dalles.

Only by coincidence did Hill have the same last name as his more famous father-in-law, Great North-

Sam Hill, as he appeared in his later years.
Maryhill Museum

ern mogul James J. Hill. At St. Paul in 1888, young Samuel had married J.J. Hill's eldest daughter, "Mamie" (Mary Frances). The marriage, however, was on a thin thread when Samuel brought his beautiful wife out west in 1901. By spring 1903—a month before Olmsted arrived for Seattle park work—Mamie departed for St. Paul and points east, never to return.

Hill poured attention on western business matters and needed an impressive residence to go with his status. In 1902, he had purchased a precipitous hillside lot on the west slope of Capitol Hill and convinced prominent friends to buy nearby. Just a few blocks west of new Volunteer Park, the hilltop mansion remains today at 814 E. Highland Drive, a reminder of the extravagance allowed by railroad and other entrepreneurial wealth a century ago.

In 1905, when asking Olmsted to design his wife's summer property in the rolling hills around Stockbridge, Massachusetts, Hill boasted of being one of the men summoning John Charles to Seattle two years earlier. "I have not met you but have known of you by reputation for many years and was among those who urged that you be invited to Seattle," Sam Hill began his September 4, 1905, letter to Brookline.

Establishing his credentials (but yet to mention his more famous father-in-law), Hill outlined the exacting requirements for an expected Olmsted visit to the Berkshires. "My wife has a farm here [in Stockbridge] and before her final plans are carried into effect I am anxious you be consulted." A flurry of telegrams and two Olmsted site visits that autumn generated much paperwork and expensive advice.

In Seattle in 1906, Sam Hill buttonholed John Charles during and after meals at the Rainier Club, convincing the visiting landscape architect to inspect the newly fashionable district just below Volunteer Park. While Olmsted tried in vain to discourage taking on private commissions during his first weeks of AYPE work, Sam Hill and his Leary and Ferry neighbors prevailed.

Modern photo of the mansion Sam Hill eventually built on "Volunteer Hill."

together and needing a design providing for a better auto turnaround and privacy between them. The narrow curving drive down the slope between the brother and sister's front doors caused Olmsted to comment that even buggies had trouble negotiating the twists and turns.

A coal storage out back and a barn in the ravine below likewise received detailed comment in Olmsted's report to the pair. Also, a sloping lawn behind Mrs. Leary's house, which would require a pull-up operation to retrieve the lawnmower after each downhill cut, drew Olmsted's criticism. Instead, he advised leaving a little lawn on a level plot nearer the house, and planting the steep slope in vines.[5]

Sam Hill's project around the corner had even more extensive ravine and bluff considerations to take into account. Calling in several experts and summoning both Olmsted and architect Kirtland Cutter, Sam Hill led this group of professionals during a long inspection of the property on the afternoon of November 5, 1906. "The sunset will be great feature from these lots," Olmsted reported to his office.

In the four page report to Brookline, he concluded that Hill "was very quick to grasp plans and ideas and very prompt in his decisions but willing to change if good reason appeared."[6]

Hill eventually changed his architect for the project, settling on the Hornblower and Marshall firm of Washington, D.C., instead of the Northwest favorite, Kirtland Cutter. Perhaps this was suggested by Hill's wife, who was not enamored with the Pacific Northwest and was then living in the nation's capitol. Olmsted, however, would find many other opportunities to collaborate with Cutter, who designed the nearby C.J. Smith home, just to the southwest of Hill's property.

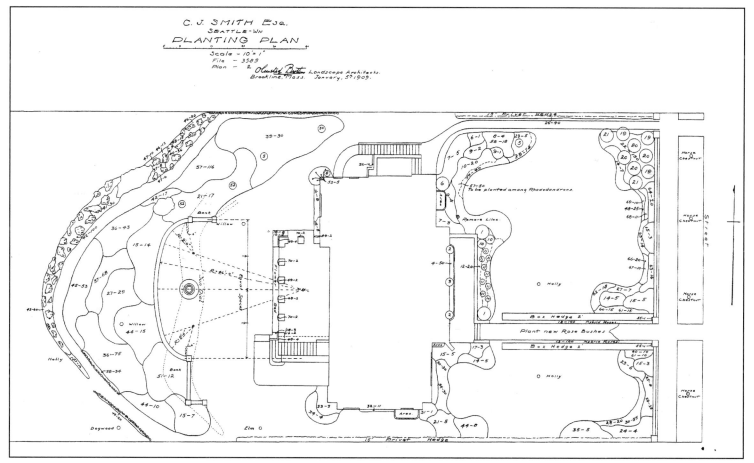

Olmsted prepared this garden plan for C.J. Smith's home adjacent to Sam Hill's property along the western ridge of "Volunteer Hill." The house and garden are protected today in the Harvard-Belmont Historic District. *Fairsted*

Down the tree-lined street to the south, the Horace C. Henry estate also borrowed Olmsted themes, likely gleaned from verbal advice coming either directly or indirectly from Olmsted himself. Henry served as the Rainier Club president on several occasions and was an avid art collector (today, a UW art gallery is named in his honor). He also served on the AYPE executive board.

Henry likely crossed paths with Olmsted often enough—at the Rainier Club and elsewhere—to be influenced by the landscape architect's advice.[7] Today, most agree that the Henry garden just south of the other "Volunteer Hill" properties exhibit Olmsted's influences. (The present-day owner of the Henry garden recently donated it to Seattle parks.)

Olmsted's old associate, C.J. Smith, then serving as head of the AYPE buildings and grounds committee, asked Olmsted to plan a small town garden surrounding

C.J. Smith. *Curtis Collection, Rainier Club*

the Seattle banker's imposing mock-Tudor house designed by Kirtland Cutter's firm. Sited on the west edge of Capitol Hill, the home sat very near a slope, making back-lot development difficult. The Olmsted Brothers final plan advised projecting above the slope and holding the hillside with a permanent retaining wall.

Relatively little space was available for front garden finery as well, between the main entry and the street. But the formal Olmsted plan effectively fit the site. (Today, the Olmsted planting plan can be studied to reveal what was fashionable and recommended for Northwest town gardens in the early 20th century.)

Correspondence is scant between Olmsted and Smith. As the AYPE site committee chairman, C.J. Smith's days were extremely busy before the exposition opening in 1909 and he had less time to fuss over house and garden details as Hill had in 1906. The results, however, were handsome and just as visible today as for the other restored properties farther north on old "Volunteer Hill."

Olmsted and Smith often crossed paths and frequently conversed in Seattle. Consequently, the voluminous client correspondence normal for many other jobs is largely absent regarding this particular assignment. In March 1909, Smith simply wrote John Charles a quick thank-you on Washington Trust Company stationery: "I am very much pleased with it."[8]

Golden Gardens, Northwest of Downtown

A plan for the Golden Gardens development, located near the Puget Sound shoreline south of The Highlands, also received Olmsted's attention. However, the final result—though he dealt with only one client here, instead of many individual ones as at The Highlands—pleased him less when it was completed later in 1907.[9]

With too many alterations for Olmsted's taste, he felt the finished work never matched the appeal of the final Highlands' community plan. After visiting the shoreline bluff with Harry W. Treat, the residential development's principal owner, and his engineer, Olmsted confided to Sophia on December 19, 1907: "I enjoyed the trip to Golden Gardens yesterday—I mean the place itself—the trip is rather tedious. Mr. Cox [the engineer] has followed

View of C.J. Smith home from front walkway.

some of the ideas of my plan of last Spring, has changed others and omitted some…Mr. Cox was very liberal in according even too much of the credit to my advice and plan considering how much he has changed it and how much he has devised himself."

The overall Golden Gardens site, in Olmsted's view, was as splendid as The Highlands properties farther north up the shore, but future lot divisions would bury Olmsted's landscape work, he predicted. He consoled himself with the beauty of the place, but hoped that one "country place" might materialize on the bluff, rather than many little lots side by side.

"But anyway the large trees and evergreen undergrowth and the commanding views of the Sound and Olympic Mtns. (when visible) are very admirable. It all makes our Deer Isle scenery so tame and picayune. The bluff proper is much higher and far more handsomely wooded than the [Highlands] Country Club. But because of the woods the view is not so open. They are crazy to cut every piece of land up into lots."

Sheffield's Humble Island Retreat

AYPE secretary William Sheffield asked Olmsted to make an overnight trip to Sheffield's summer house on "some island, I have forgotten the name," John Charles wrote in Seattle on November 13, 1906. "I think it is hardly worthwhile but he asked me several times so I hardly liked to refuse any more."

The November 14 outing west across Elliott Bay to the southern end of Bainbridge Island produced the same thorough results as for other Seattle clients to follow. Olmsted also wrote with enthusiasm about the boat trip to the island. He compared the Puget Sound vessel he rode on with a familiar Penobscot Bay steamer often taken by the Olmsteds to their Deer Isle, Maine, summer home.

Writing so Sophia might easily imagine the boat trip that day, he said: "The steamer was of the type of the *Katherine* but not so commodious. She seemed longer but narrower and not so high out of water. She is owned & run by her captain & mate and engineer & has been for 18 years. She only makes one trip a day. We landed at a small wharf…It took 50 minutes to get there so it is nearly as far as from Rockland [Maine] to North Haven [Island, in Penobscot Bay]."

Sheffield's property was rather modest. Obviously, Olmsted's recommendations for it would be of a rather small scale. Since he had only previously visited the Northwest during springtime, however, this field trip gave him a sense of November weather and conditions away from the city. Of course, the island scenery appeared so similar to the shorelines back in Maine.

Mr. Sheffield "had intended that we should sleep in his tent which has a floor & frame & is 18'x 24' but he found it rather damp, so we slept in the house of a friend which had been placed at his disposal & where we dined. There we had the furnace going & also an open wood fire so it was very hot for me with my thick woolen underclothing. I had on rubbers & rubber leggings & we walked the length of the little settlement and back before dark.

"I slept well but…woke fairly early as the servants made considerable noise after they got up…It was so rainy and misty that I could see but little across the water until this morning when it cleared off considerably. The steamer was late this morning so I did not get to the office till 9:30 a.m."[10]

Within a short time of arriving back in Seattle, Olmsted "tramped about" one "wooded ridge next [to] Lake Washington" on the Mt. Baker Park Subdivision property with a city engineer, telling his wife that night: "I am a little tired with the walk & climbing over logs but not very much so." Similar excursions for clients in soggy conditions and scrambles in the woods would fill many of his days in the years to come.

Sheffield's on South Beach eventually changed hands, but other Bainbridge Island clients would call on Olmsted, too. As early as the following spring, some original country club families at Restoration Point invited him over.[11]

Other Small Jobs

Though primary demands in Seattle, Portland, Victoria, Spokane, Walla Walla, and Kennewick would occupy all but a few of Olmsted's working days in the Northwest, Olmsted occasionally accepted smaller jobs, but sometimes regretted it later. On the corner of Madison at 38th, Olmsted found himself planning grounds-work and a simple retaining wall at the neo-classical Samuel Hyde house, built in 1909–10. Hyde's architect, Charles Bebb, had convinced Olmsted to get involved.[12]

Rose Lodge, south of Alki Point in West Seattle. *Southwest Seattle Historical Society*

"The house is very good and comfortable and all that but…I am very sorry I had to take up that Hyde job," Olmsted wrote to his wife on June 7, 1910. Packed with existing commitments, he added: "I oughtn't to be bothered with such a…small job. Mr. Dawson could do it perfectly well."

One reward of that "small job," however, was working with (or rather listening to) architect Charles Bebb. With his amusing stories of younger days at Adler and Sullivan in Chicago, Bebb was "good company" Olmsted wrote.

After the Seattle fair had closed in late 1909, another minor job along the beach south of the Alki Point Lighthouse had caught Olmsted's eye and imagination. But as soon as he accepted B.W. Baker's small cottage commission in West Seattle—perhaps for the novelty and seeming simplicity of it—he soon struggled with a solution to the "Rose Lodge—Woodland and Seaside Resort" design.[13]

"I can't think of much to advise him about," Olmsted wrote on December 6. "He has a story and a half house and a separate dining room and kitchen and forty three tents of different sizes which he rents in summer to boarders at an average rate of $3.30 a week, on a tract of seven acres on the south shore of Alki Point, which is the west point of West Seattle annexed about 2 years ago to Seattle."

Olmsted added: "A car line terminates at his place so it is convenient for businessmen to live there with families. About half the place is low sandy land and about a third is wooded with fir trees, and runs up to twenty feet or so in height. He is fond of nature and likes his place but I can't think of anything much he can do…he claims that the 'season' is getting longer every year and that they could get more rent with the bungalow."

"I spent a good part of this morning studying a scheme for placing the tents at Mr. Baker's Rose Lodge. I put them in the shape of a W…Each now is 8' back of the one in front. The front ones are 12 x 14, next 10 x 12 & the rest 8 x 10. You see by this trick they got a wider view (except the 3 back ones) than they would in two straight rows 8' apart in each row. Ever your loving husband."[14]

Thornewood, Outside of Tacoma

Some of the vast Thornewood estate—a far grander commission—endures to this day on American Lake, south of Tacoma. Based on visits to the property in June 1908 and January 1909, Olmsted developed an extensive design for the broad grounds of the new Tudor-gothic Thornewood home, a Kirtland Cutter design built in 1908–12. At Thornewood, Olmsted's massive garden arrangements and Cutter's plan for the large stoned faced mansion with more than 50 rooms would come off as companion projects.[15]

During his first visit to discuss plans with prominent banker Chester Thorne and his wife Anna, John Charles provided a snapshot of both the American Lake area's scenery and the grand dreams for the locality. From Tacoma, where the family then currently lived, Mr. Thorne "took me out in his large auto with Mrs. Thorne and their neighbor Mrs. Rice, who is thinking of becoming also their neighbor out in the country [near American Lake]. The first half of the way was over streets and heavy traffic roads and not very good although dry. The last half was on the Prairie roads which are excellent as the soil is dry and gravelly & not enough heavy teaming to hurt them.

"While it is called prairie it is not bare as the real prairie but has enough trees to make a beautiful park like effect— fir & spruce usually in groves or irregular patches of wood and oak…Some are large but they seem to perish mostly from drought I suppose—the smaller ones are usually in bunches.

"Mt. Tacoma (Rainier) showed up grandly high. We passed a few country places and then came to the Country Club (really only golf is played) through which we passed to Mr. Thorne's proposed purchase about 1/3 mile S.W. of the W. end of the club land—both on American Lake some 3 miles long and shores wooded almost uninterruptedly.

The prairie comes within 300' or 400' of the lake though. The soil is dry and gravelly and full of cobblestones.

"The lake is nice and the proximity of the club makes it desirable for families [to move here] as they can see so many friends. I lunched & dined with them at the club."[16]

During his second visit—early in 1909—Olmsted spent a memorable weekend with the Thornes at their residence in Tacoma—a rarity for John Charles, who seldom accepted such invitations from clients. (He always preferred to stay at private clubs or business-oriented hotels, where stenographers and pianolas were in ready supply.) Due to his long talks with the Thornes, automobile rides out to American Lake, and dinner parties at the Tacoma residence, this was a rare instance when Olmsted did not find time to write Sophia before retiring in the evening. The work and social schedule prevented it.

Once settled in Portland after the long, busy weekend with the Thorne's, however, Olmsted would relay the news from Tacoma and American Lake. "I was disappointed at skipping two days in my writing to you," he began in his 4-page letter. "I seemed to be occupied with them [the Thornes] so closely that there was no good time to write. I arrived about ten Friday evening [in Tacoma]. Mrs. Thorne was at a show. After she returned there was lots of talking until others left and then she talked plans &c with me till after twelve. Naturally I had no desire to get up early Saturday morning."[17]

Olmsted's automobile ride on Saturday with the Thornes, however, provided country views valuable for planning the property's vast gardens. Continuing with the letter to Sophia: "After perhaps a mile of paved street the road was very muddy, with ruts & holes and plank sidewalk crossings for 4 or 5 miles. About then it gets up on the prairie as they call it where the soil is so gravelly that the roads are fairly good especially where there is very little traffic. We did not get back until just before dinner. No time for writing. Sunday was the same except that Mr. Thorne went out with me as far as the golf grounds & Mrs. Thorne came out later in the automobile. I had time before dinner to go and hunt up Jack Olmsted [a relative]."

Over dinner at the Thornes, stories were exchanged with the guests. "Mr. Macomber [the Thorne's gardener] returned with us and is a fluent talker. Later a gentleman from Seattle called and then…three [of the] gentlemen conversed assiduously about golf and so loudly no one else

could talk so Mrs. Thorne, Mr. Macomber, Jack [Olmsted] & I had to sit still and listen…Mr. Macomber lives in a log cabin which he built for $90…Macomber seems to enjoy the job very well. Mr. Thorne told as a joke how Macomber wore a bowie knife and pistol on his belt for some months after he arrived—until he was jollied out of it. It tended to show, you see, that his ideas of the West were founded on novels and magazine stories and Wild West shows."

In regard to the Thornewood project, which involved a considerable work effort, Olmsted noted: "A great amount of 'cleaning up' some road grading and stoning and considerable collecting of wild trees and shrubs and the work to date has cost some $10,000." He added: "It is a picturesque place on American Lake with the Country Club only a mile away."

Mrs. Thorne continued to call on Olmsted as the commissioned work progressed. On one occasion, only 10 days after the AYPE had opened, John Charles interrupted his busy schedule: "Mrs. Thorne wanted me so I went. She told me of some shrubs and flowers & trees she wanted. She is observing them about town [Tacoma and environs] and deciding which please her. The rhododendrons that Macomber planted all lived but most of the wild plants & shrubs he collected died. It is possible some of them might have been saved if they had been watered & cut down but they haven't got the water pipes nor pumps in yet. I dined at the club in Tacoma with them & came here by 'The Flyer,' as I like it better than the electric train. She must go twenty miles an hour. I had to go inside it was so cool although Mr. Thorne said this was as hot a day as they ever have…I have had an easy day of it. I couldn't see that I accomplished anything worthwhile." Thus Olmsted wrote from his Seattle hotel room after returning at 10 o'clock that night.

Seattle Parks Individual Clients

Seattle park commissioners Ferdinand Schmitz and J.M. Frink also called on Olmsted for private work either on, or adjacent to, the parks named in their honor. Frink's personal property above the park land he donated occupied Olmsted associates after 1911.[18]

Cowen Park displayed an Olmsted-designed arbor over its wood palisade entrance, after its donor requested a special "Cowen Park" announcement in wooden letters.

Both Ferdinand Schmitz and Charles Cowen considered the entryways to the parks as important; they were quite willing to contribute personally for Olmsted-designed entrances that otherwise would have been too costly for the park budget.

Olmsted admired Schmitz's private grounds and appreciated his advocacy for West Seattle's abundance of park land. Because of this, he indulged Schmitz's every whim (including Schmitz's gift of tropical birds to the city, for which a special display facility in Woodland Park would be required). Schmitz was one of Olmsted's last Seattle clients, before John Charles took ill in 1912 and cut back on his western work.

Charles H. Black House and Gardens

One of John Charles' first private clients in Seattle was Rainier Club member C.H. Black, whose new home on the southwest crest of Queen Anne Hill dominated its surroundings (as it still does today). The property occupied an entire city block and commanded a fine view of Puget Sound. With the panorama and splendid location, however, came extensive landscaping challenges for Olmsted to resolve.[19]

C.H. Black home as it appears today on the crest of Queen Anne Hill. The gazebo suggested by Olmsted remains intact and the garden open to viewers passing by. *Peter S. Hockaday*

Accustomed to the most demanding clients, Olmsted set out with Black on November 10, 1906, on what would be the first of several site visits between 1906 and 1909 for the Seattle Hardware Company executive. In the process, Olmsted would learn more about the success rate in saving native madrona trees (low indeed), and about slopes and seepage, soft falling precipitation in winter and little rain in summer,

Preliminary plan and typed notes sent to Brookline—

Mr. C.H. Black.
Notes by John C. Olmsted—10th November, 1906.

Conservatory attached to stable. Planting plan and roads and walls, etc., $150. and expenses. Log cabin for girls, 7-year-old twins. One boy Hotchkiss School in Pennsylvania. Summer house for view not rustic. Hot water heater for stable. Manure pit. Wants place for compost. Will use small shrubs for economy, not too many evergreens, flowering shrubs. Wants shrubs a few feet in front of basement windows. Boag, florist, was head foreman at U.S. Navy yard at Bremerton, will execute planting plan. 4 cherries, 1 plum, 3 pears, 1 Am. Chestnut.

Olmsted's sketch at bottom represents a suggested gazebo for the southeast corner of the property. *Library of Congress*

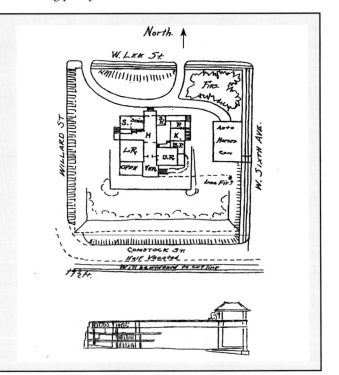

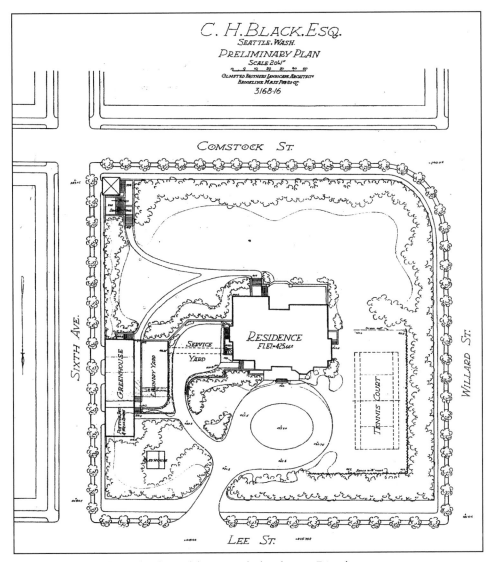

C. H. BLACK. ESQ.
SEATTLE. WASH.
PRELIMINARY PLAN
SCALE 20=1"

OLMSTED BROTHERS LANDSCAPE ARCHITECTS
BROOKLINE MASS PEB 20-07
3168·16

COMSTOCK ST.

SIXTH AVE.

RESIDENCE
FL.EL=425.66±

SERVICE YARD

GREENHOUSE

LAUNDRY YARD

TENNIS COURT

WILLARD ST.

LEE ST.

The final C.H. Black plan, with redesigned driveway and other changes. *Fairsted*

Olmsted fully realized just how much work this would require. In his more precise 4-page field notes sent to the Brookline office—typical for many of Olmsted's complicated private commissions—he detailed the job in its entirety. He provided the draftsmen and associates with fully sufficient information to proceed even without his presence. The overall design was Olmsted's first order of business. Now with several months of Northwest experience under his belt, plus having made an initial quick study of landscape conditions in Seattle, he worked fast in his decision-making.

A full circular drive with two street cuts requested by Mr. Black (and as initially sketched by Olmsted) would result in the taking of a group of fir trees in the property's northwest corner. Olmsted regretted this. Instead, he suggested one curb cut and drive entry, with a circular turn well within the grounds. Black accepted the alteration, which the property retains today.

In one exchange of ideas during their November survey, the client and landscape architect combined concepts for the sloping southeast corner. Olmsted wrote his office saying that Mr. Black "would like stairs down at S.E. corner. I suggested a gazebo or summerhouse on corner and he liked the idea."

He deftly avoided some clients' ideas—and there were many that Olmsted had to handle with extraordinary patience. "He wants to plant sidewalk with elms which he says are fine in Detroit where he comes from but I told him they would destroy his fine view and 'topping' would spoil their special beauty," Olmsted had advised on the spot.

and a range of other things affecting soil conditions and long-range garden planning in the Pacific Northwest.

In the evening following the first visit to the site, he wrote to Sophia and to the office back in Brookline recording his overall impressions. "It is a great deal more extensive than Corey Hill and I should think higher," Olmsted wrote to his wife before dinner that evening. He referenced Corey Hill, an eastern feature known to Sophia, so she could put Black's hilltop property into perspective. "He has got to spend a lot for retaining walls though, because his land is so high above the street."

"He wants a tennis court which he thought would be between the house and the lone fir tree [this was not to be; the tennis court ended up on the opposite side of the property]. He wants 4 cherries, 1 plum, 3 pears and 1 Am.[erican] chestnut, no apples because of pests. He wants shrubs a few feet in front of cellar windows so as to disguise the stilted effect without shutting off light. Does not care for many evergreens but would like showy flowering shrubs massed or in borders. Is anxious to have a compost heap and suggested middle of young fir grove. I said it would breed flies and he said he would keep it covered with 4" layer of earth."

All the requests were carefully recorded in the field notes, either for attention in the near future, or for consideration in later revised plans. "I asked if he would have a playhouse for his girls (7-year-old twins) and he agreed."

Construction of the 33-room house, designed by architect Charles Bebb, was in process when Olmsted visited the property. The home sat just south of center on the lot, and Black wanted to keep it in open view from the sidewalk and street. "He wants his lawns steep enough so the house will show fully to the base from neighboring streets. He does not want to be secluded by hedges or plantations or walls or parapets and wants everyone to enjoy views over the place and to watch him and his family using the grounds." The Olmsted firm adroitly fulfilled these requests.

The Highlands

For well-to-do residents in Seattle's core area, who no longer wished to reside on limited lots facing the city's wooden-planked streets or experience the nearby and never ending re-grading projects (necessary as it was), there were possibilities for spacious residences and estates in land developments farther afield. The growing prosperity of these people, too, would allow them to build ever finer and more expansive homes, away from the hurried bustle of downtown.

The Highlands, one of the most prestigious of the new residential areas, was being developed four miles north of Green Lake, next to Puget Sound. The design plan for the exclusive neighborhood—in its entirety for 60 lot owners—came off the Olmsted Brothers drafting board after John Charles secured these client connections in 1907.

His first site visit in the spring of 1907, and subsequent meetings with all the lot owners, brought to the surface rewards and setbacks in working with so many land owners all at once. While individual Olmsted Brothers garden designs materialized there over the next quarter century, the initial raw landscape and joint ownership problems were clearly outlined in John Charles' early letters home to his wife.

On April 21, 1907, Olmsted wrote Sophia about his visit to The Highlands (he called it the "new country club" at the time). "The country club people came about 9 and

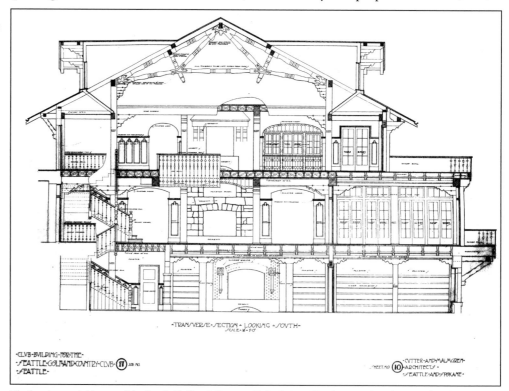

The handsome clubhouse of the Seattle Golf and Country Club, designed by Cutter and Malmgren of Spokane, was an enticement for families to move to The Highlands north of town. *Museum of Arts & Culture, Spokane*

we went in an automobile out to the property. Everything as I supposed is very crude. The large trees were cut off long ago. What are left the lumbermen did not care for at that time. We should call even those large trees…Then young fir trees and alder trees sprang up and now generally cover the land. But this place will easily be made beautiful."

(Only a week earlier, Olmsted had visited another enclave on Bainbridge Island's Restoration Point, calling it the "country club." Consequently, he referred to the development north of Seattle as the "new" country club, until The Highlands name took hold.)

The property, he noted, "is about 450' high and slopes down to the Sound." Continuing with client news: "We went down to the farmhouse and left the auto and walked down to the R.R. [railroad] & shore and N. along the shore to a beach. When we got back some ladies & gentlemen had come. A number of men walked with us N. along top of bluff & back. Then more ladies and gentlemen had arrived and there was a nice picnic."

Whenever the weather turned pleasant or the mountains came "out," Olmsted often relayed this news to Sophia. "It was a mild sunny day & the snow clad Olympic Mtns made a very fine view, so all enjoyed it."

"We broke up at 2 and started back at 2:17—We came along at a great rate in spite of humps and hollows in the road. It was a Franklin & in spite of a tremendous grade getting up from the farm house 12 horse power seemed to be plenty strong enough. Ever your loving husband."

On May 9, Olmsted reported that he "worked all day on the Country Club," making "very good progress with the plan as a preliminary study…I shall have to go on the ground and test it. Then there will prove to be need of lots of changes—no doubt. Chiefly, I guess in getting the outlooks of the houses in the right direction and the lot lines adjusted."

Five days later, Olmsted walked the grounds alone. "Except for pushing my way through undergrowth some of it dead from fires and often horridly dense, I had a rather enjoyable day of it." He noted that "the new owners will gradually clean up the dead logs & rubbish and open up the thickets enough to get views and in time it will become a very beautiful place."

The high bluff, he noted, deflected the "sound of trains" rumbling along the shoreline, "so the noise is not serious," adding, however, that "the smoke is likely to prove annoy-

ing but it is possible oil may be used for fuel before many years" (a prediction for diesel locomotives that proved true).

As for the country club name, "so called" as Olmsted wrote that night, "it is really only a cottage community or residence park proposition—not a real country club like that in Brookline."

With his other Northwest work, particularly the AYPE, bearing down on him, and having promised to return east in late June for a family gathering in Maine, Olmsted's letters took on an urgent tone. Developing The Highlands design for anxious owners, his meetings with University of Washington trustees regarding the exposition, and the pending Golden Gardens plan all added to a quickened pace.

"I went out by the 8 o'clock [electric] car to the new Country Club and returned so as to get here at 7:20 p.m. which made a rather long days work," he noted on May 27. "My aim has been after making a plan on paper, to visit each of 60 house sites and adjust them to the ground. That I could easily do in open land with a good map & plenty of stakes to pace from. But here all the conditions except weather are against me.

"I doubt if I have identified half the house sites and I don't see how I can find time to do any more before I leave," Olmsted complained to his wife, a week before the landowners called a meeting to draw for lots.

"It was extremely troublesome getting about today— the brake ferns have grown up so as to conceal the logs & stumps and holes & I tumbled about and was afraid of breaking a leg. Besides it was very slow and hot work climbing over and under logs, pushing through dead branches and slipping & stumbling. Some stumps have burned out leaving deep holes into which I sometimes stepped and fell…Many slopes are like the roof of a house for steepness & run up 200 or 300 feet. The surveyors must have had a hard time too. Now it is 10:30 & I shall be glad to be in bed. Ever your loving husband."

Gathering at Judge Burke's

A raucous meeting regarding The Highlands properties ensued on Friday, May 31, 1907, in Judge Thomas Burke's office. Burke, a most distinguished Seattle legal pioneer and entrepreneur, was one of the prospective lot owners. He also was a founding member and past president of the Rainier Club. (His home, then in town, was filled with

Indian artifacts, which today form a nucleus of the Burke Museum of Natural History and Culture on the University of Washington campus.)

On the night of May 31, however, John Charles' hopes for punctuality and unanimity were dashed when the landowners gathered to see his preliminary plan in Judge Burke's office. "I got there promptly at 8 and no one was there but a clerk. They came in gradually," Olmsted wrote his wife two days later. "I explained [the] plan some but could not do so to advantage as everyone talked loud & all together and fired questions at me and argued with each other."

"However, they seemed pleased with my plan," but he also noted that the roadway required alteration across cut banks.

The landowners were in a hurry to choose lots, which was made clear to Olmsted. It was "urgent to get the plan quickly, so I had to promise to get it done in 2 weeks. It bothers me to be so rushed."

The owners "couldn't even wait for my revision of the plan but told the engineer to go on and stake the roads & house sites and lot lines of this plan so they could begin choosing house sites even if some had to be changed later."

The Highlands' complicated plat rather confounded Olmsted and future lot owners as well, as the new purchasers hastily drew lots before Olmsted could fully advise them.

With a week's work in Victoria scheduled to begin in two days, and with more Portland and Spokane projects already arranged, Olmsted squeezed in two more Highlands planning days when back in Seattle two weeks later between his Victoria and Portland commitments. He phoned one Highlands owner, who then called "several others," and "7 or 8 gentlemen of the Country Club came to look over my plan and discuss it and what to do next. They made no further suggestions so I can call the plan done for the present."[20]

These early "Country Club" clients—and including H.W. Treat, on the AYPE buildings and grounds committee—were Rainier Club members. They would remain loyal clients to Olmsted and his younger associate, Fred Dawson, for many years to come.

Judge Thomas Burke whose office hosted, in Olmsted's opinion, an unruly meeting of Highlands landowners. *Curtis Collection, Rainier Club*

Garden for the "Father of Seattle Parks"

Having designed the large Highlands enclave—still one of the most handsome residential plans near the Seattle shoreline—Olmsted then advised individual owners, one at a time, on site and garden design. The Highlands, along with The Uplands neighborhood near Victoria, proved Olmsted's mastery of his trade. Convincing clients to follow plans accommodating the contours of the land and to retain more natural landscapes overall were his greatest accomplishments in neighborhood planning out west.

E.F. Blaine, the "Father of the Seattle Park System," eventually became a private Highlands client, too, in 1909. In April 1907, Olmsted became reacquainted with Blaine at the Rainier Club. "I was greeted by Mr. E.F. Blaine while I was at dinner," Olmsted wrote Sophia. "He was friendly and glad to see me. He was formerly the President of the Board of Park Commissioners here. That was when I was here three years ago."

Olmsted also reminisced positively about Blaine's past park presidency, as compared to the current president, who he called a "barber shop and Turkish bath keeper" leader. "They seem to have adopted a policy of rotation in office, which seems to me to be a bad policy. The best man should be president. Now the president is…a good honest man in his way but not as broad-minded and as experienced in park matters as Mr. Blaine."

No longer president but still a member of the park board, Blaine had supplied Olmsted with more city parks work before he called upon the landscape architect to design Blaine's own lot at The Highlands in November 1909. At this time, Olmsted was surprised to learn that members of the country club—or particularly their wives—were reluctant to pull up stakes from their city homes and set up year-round or even summer housekeeping on the then-remote northwestern shore above Seattle.

"I had a talk with Mr. E.F. Blaine as to his lot at the Country Club. It seems strange that so few are building there," Olmsted wrote Sophia on November 26, 1909. At

Bridge in The Highlands.

recalled his visit to the soggy site shortly thereafter: "Mr. Blaine called for me at 8:50. I think it took us nearly 45 minutes to go out…He had a covered automobile which was good as it rained almost steadily all day—at times a real rain but mostly drizzle and drip from the trees. He had apparently not arranged with Mr. Ainsworth, who is to share the lot with him, to be there, or come there, but Mr. Ainsworth lunched with us at the clubhouse. It looks as though he was 'roping in' Mr. Ainsworth. The latter evidently was in no hurry to do anything on the lot."

(However, E.E. Ainsworth's cannery business partner, Arthur G. Dunn, was most willing to have a garden designed by Olmsted Brothers a decade later, on his property outside The Highlands gate.[21] Today, Dunn Garden is open for tours.)

Olmsted also "looked at the Hughes, Edwards, Smith, Clark[e], C.D. Stimson, Fred Stimson and Hogue [Hoge] lots" and mentioned that C.D. Stimson's son met his party on the site of Stimson's "little bungalow."[22]

John Charles' field notes sent to the Olmsted Brothers office—identified by individual client and job number— provide a more intricate description of each site visit than the broad sweep of daily activities described in letters to Sophia. A typical example of this exacting detail can be seen in a report regarding Blaine's property at The Highlands.

"It is lot 38 at The Highlands. He sketched outlines of lot & described it & sketched site of his house and that of Mr. Ainsworth & the joint garage. It is the lot below, S.W. of the little reservoir at the second bend of the north road down the hill. He said they had done a little clearing & had graded a path down the ravine but that I could change that if I liked. He is satisfied with his site but Mr. Ainsworth is undecided between a site immediately S. of his & one on the spur of the S.W. side of the ravine."

After actually touring Blaine's property in The Highlands, Olmsted recorded in his field notes:

"Mr. Blaine showed me his boundary stones. We walked up the trail he has made up the ravine. It is decidedly winding but I did not make any criticism of it. There are some other trails in the upper part of the lot and perhaps made by surveyors. He has cleared brush from a space for his own house from a space for a garage and from two spaces for alternative sites for Mr. Ainsworth. The steep bank below the north road has had a series of logs about 8 feet

a Rainier Club luncheon that day, "I expressed this idea to Mr. [E.C.] Cheasty [the park board president] & he said it was because they had houses in the city & did not care for country life as it is too lonesome and the Country Club too far and the roads not good enough."

Recalling his own trolley trips there in years past— "twice I remember missing the connection at Ballard & had a long wait"—he agreed that the site stood far from city luxuries. "They agree that it is a fine place when they do get there and lots of them enjoy going to the club itself & to play golf there, but don't care to live there even in summer," Olmsted relayed from Cheasty. "Many do not like what they call 'pioneering.' I guess the men would nearly all like to live there but their wives do not want to I guess."

Blaine, owning a handsome lakeside house nearer town, also was reluctant to "pioneer" on his own, so he hoped to lure salmon packer E.E. Ainsworth (of the Ainsworth and Dunn cannery) to share a lot at The Highlands. Olmsted

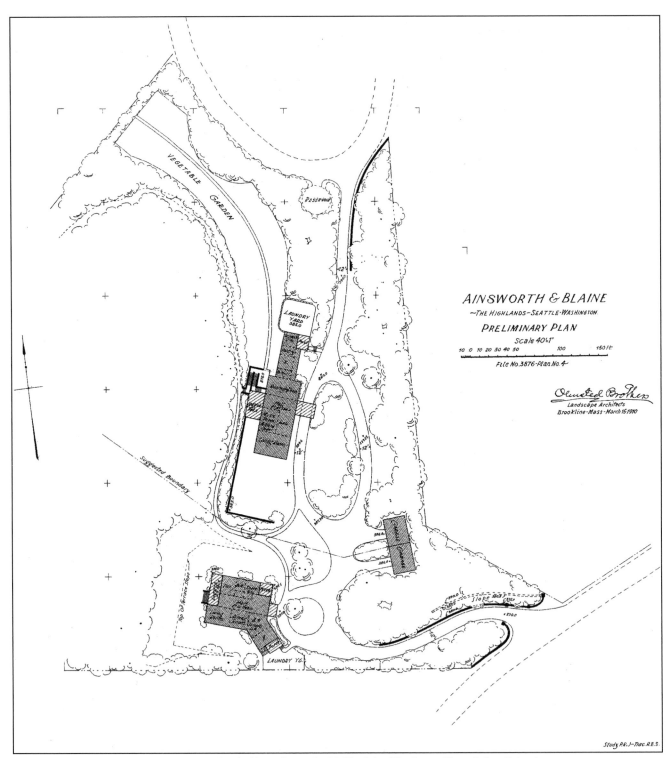

Elbert Blaine tried to entice partner E.E. Ainsworth to build together on this Highlands lot following an Olmsted plan. *Fairsted*

or 10 feet apart running directly up the bank which is bare coarse sand and gravel…He says he intends to cover bank and logs with ivy. The steep natural slope west of this log slope he says he will cover with a berry bush garden. The steep slope south of it he plans to use as a vegetable garden. I suggested that as it was about 2 on 1, it would have to be terraced to be usable. He said he should not do that as it had been demonstrated to be a mistake for such light sandy soil as the outer side of the terrace got too dry in summer. It was all right for clay, he said. I advised him to at least form narrow contour terraces by means of logs for paths or trails to get at the vegetable beds comfortably. He said his house would be a long narrow one with a hall and two wings standing at a slight angle with it so as to follow the contour and conform to the ravine. The house would stand nearly at the level of the reservoir and north road but rather lower. His drive will enter above the reservoir. He advocates covering the reservoir with a light iron frame and covering that with 1/4" to 1/2" galvanized steel mesh to keep out leaves. I suggested a concrete cover but he said it was not necessary to keep the water dark as algae did not grow in it. It is ugly and ought to be hidden by shrubs & vines…I preferred… better view of ravine and Olympic Mtns. We looked at the extension of lot to the road on S. I asked if owner of next lot N.E. (Henry) would be likely to permit slope on his land. He thought there would be no trouble about that. He will have his kitchen wing at N. end of house. Ainsworth he said would have his at S. end. I thought but did not say that it might better be at E. end. He said Mr. Ainsworth had an idea that he would not want the drive to come directly up to his front door, but would prefer a walk from drive to garage. He said Mr. Ainsworth wants his main lawn on side of house toward view. The spur lends itself to that idea so I made no objection. What little lawn he has he says will be on E. side of house. He will keep W. side quite wild. He could terrace out along contour S. of house & have lawn there if he wants to go to the expense, thus connecting his house and lawn with Mr. Ainsworth's. His idea is that the lower wild part of the place will always be held jointly & while upper part will be owned separately he proposed no fence or screening plantation between & they can use the drive in common. He says he will have a dance hall in his basement. He spoke of a living room & billiard room & will have hall running through. They do not expect to build for 2 or 3 years maybe. In fact nearly all the owners of

lots are holding off from building as they do not want two houses & at present prefer to live in the city. He expects to keep the tall fir trees by topping them."[23]

For the present, Blaine kept "roping in" Ainsworth as a partner to jointly build on lot 38 at The Highlands.

Judge Burke's Highlands Property

In January 1908, Olmsted had visited Thomas Burke's two lots at The Highlands and wrote to the judge's secretary on the 25th. "It is evident that we can give advice of value to Judge Burke in connection with his place. The next step now is to get a good detailed topographical map."

He advised which engineer to hire: "I recommend, as Judge Burke has authorized a detailed map to be made, that you employ Mr. L. Hussey, a young engineer who had done…what appears to be a very satisfactory topographical map of Mr. George Donworth's place last week for our use."

Olmsted wrote enthusiastically about the outing to his wife. "I have had an enjoyable break in my routine of indoor work. I went out, by carriage, to the Country Club today with Mr. Dawson and Mr. [Samuel] Lancaster [a renowned roadway engineer, and consultant to the city and part-time to The Highlands]. We started at 7:40 & left about 2. It was a fine day—one of the finest we have had and we enjoyed the mountain vistas very much. Even Rainier was in full view & Mt. Baker too. The woods were beautiful especially on a property that has been added to the club since I made my plan. Coming back we visited the Exposition Grounds and the mountain views there were very fine."

Olmsted had free reign on Judge Burke's property while his client traveled in Europe. However, he found that development of the property raised troublesome concerns with neighbors. Olmsted's report and preliminary plan sent to Burke on April 15, 1908, left little doubt that developing driveways to this property on a bluff was problematic.

"The boundaries of your lot are such that at present the only possible place for the approach drive to enter is at the extreme northeast corner. As this will be a decidedly roundabout way for you to get to and from the Golf Club house and to a less degree to go to and from the city, we strongly urge you to make an arrangement with Mr. M.F. Backus, owning the property next south of yours, or if you cannot

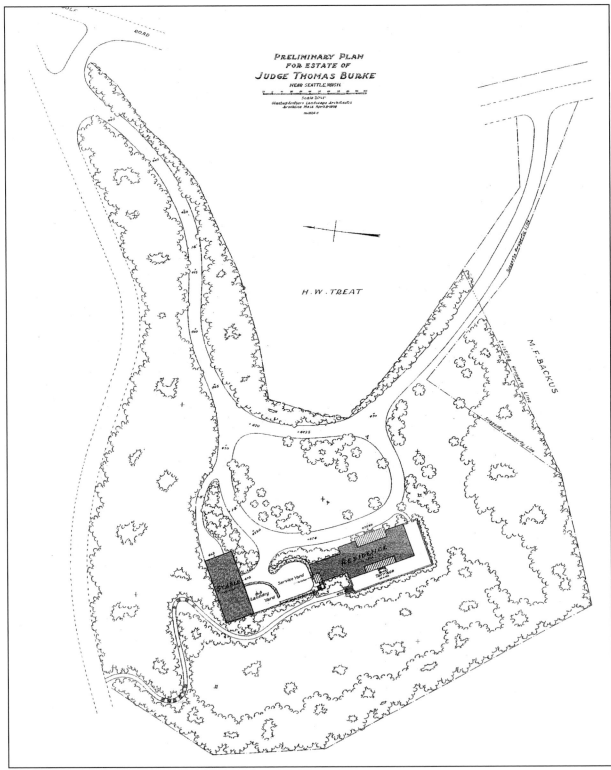

deal with him, with Mr. H.W. Treat, owning the property east of yours, by which you can secure a right-of-way for an entrance drive from the Club road east of the places of Mr. Backus and Mr. Treat. We have shown on the plan such an entrance drive in an irregular piece of land to be purchased if possible from Mr. Backus."

Olmsted, being confident of his capabilities and national prominence as a landscape architect, did not mince words when explaining a conflict between neighbors. "Mr. Treat has been somewhat exercised as to the effect on his view of the erection of buildings on your property. We therefore call your attention to the fact that by suitable clearing of trees his best view (that of the Olympic Mountains) would be on a line passing south of your residence. You will see that in sketching the foliage on our plan we have left the little valley south of your home nearly free of trees, partly for this purpose."

Also, the club road as configured "ought to be considerably changed owing to the violent up and down contour of the ground" Olmsted pointed out. Realizing Burke was held in high esteem by his neighbors, Olmsted then asked him to "take an interest in the [road layout] matter and use your influence to have the location of the road improved."

As in new neighborhoods everywhere, the first lot owners had the pick of the place—and, in the Seattle area, also the best mountain views. Judge Burke, in the second wave of purchasers at The Highlands, needed to pay heed to blocked views and the impact of irregular roads leading in and out of his property. John Charles found himself mediating between Highlands neighbors in these stages of the design plans.[24] In the end, Burke did not build.

Stimson Family

For the Olmsted Brothers, responding to the needs of the expanding families of clients became routine over the years. The Stimson family in The Highlands, beginning with Rainier Club members Charles D. and Fred S., provides a case study. John Charles' work with the Stimsons began in 1908 and continued for years.[25] Then, after John Charles' death in 1920, the Olmsted firm would be called upon again for more Stimson family work.

Olmsted's first visit to the Charles D. Stimson property came after a casual encounter at the Rainier Club in May 1908, a month after sorting out difficulties on the Judge

Burke estate. "I had another little job offer today—may go out to the place Wednesday. It is at the Country Club," Olmsted wrote his wife on the 25th. (At the time, the C.D. Stimsons' also were owners of a fine home on First Hill in the city. Today, the Stimson-Green Mansion is a designated Seattle Landmark.)

Seeing the country club area in springtime, rather than during winter, gave Olmsted a better idea of his clients' ground clearing projects. "I have been out all day at the Country Club for Mr. Clark[e] and Mr. Stimson. It was delightful being in the woods although dull and cloudy with several sprinkles, some enough to require my umbrella to be up."

Olmsted sometimes wrote critically of his clients' views, but these comments usually only appeared in letters sent home. Writing in this regard on May 28, he told Sophia: "It seems especially queer that they cannot appreciate the beautiful evergreen undergrowth they have here—the Oregon grape, the Sallal and the evergreen huckleberry."

On the other hand, Olmsted thought the property of prominent lumberman and real estate developer C.D. Stimson was handsome, with more sunlight allowed in to give undergrowth a chance to flourish. With huckleberry and madrona, "Mr. Stimson has acres in very fair condition as the trees are sparse so the bushes have had plenty of sun."

The wives then presented their garden ideas, not always endorsed by Olmsted. "Later Mrs. Stimson…came out and I told…what I had advised Mr. Stimson, but it appeared she wanted a little formal garden."

Olmsted, nevertheless, was fully open to these clients with another of his criticisms. "They want an old New England farmhouse bungalow 2 stories high, with plenty of verandas and a big second story sleeping porch. Now a New England farmhouse never had verandas & never a

Charles D. Stimson started his extended family's long association with the Olmsted firm. *Curtis Collection, Rainier Club*

"View to entrance of property"

"Cottage."

"Tea house on the edge of the cliff."

Olmsted's own photo album maintained in Brookline showed the development of Stimson family property throughout the 1910s. *Fairsted*

second story sleeping porch & a bungalow is strictly one storied & with much veranda. I told them to have what they want but not to call it by the wrong names."

Stimson family members—Charles D., Fred S., C.D.'s son Thomas, and then later, the married children—would contact the Olmsted firm for more work through the decades. Warm client relationships helped keep clients in the fold once they were secured by the prestigious Olmsted office. John Charles' extensive and intricate field notes eventually were followed with the briefer and less detailed notes of his younger associate, Fred Dawson.

Early on, John Charles had realized that clients only occasionally ignored his recommendations and opinions. No small part of this was due to his formal and forthright manner in dealing with people. However, Northwest clients also often asked Olmsted to scale back on expensive advice for large and small works alike.

Notes

1. Olmsted job #3206, W.G. Jones; Library of Congress.
2. Letter, October 23, 1906.
3. Letter, November 12, 1906.
4. Olmsted job #3273, Robert Moran, Orcas Island; Library of Congress.
5. Olmsted job #3207, Mrs. John Leary; Library of Congress.
6. Olmsted job #3205, Samuel Hill; Library of Congress. For references regarding Sam Hill's career and the Great Northern Railway, see Enoch A. Bryan, *Orient Meets Occident: The Advent of the Railways to the Pacific Northwest* (1936), Michael P. Malone, *James J. Hill: Empire Builder of the Northwest* (1996), and John E. Tuhy, *Sam Hill: The Prince of Castle Nowhere* (Maryhill Museum of Art, 1991).
7. There is no Olmsted-designated Horace C. Henry job file in the Library of Congress holdings.
8. Olmsted job #3589, C.J. Smith; Library of Congress.
9. Olmsted job #3348, Golden Gardens; Library of Congress.
10. Letter, November 15, 1906.
11. Olmsted jobs #3208, W.M. Sheffield, and #8207, Bainbridge Island Country Club; Library of Congress.
12. Olmsted job #4070, Samuel Hyde; Library of Congress.
13. Olmsted job #3871, B.W. Baker; Library of Congress.
14. Letters, December 6 and 7, 1909. The Southwest Seattle Historical Society at the Log House Museum, 3003 61st Ave. SW, holds an early postcard collection depicting the Rose Lodge resort during its prime period of use.
15. Olmsted job #3495, Chester Thorne; Library of Congress.
16. Letter, June 8, 1908.
17. Letter, February 1, 1909.
18. Olmsted job #4083, J.M. Frink; Library of Congress.
19. Olmsted job #3168, C.H. Black; Library of Congress.
20. Letter, June 13, 1907.
21. Olmsted job #6171, Arthur G. Dunn; Library of Congress.
22. Letter, November 28, 1909.
23. Olmsted job #3876, Ainsworth and Baines; Library of Congress.
24. Olmsted jobs #8243, Highlands, and #3324, Thomas Burke/Country Club; Library of Congress.
25. Olmsted jobs #3491, C.D. Stimson, and #3590, F.S. Stimson; Library of Congress.

6

University Campus &
Alaska-Yukon-Pacific Exposition

I walked over the part [of the UW campus that] the exposition is to occupy. The growth on the ground is so dense…the land has never been cleaned up…still some groves and scattering original fir trees left…[look like] very biggest we ever had in Maine. They are tall and straight & would make fine masts.—October 20, 1906

Thomas Kane served as UW president, 1902–13. He showed Olmsted around campus in 1903 and remained loyal to the Brookline firm through John Charles' last visit in 1911. A Latin professor before elevation to the presidency, Kane's inside knowledge of campus capers and plans helped Olmsted sort priorities for university officials, faculty, and students. *Tyee*

The spring 1903 visit in Seattle included only park work at the outset, but park board president E.F. Blaine urged Olmsted to meet with Alden J. Blethen, president of the University of Washington Regents, in late May. Blaine and Olmsted wanted assurance that the new university campus (1895) on a hill above Union Bay would fit in with parks planning during this crucial period of growth.[1]

Along with park commissioner Blaine, Alden Blethen (the *Seattle Times'* editor-in-chief) would become a key supporter throughout these planning years. Into the next decade, John Charles sent sketches, wrote reports, planned portions of the campus, and offered advice, as the university expanded at a rate inconceivable today.

From working on the campus's early oval design (in place upon his arrival), through extensive re-grading of the undeveloped central portion of the campus for the 1909 Alaska-Yukon-Pacific Exposition, to a final plan requested by President Thomas Kane two years later, Olmsted's asso-

ciation with the regents and faculty remained cordial and politically important throughout the decade.[2]

During the first tentative visit on May 21, 1903, Olmsted and Blaine presented the Seattle parks case for joint planning at the campus site. A full campus plan by Olmsted was postponed at the time, but he was asked on the spot to prepare a preliminary report about the state of the current campus.

The report to the regents in early June was mixed.[3] "The size of this oval campus and the [wide] spacing of the [five primary] buildings is uncommonly liberal for a university," while the diagonal orientation of the oval design, against the natural fall of the land, "proves to be decidedly embarrassing."[4]

Three months later, with timely advice in a letter from trustee Blethen, Olmsted was on his way to designing a full campus plan, after the financial arrangements—always a sticking point out west—were put to rest. Blethen, in his August 28 correspondence,[5] noted, "it is fair for me to tell you that probably a majority of the Board do not feel like paying $2,000 out of the $10,000 appropriated—

Seattle Times editor Alden J. Blethen provided Olmsted with crucial confidential advice to get the UW plan presented to the trustees. *Seattle Times* reporting also gave blessing and support for Olmsted projects. *Curtis Collection, Rainier Club*

because they feel that they will be criticized by the next legislature for expending 20 per cent of the entire [state] appropriation in the mere plans of landscape gardening advice. Whether right or wrong, it is difficult to overcome such a sentiment."

In short order, Olmsted sent a telegram from Boston agreeing to a lesser fee that Blethen strongly suggested in the personal letter. Consequently, the regents hired John Charles to provide more precise suggestions regarding the arts and science quadrangles and the placement of boathouses, gymnasiums, dormitories, and faculty and fraternity houses on and off campus, as well as recommendations for future campus expansion.

Olmsted's resulting January 1905 sketch, with its accompanying 41-page report, provided a blueprint for university planners. He also reminded the regents of the Olmsted firm's involvement with numerous other campuses across the country. "We will call attention to the great importance of insisting in the design of all buildings upon a reasonable degree of harmony of design…As is well known, there are two radically different architectural styles in general use by the universities of this country; namely, the…Old Colonial, and the Gothic, as exemplified by some of the recent buildings of Princeton, Pennsylvania, Bryn Mawr and Washington University of St. Louis…Both styles have their admirers and there is much to be said in favor of each. However…it is of vastly more importance to adopt one of them and stick to it than it is to discuss the question of which is best."

Olmsted continued this theme in concluding the report. "The failure on the part of college and university authorities to recognize the importance of sticking to one style has been almost universal, and has led to what can be fairly called a hideous jumble of buildings in the case of most of our leading universities. It is possible to understand how intelligent and cultivated men such as college presidents… may fail to grasp the importance of sticking to one style,

Cheerleader from the 1904 campus yearbook, indicating the school spirit just taking shape on the Montlake campus. The early *Tyee* yearbooks tell the emerging story of Campus Days, the AYPE, new professors, and construction on the hill. *Tyee*

but it is difficult to comprehend how architects, who make a life work of studying the esthetic [sic] relations of buildings, should not only consent to design buildings utterly out of harmony with previously erected buildings with which they are to be closely associated, but should even in many cases vigorously urge such departures from the style previously followed. This has become such a marked abuse that we cannot too strongly urge upon those in authority the necessity of insisting at all hazards upon the preservation of harmony in the architectural style of all buildings that are built in close relationship with each other on University grounds."

Olmsted's campus planning advice and prophetic words, however, appeared to go unheeded for months. In May 1905, he wrote to the new president of the regents: "Be so good as to communicate with us in this matter." Another half year passed, however, with no official word coming from either the regents or the president's office.

Architect Charles Saunders—one of Olmsted's park board supporters—designed the observatory, among the first buildings at the new Montlake campus. The university had recently moved from its hemmed-in downtown site to a hillside above Lake Union and Lake Washington. *Fairsted*

In Olmsted's day, upscale downtown hotels provided traveling businessmen with all their office needs, including stationery and envelopes, pens, typewriters, desks, mailing service, and access to professional stenographers. *Harvard GSD*

Alaska-Yukon-Pacific Exposition, Seattle, Washington, June 1 to October 15, 1909. "The Fair that will be Ready."

In February 1909, Brookline received this postcard from staff members working in Seattle during the final months before the exposition started on June 1. Sleepless nights and endless worry would precede the opening, but this image signaled the glory days ahead. Note the older university building at bottom left, dwarfed by the brighter, magnificent, but mostly temporary AYPE buildings. Olmsted's "Rainier Vista"—his most lasting landscape feature—stands out at center stage. *University of Washington Libraries*

A century later, Olmsted's Rainier Vista continues to inspire the viewer on the University of Washington campus.

Olmsted tried convincing the AYPE's architects to design a Russian-themed fair, but met with little excitement for such an unconventional concept. Here, Howard & Galloway sketched an exotic facade for Olmsted, but it exists in watercolor only. *University of California, Berkeley*

The Washington State Building.

View from the Geyser Basin, looking eastward across Union Bay.

Court of Honor and Rainier Vista postcard, with the mountain's size enhanced to appear closer.

Aerial view of the AYPE overlooking Lake Washington to the south. *FSOP*

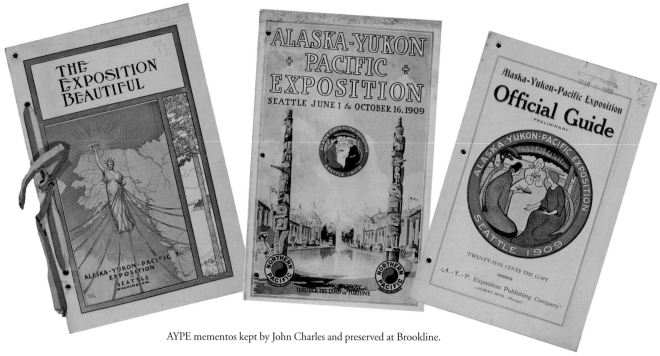

AYPE mementos kept by John Charles and preserved at Brookline.

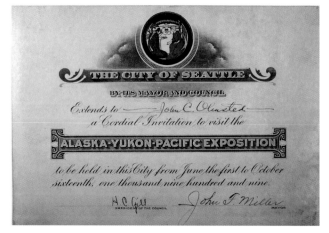

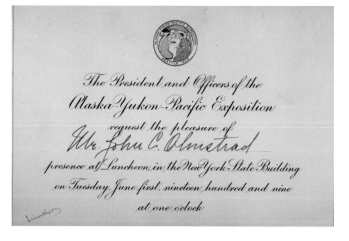

In 1903, when Olmsted and assistant Percy Jones visited the campus and took these photographs, a half-dozen new buildings sat forlorn in their surroundings after construction. The oversized campus "oval" was too vast and out of scale for the surrounding buildings and student requirements, Olmsted wrote trustees. However, remnants of the early perimeter path in this part of the campus remain today, adjacent to Denny, Parrington, Clark, and Lewis halls.
Frederick Law Olmsted Historic Site, Brookline (Fairsted)

Campus "oval," looking west with the Charles Saunders designed Administration Building (Denny Hall) to the right.

Science Hall (Parrington Hall).   Men's Dormitory (Lewis Hall).   Women's Dormitory (Clark Hall).

In January 1906, Olmsted wrote the regents a final (or so he thought) brief letter. "We conclude that either the whole matter has been dropped and is no longer of interest to the Trustees, or that they have no suggestions of consequence in connection with the further improvement of the plan…there seems to be nothing further that we can do under our agreement."

That October, however, the organizers of the Alaska-Yukon-Pacific Exposition (then in the initial planning stage), asked Olmsted to design the exposition grounds on a steep, unused portion of the UW property just south of the existing oval campus. The AYPE had just leased this land from the university trustees. This provided another opportunity for Olmsted to design the campus and plan for major growth using the exposition site as the key focus.

Meanwhile, the students and faculty at the University of Washington, driven by the enthusiasm of Edmond S. Meany, a noted Northwest author and history professor, were improving the campus grounds to make it a more appealing place. Beginning in 1904—and once a year until the 1930s—students pitched in on "Campus Day," clearing out stumps, debris, and unwanted vegetation (and some of the undergrowth so beloved by Olmsted). In 1904 and the years immediately following, they gradually cleared up the area around the main campus oval in anticipation of the great 1909 exposition.

Trees and underbrush Olmsted so admired—including here salal—falling under the axes of male students during the first Campus Day cleanup in 1904. *University of Washington Libraries*

Edmond S. Meany addressing students during the 1907 Campus Day, with the Men's Dormitory (Lewis Hall) in the background. Olmsted valued Meany's awareness of preserving native vegetation and expressed support for his efforts. *Campus Days #880, University of Washington Libraries*

Outdoor lunchtime on Campus Day, 1906, with the new Administration Building (now Denny Hall) in the distance. *University of Washington Libraries*

Professor Meany's letter to Olmsted, April 14, 1907—
"My dear sir: We are trying to establish a custom that will, I hope, develop into a true college tradition. On next Friday we will celebrate the Fourth Annual Campus Day. All the students and professors put on old clothes and devote the whole day to the work of beautifying the campus. We do not aim to destroy any of the natural beauty but we do try to make it more accessible by cutting paths, building rustic seats and cleaning up trash and debris. I wish to encourage the workers by words of comment from men who count. Will you please send me a letter addressed to the Faculty and Students of the University of Washington giving your opinion of such a custom? Yours faithfully, Edmond S. Meany."[6]

Olmsted Hurries West

Summoned in haste in the fall of 1906, Olmsted canceled a planned visit to Louisville in favor of Seattle's request. On October 1, 1906, AYPE secretary William Sheffield had written to Brookline and the letter was forwarded to Olmsted's hotel in Chicago. "I am directed by the Board of Trustees of the Alaska-Yukon-Pacific Exposition… to ask if it would be convenient for your firm to lay out the grounds…We would want to know, in the event that you accept, how soon a member of your firm can come to Seattle...

"The site of the Exposition is located on the un-improved part of the campus of the University of Washington, with

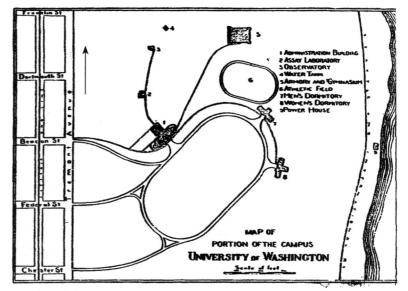

Olmsted submitted a preliminary campus design to the trustees in early 1905, but the new 1906 AYPE planning for campus land south of the original "oval" rendered it out of date. The darkened building profiles in these two sketches indicate existing buildings in 1898 and 1905. *Norman J. Johnston,* The Fountain & the Mountain *(UW Press 2003)*

Pre-Olmsted plan, 1898.

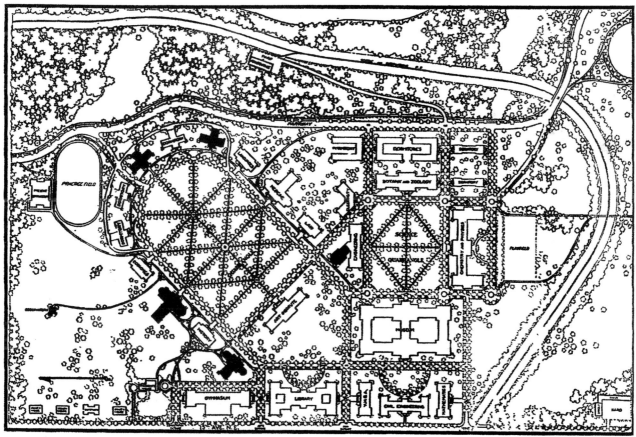

Norman J. Johnston, *The Fountain and the Mountain* (UW Press, 2003).

which you are doubtless familiar because of the work which you did in laying out the University Grounds. About two hundred and fifty acres of the campus have been leased to us for exposition purposes. This is the South area bounded on the East by Lake Washington and on the west by Lake Union. On the North are the buildings now occupied for University purposes, which have been excepted from the lease…

"You will be expected to lay out the grounds so that the Board will be able to form a pretty definite idea how they will look when improved. You will be expected also to furnish plans from which the Board will be able to award contracts for the landscaping, the grading, and the various boulevards, paths, driveways, etc. We will also expect the plan to show where the main buildings of the exposition will be located. If any suggestions or recommendations are desired, in regards to the architecture of the buildings, that matter will be taken up with you when you come.

"I will thank you for an early reply to this letter, and if you think it advisable you may wire me at the expense of the Exposition, saying when you can come to Seattle. Yours very truly, William Sheffield, Secretary."[7]

Rushing to change course, Olmsted quickly accepted, sent off a hurried letter to Sophia, and then boarded a cross-country train for his second visit to the Pacific Northwest. During his extended stay—this time at the Rainier Club and sponsored by exposition organizers—he would look the city and campus over again in even more detail than during the month-long stay in 1903.

With the hasty departure from Chicago in October 1906, some personal needs required attending by his wife. "Now I am wondering whether you mailed my trousers and cigars last Monday. I have two cigars left which will carry me through tomorrow and then I shall have to resort to what the club sells unless mine come."

The rolling and wooded AYPE site—a broad undeveloped slope south of the existing main campus oval—would cause more perplexing design challenges than at Portland's exposition grounds. During the planning for the Lewis and

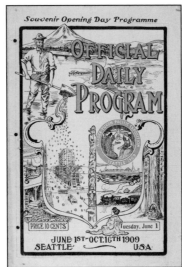

John Charles kept this opening day souvenir in his AYPE album in Brookline.
Fairsted

Clark Centennial Exposition, Olmsted served as "consulting landscape architect" only, and was employed just two weeks in laying out and advising the organizers at the relatively flat site. Olmsted's recommendations also had taken a relatively short time to be fulfilled, since a team of Portland engineers and architects already were in place to carry out the plan.

The University of Washington site, in contrast, was wilder and steeper. Adding complexity was the fact that the entire site would revert to the university after the exposition closed, with the grounds and some of the AYPE buildings being permanently retained. Planning for this was challenging, but also allowed Olmsted to take in a long view, a rare opportunity for exposition designers early in the century. After most fairs closed, the buildings were quickly razed and the grounds altered as other development immediately followed.[8]

Furthermore, Olmsted and the AYPE's main supervising architect, John Galen Howard, would shoulder difficulties attendant to design by AYPE committees in 1907–9. However, this proved to be an inspired partnership. John Galen Howard (of the firm Howard and Galloway) had served as the supervising architect at the equally hilly University of California campus in Berkeley, for which Olmsted's father had submitted a blueprint in 1866.

There was another interesting coincidence—during the 1880s, Howard had worked in the Brookline, Massachusetts, office of architect Henry Hobson Richardson, located just up the hill from Olmsted's own home and office. After graduating from the Boston Latin School, Howard had studied at MIT, and toured in Europe, as did Olmsted. Howard's Beaux-Arts schooling overseas ultimately separated his design views from those of Olmsted's, but this proved more a matter of personal debate and did not alter their fine working relationship.

For relief during their busy work schedules, the two men and their associates would attend Seattle theatrical productions and enjoyed meals together, thus breaking Olmsted's work-around-the-clock routine. The two men, however, differed in their writing styles. Howard's intermittent letters home to California exposed a lyricist at the core, whereas John Charles' nightly letters sent to Boston revealed a workhorse of the first order.

Work Begins

"The problem is very complicated," Olmsted wrote Sophia regarding the AYPE site, the day after he arrived in 1906.

The California architect, too, agreed with this assessment when he arrived in early 1907. He admitted to his wife: "I am to meet the regents of the University about the permanent exposition buildings which are to be made to conform to the dual purposes of show and learning—rather a hard task—especially in the case of the Chemistry Building, which is to be used by the show as a Fine Arts Museum! Such transmogrification [sic] requires some species of magic which I doubt I…possess."[9]

Howard also told his wife that the Hotel Butler's "hideous" stationery and "stabby pen" prevented him from corresponding each day. Over at the Rainier Club, meanwhile, Olmsted only occasionally complained about a lack of proper linen paper when writing his nightly letters.

Not having an Olmsted Brothers draftsman on hand (clients often were unwilling to pay for this added expense), John Charles borrowed a city draftsman, who proved not fully up to the job. On October 31, 1906, he informed Sophia: "The plan goes slowly. The draughtsman is not as

Scraping crews with horse teams leveled the terrain before planting the gardens. These "official" AYPE photos were either presented to Olmsted or sent by the staff for his photo album coverage of the AYPE job. *Fairsted*

good as he should be…Well, in a way, I am enjoying the solution of the problem, so from that point of view, I do not regret the delay here. I think the best place for me now will be bed. Ever your loving husband."

Architect Howard, on the other hand, had arrived in Seattle with an assistant, who set up shop for the duration. Olmsted, too, eventually received an appropriation for three assistants.

Architectural Themes

Olmsted suggested an overall Russian theme for the exposition, to honor Alaska's historical heritage. At a University Club dinner in November 1906, he announced the concept to several architects but found them split in their enthusiasm for Russian domes and spires in Seattle. "I told them I had recommended the Russian style for the Exposition. I thought [Charles] Bebb[10] was pleased with the idea but [W. Marbury] Somervell had studied in Paris & I imagine thinks there is no architecture worthy the name that is not pretty pure classic or French Renaissance."[11]

Over the winter, he sent Howard a list of Russian architectural books for reference, should the committee choose to adopt a Russian theme. Howard replied on March 2, 1907, indicating he ordered the books and his partner, Howard K. Galloway, made some sketches, but, in the end, forces were against the idea. "We have decided to bring

> into association with us a group of Seattle men and the question of getting up the design of the buildings in a wholly unfamiliar style, as a work of collaboration among a group of men whose individualities are necessarily more or less problematical, would seem a very serious one." The "Seattle men" were the associate architects, hired to design individual buildings, and who, Howard gently told Olmsted, needed more freedom at the drafting table.
>
> John Charles also told Howard he would send other architectural suggestions, as depicted in photographs he had taken during a visit to the Jamestown Exposition that September. "I shall look forward with pleasure to receiving the photographs…which I am sure will be of great interest," Howard replied to Olmsted, who at that time was back in Brookline.
>
> During the early exposition planning, Olmsted had the opportunity to produce his overall landscape

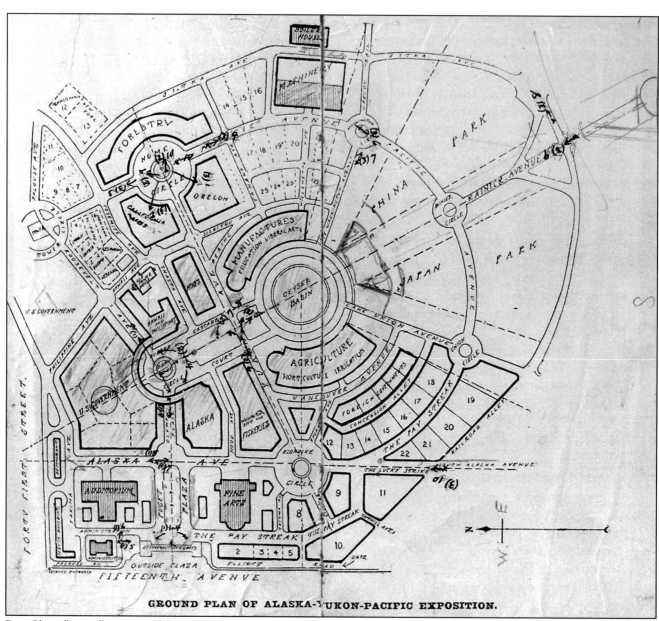

GROUND PLAN OF ALASKA-YUKON-PACIFIC EXPOSITION.

From Olmsted's own album preserved in Brookline, this sketch of the exposition grounds, showing proposed buildings and layout, is one of many that came off the drawing board before opening day. He revised the plan many times during the two years of planning allowed before the AYPE opened. See the end of this chapter for an example of the Olmsted Brothers' final plan. Handwritten numbers and arrows on this May 1907 drawing indicate photographic shots taken to gauge design progress *Fairsted*

design before Howard was brought in. On October 27, 1906, he explained to Sophia: "As they did me the honor to employ me before they employed their architect…I felt they ought to see and discuss the plan with me here, and not merely have a plan sent them from Brookline which might not suit them. I concluded it was my duty to stay and try to satisfy them."

Three days later, he added, "I want to leave a plan that will be worth something." (Indeed, his Rainier Vista, created that autumn, endures to this day.)

The main architect and the primary landscape architect proved a most complimentary team, working through their designs together, and relaxing together in the rare moments when they escaped the demanding project. Years later—

in 1911—John Charles would ask Howard to return for the Olmsted Brothers' third University of Washington campus design project. "My firm has been engaged by the Regents…to make a general plan for the university grounds…I…strongly recommended that they employ you as consulting architect," Olmsted wrote on June 13, 1911.

Howard replied on June 23: "It would give me very great satisfaction to take up such work in conjunction with you…Let me take this opportunity of saying to you that my association with you on the Seattle Exposition was the most satisfactory association that it has ever been my good luck to have."

Media Attention

Media interest—and publicity for the AYPE—increased with Olmsted's presence in Seattle. "I do hope I can get… [a sketch and] report ready for the newspapers on Sunday a week from tomorrow," he worried on October 27.

Realizing a bond existed between John Charles and publisher Alden J. Blethen at the *Seattle Times*, the rival *Seattle Post-Intelligencer* had sent a plea to Olmsted at the Rainier Club on October 21, 1906. "Dear Sir: The *Post-Intelligencer* will appreciate it as a personal favor if, when your first sketch of the grounds for the Alaska-Yukon-Pacific exposition is complete, you will allow us the privilege of reproducing same.

"Inasmuch as the A-Y-P expo. is a matter in which all persons and all newspapers in Seattle are identically interested, I would suggest that you prepare the sketch and have it released for publication in the Sunday papers simultaneously. I suggest this also for the reason that I know you will be urged by other newspapers in the city to release for their use exclusively, which, of course, would be embarrassing for all concerned, particularly the newspapers that had been overlooked.

"While I am writing, might I request that you furnish us with your latest photograph. The one we have in stock was taken on the occasion of your first visit to Seattle, I think, in connection with our park system. If you have not got a picture here, the photographers, James & Bushnell, will give you quick service under instructions from us. Their studio is in the Arcade building. Thanking you in advance, Yours very truly, F.P. Goss, City Editor."

The Olmsted plan, indeed, was presented to Seattle readers in the November 18 editions of both newspapers. "I enclose newspaper clippings giving my plan for the Exposition & extracts from my report," Olmsted wrote Sophia that night. "Both reproductions are poor—partly because the lines of my drawing were not as strong as they should have been for newspaper work." After admitting this shortcoming, he then took on the newspaper quotes as not accurately his own words. "A good deal that purports to be quoted was written by a reporter," he said, citing as an example the 400-foot-wide fountain basin being reported at only 200 feet.

Deficiencies in typesetting, quotes, or image quality aside, he worried that night about releasing his early site design at this time. "I question the policy of publishing this plan now, and later working to one covering less land and cheapened in various ways."

Olmsted was correct. Within the week, a scaled-back plan was in the works. He noted on November 21: "I am disgusted that I took all the time and trouble to trace my first exposition plan only to have it discarded because too expensive. Architects I know are continually doing that sort of thing and I always wondered why and here I have gone and done it myself."

The spate of publicity over the AYPE—with the *Seattle Times'* Blethen on record as one of the key supporters—enhanced Olmsted's reputation, which to his surprise took on celebrity status. On an errand the following spring at the Seattle post office (mailing off a Portland client plan), Olmsted was astonished when "the clerk who weighed it for me looked at the name & asked me how I was getting on with the Exposition plans. So you see I have been well advertised here," an amused Olmsted wrote Sophia on May 25, 1907. At the time, he was in his second two-month AYPE engagement.

Interaction with Architects

When working with the exposition's newly hired architects, Olmsted made sure his landscape plan—which the fair planners first had in hand—remained as pure as possible in its principles for adaptation to the sloping site. Each proposed structure fit into a whole scheme; thus, any change in building size or realignment meant revisions in the landscape design. He was consulted when proposed alterations in the configurations of buildings intruded on carefully prepared walkways or blocked essential avenues.[12]

Discussion over one structure alone—the Forestry Building, designed by Saunders and Lawton of Seattle—generated voluminous correspondence. For example, architect Charles Saunders replied in June 1908: "Received a letter a few days ago…stating that our design for the Forestry Building, if placed on the site allotted to it…a change would be necessitated in Sitka Avenue."

Letters to exposition officials and Saunders ensued from the Olmsted office, stating regret at the impact on that portion of the landscape plan and the disruption in the pathway pattern. The most significant loss in the eyes of the Olmsteds, however, was that a smaller semi-circular Forestry structure would not adequately fit its allotted half-circle in the overall grounds plan.

"We are extremely sorry to see this building reduced to the size indicated on the plan sent us by Mr. Allen [executive engineer for construction] and are sorry to see that the Commission would not accept our suggestion for having a large Forestry Building on circular lines," the Olmsted office replied to Saunders on June 29.

In this particular case, the landscape architect point-of-view would not prevail.[13] Nevertheless, the Olmsted Brothers continued to effectively interact in the planning details regarding the new buildings, thereby retaining the integrity of the overall grounds design. Throughout, John Charles remained at the center of this precise decision-making process.

Planting Plans

With time running short before opening day on June 1, 1909, the Olmsteds also turned their attention to which trees to save, acquiring rhododendrons, moving sod from Woodland Park to fill in scraped earth from the construction activity, and other planting needs. The landscape firm's reputation would be on the line if the grounds looked scruffy on opening day.

Years later—in 1923—a Seattle writer noted that C.J. Smith, chairman of the building and grounds committee, "stated that the exposition would be ready on the opening day, and he kept his word. There was not a loose stick on the grounds and the whole affair was a fairyland of beauty and a model of planning and execution."[14] Little did the author know just how much effort the Olmsted Brothers expended in making Smith's promise a reality.

As early as November 1906, in his 19-page report, Olmsted strongly advised exposition planners to immediately begin tree selection and transplanting. "With regard to planting, very little that is satisfactory can be accomplished with trees unless they are planted a year in advance, as they almost invariably have a stunted and feeble appearance the first year after transplanting."

With the design of other World's Fairs under the Olmsted banner, John Charles provided advice gleaned from past experience. "Almost every visitor to expositions has found the heat from the sun very annoying and has deplored the lack of shade. If a few thousand trees could be selected and root-pruned this fall and moved into position at the proper season as rapidly as the grading should permit, and at any rate, not later than the spring of 1908, and if they are well watered and cared for and planted in good soil, they would make good-looking trees by the time the Exposition opens."

Constant reminders to AYPE officials resulted in the selection of Olmsted's hand-picked Seattle park superintendent, J.W. Thompson, as part-time director of planting. This was later followed by acceptance of John Charles' request for a direct Olmsted Brothers representative, who

Flowers blooming in a parterre during April—whether all of the thousands of flowers survived to opening day was another story. *Fairsted*

With few people about, the planting crew could get on with the opening day preparations. This view is down the main court from the European Building, April 22, 1909. *Fairsted*

Olmsted's contract required his presence in Seattle twice a year, while Fred Dawson stayed for extended periods. To John Charles' delight, Dawson worked well with the construction supervisor, Frank P. Allen Jr. In June 1908, he reported: "Mr. Dawson has gone out to dinner. He will make friends easily because he is tactful…He seems to have won Mr. Allen who seems hard to suit in some ways."

Dawson remained entrenched in Seattle for months at a time, but on occasion returned to the Brookline office to finish up other work. He also accompanied Olmsted on visits to clients in Portland, Spokane, and on Orcas Island. His main contribution in this period, though, was his exposition planting management and client follow-up in John Charles' absence.

would remain on-site for months at a time leading up to opening day. The young associate, Fred Dawson, filled this plantsman position on a semi-permanent basis.

It was Dawson who reported, after the exposition, a crisis that occupied the attention of every groundsman and nurseryman at summer's end in 1908. With less than a year to go before opening day and 20 men employed in just sowing sod, "it was discovered that the [194,000] plants in the nursery had been retarded to a considerable extent on account of the amount of resinous matter in the soil, deposited by the fir trees whose roots had occupied the soil for a great many years."

The solution was swift. "Immediate action had to be taken to counteract these soil conditions. Several carloads of slaked lime were immediately purchased and spread over all areas which were to be seeded with grass or otherwise planted. This had the effect of liberating the plant foods in the soil that were being held by the resinous matters."[15]

Planning for the buildings started in early 1907, and in 1908 new structures began appearing alongside the paths and vistas. "Today has been a day of architects;—architects this morning, architects this afternoon, architects this evening, and I have just said good night to one of them after oysters and a high-ball," John Galen Howard had written to his wife from the Hotel Savoy in January 1907.[16]

Dawson sent this photo with a detailed description of rhododendron copses and sequoias hedges. Many of the shrubs were plucked from nearby landscapes before the exposition opened. *Fairsted*

Olmsted's six trips west to supervise the AYPE work revealed both progress and disappointment. Soggy wintertime visits in December 1908 and in January 1909 highlighted both. On December 31, he told Sophia: "I went out to the exposition this morning…They seem to be short of money. Mr. Dawson asked for an additional appropriation for landscape work of $35,000 and they cut it down to $20,000…such work always (almost) does cost more than the estimate if one does it as one would like to do it." But he then added: "The prospect of being ready on time is good."

Three weeks later, a gloomier picture emerged. "I went to the Exposition & spent the morning there. Little progress has been made in the 3 weeks I have been here because the weather has been so bad. The mud is horrid. I wore my arctics—rubbers wouldn't have been high enough and would have pulled off."

Opening Day, June 1, 1909

Nevertheless, when returning four months later in preparation for the opening ceremonies, Olmsted was dazzled by what he saw. "[Dawson and I] went out to the grounds & Mr. Allen had the electric lights and water turned on for my benefit," he told Sophia on May 27.

"The grounds are very nearly completed—enough to call complete," he continued. "There are lots of flowers in bloom and everyone is highly delighted with Mr. Dawson's work. It is indeed very creditable. Now I must go to bed. Ever your loving husband."

By now three Brookline employees—Dawson, Harold Blossom, and tree expert Hans Koehler—were working on the grounds, assuring success.

On May 27, 1909, a special showing to invited guests produced this promenade picture along Rainier Avenue with its "electroliers." The use of electricity was an exciting new development in exposition planning. *Fairsted*

"Invited [Dawson]…Koehler and Blossom to supper at Mann's," Olmsted told his office on May 28.

Before opening day, Olmsted slept well, but young Dawson stayed up all night, "superintending sodding and other finishing work," Olmsted noted in field notes. "Two car loads of sod laid after 11 p.m."

On opening day—and the evening too—John Charles' time was filled up attending gala festivities and receptions, and viewing the magnificent buildings and exhibits. The presentations and displays were all grandly formal in nature, with the exception of "The Pay Streak"—an avenue on the exposition's western edge that provided carnival-like entertainment. It was not until well after midnight that Olmsted could sit down to write Sophia, describing the day's events.

"I got up at 6 a.m. I was slow getting dressed & getting out…my black cutaway. So it was after nine when I got started. While I was standing on the corner waiting for a [public transit] car Mr. Bebb saw me & said come along in a taxicab. So I went with him. It was very comfortable and only took 15 minutes to get out to the exposition. I went with him to see the State of Washington Bldg which is arranged as a social bldg purely & which he designed. Then I strolled about the grounds till I went to the Administration Bldg. I joined Mr. Dawson. We strolled some more and went to the New York State Bldg and waited there until the procession had passed. Then we went to the platform seats in the 'natural' amphitheatre. The speeches began at 10:50. At 12 the guns fired & the exposition was declared open. We waited at the New York Bldg and then had luncheon, buffet style. I also went there for dinner this evening. I saw lots of men & a few women. I

Each photo sent back to Brookline showed different scenes, from the finishing touches to the opening days. Here, the popular Forestry Building, which survived on campus years after the AYPE closed, looms over its companion buildings and presented a more Western architectural look. *Fairsted*

knew and was introduced to 50 or more but of course can't remember them. I spent the afternoon at the Art Bldg & enjoyed a fine representative collection. After dinner which began at 8:50 & ended about 12 there were speeches which were fair but not remarkable. Now to bed! Ever your loving husband"

The following night, June 2, he filled in further details from the day before, and mailed Sophia a copy of the keynote talk presented by James J. Hill, the Great Northern Railway magnate.

"I am sending you J.J. Hill's speech. It is really quite interesting though it was too long & too much language. His statistics and main ideas are good though. I was introduced to him last night [by Professor Meany] and had a short interview with him. He seemed quite interested to meet the designer of the exposition as he had set aside the day for the exposition & consequently was not busy with something else. His face is rather puffed but his eyes looked strong...I told him he had probably known or known of my father; that seemed to interest him. He was probably trying to remember whether he had met him & when. He was to me much the most interesting of all those I was introduced to—I wished I could have stood by and have

listened to his talk to others but I was whisked off by Prof. Meany. I enjoy the university and college people to talk to much more than I do the businessmen. I must put in another day on writing on that everlasting Lafayette College report. I mean a day or more. Ever your loving husband."

Three Final Reports

All three men—landscape architect Olmsted, plantsman Dawson, and architect Howard—submitted insightful reports after the AYPE closed.[17] John Charles' December 1909 wrap-up reveals his maturing—from being a basic non-compromiser, to allowing acquiescence in achieving broader group goals. Much experienced in designing campuses and exposition sites, he noted key differences in planting designs between the Chicago World's Fair and the Seattle exposition.

"It may be of interest to say that, in designing the World's Columbian Exposition at Chicago in 1893 this style of decorative landscape gardening [i.e., the extensive planting of annual and perennial flowers] was discussed and it was decided against, on the ground that the buildings and spaces to be decorated were so enormous that such amount of that kind of decoration as could reasonably be afforded would have an effect of inadequacy and triviality and fussiness which it was important to avoid. In the case of the A.Y.P. Exposition, on the other hand, the whole scale of the grounds was small enough, not only to make floral decoration artistically possible, but decidedly desirable."

The two earliest basic design elements captured by Olmsted were the curve of railroad tracks running partway around the campus land, and the view of Mt. Rainier. He actually set the vistas of the mountain and Lake Washington in place using the center of the railroad curve. "The site for the group of main buildings having to be above the railroads, it at once occurred to me that the bold circular curve of the railroad should be recognized in the design. In my first sketch I located the center of Geyser Basin on the center of the railroad curve. I then ran out from this center three broad radical avenues of plazas."

Plans to occupy land nearer the tracks, however, would fall victim to reduced budgets; consequently, planning

The Agricultural Building and Olmsted-designed pond, with some of the fir trees left after the grading crews finished their preliminary work. *Fairsted*

and construction moved to higher ground. "Several plans were prepared in succession with this object in view. While retaining the general ideas of the first plan, the group of main buildings was moved, step by step, further up the hill, the widths of avenues and plazas were reduced, the sidewalks and parking strips and rows of trees first proposed were eliminated and the roadways narrowed, the size of buildings reduced…[and] brought closer together and some were eliminated," Olmsted noted.

"By compacting the scheme, not only was there less…to be re-graded, but the lengths of water pipes, sewers, storm-water drains, curbing, electric conduits and roadways were greatly reduced. Thus was the plan gradually perfected until the estimates of cost were satisfactory to the Committee."

The Plantings

Fred Dawson noted the astonishing number of plants collected from the wild (including on the campus itself), at commercial nurseries, and from a nursery south of the tracks. "About the first of May 1908 the Rainier Vista, centering on Mt. Rainier, the most important of the three vistas, was moulded into shape, and the work of planting the hedges on each side was started," Dawson reported in February 1910.

"These vistas were created by cutting down broad stretches of immense timber, thereby forming magnificent pictures framed on each side by fir trees. Both sides of Rainier Vista and on the sides of Union Vista and Lake Washington Vista …hedges of Douglas Fir were planted, partly to conceal the steep slope back of them and partly to frame in the vista with a solid wall of green. These hedges consisted of trees from 15 ft. to 20 ft. high and were transplanted from various parts of the Exposition grounds where they were growing naturally."

The native Douglas firs bordering Rainier Vista in the Science Quadrangle were enhanced by thousands of native rhododendrons, which Dawson placed alongside the buildings. "At the base of all the buildings encircling the main court were planted about 10,000 native rhododendrons. These plants were not used entirely for their blossoms but principally for the effect gained by their dark rich green foliage against white buildings." Weather played a role: "As it happened, the season was later than usual and the Rhododendrons came into full bloom a week after the opening."

Much of Dawson's effort was focused on a long pool with a series of short cascades along Rainier Vista. "Many thousands" of Dorothy Perkins and other rambling and climbing roses were planted. (Only recently introduced by the American growers Jackson and Perkins, the "Dorothy Perkins" rose would become an old favorite, despite the introduction of scores of similar roses in later years.)

In separate gardens, 5,000 roses were planted, but only including 10 varieties "suited to the climatic conditions." Dawson did not indicate all the varieties. Beneath the roses, 80,000 English Daisies also were planted to extend the flowering season—and which scattered seeds into many nearby nooks and crannies, to grow for years to come.

The Architecture

John Galen Howard turned his final 13-page typewritten report, as might be expected, into a lyricist's view of the enormous work just completed. "Collaboration—that has been the keynote of the work of preparation…Whatever success the Alaska-Yukon-Pacific Exposition achieved as a work of art is to be attributed to the singular degree of unanimity and of loyalty which characterized the efforts of all concerned, whether as administrative officers of the exposi-

Olmsted noted that formal gardens with "bedding out" in abundance were more appropriate for the smaller AYPE than for Chicago's vast "White City" fair designed by his father in the 1890s. *Fairsted*

of the grounds which were now to be occupied by the exposition.

"The landscape architects' first step therefore was to establish in the new region certain main axes and vistas…The principal axis-vista was laid out in such a way as to run from the highest point of the site in the direction of the lofty peak of Mount Rainier, sixty miles away, but plainly visible in clear weather, its snowy slopes gleaming in the sun, or melting into opalescent mists."

Olmsted's design came into play during the entire architectural design process, as Howard noted. "The study of the scheme of the exposition as a whole was a work of collaboration by Olmsted Brothers…and Howard and Galloway, Supervising Architects and Engineers of the Exposition, the preparation of the drawings being under the direction of

tion company, as committee men, as landscape designers, or as architects. The difficulties and obstacles were overcome, the conflicts and frictions were eliminated, by the spirit of 'pull-together'; and this is so rare a degree that, in spite of the immense labors that went to the making of the whole, the show, when it opened, seemed to have taken shape over night, out of nothingness, and to have been evolved without appreciable effort as by the rubbing of an Aladdin's lamp."

He described the site itself, before bringing in the Olmsteds. "The fact that the very beauty of the park-like grounds in their original condition of virgin forest (which it was obviously desirable to preserve so far as consistent with the purposes of the exposition), made the task one of exceeding delicacy, especially as the ground was irregularly sloping and, in places, steep…

"The exposition was fortunate in having the invaluable advice and assistance of Olmsted Brothers, Landscape Architects, throughout the work in the preparation of the design, in the planting and gardening and in all landscape work. These gentlemen had many years before established the main lines of the University of Washington, on a basis which was at that time [1903–5] thought to provide ample accommodations for future development. The area covered by their early plan, however, was only a comparatively small portion of the whole property, and left open the question

Modern view of Lewis Hall, one of the original campus structures when AYPE planning began in 1906.

the latter, but in constant advice and suggestions from the former.

"In this long and complicated labor…Every detail was thrashed out and argued with the last degree of care, adjusted and readjusted till its final repose was found, by a process akin to the settling of water to its level…

"The joy of the work came largely from the fact that it was done together; and no word is so appropriate with which to conclude this brief account and characterize the inner and essential note of the A.Y.P., as that with which these lines began,—Collaboration."

After the Exposition

From its opening, June 1, 1909, to the final day, October 16, 1909, over 3,700,000 people attended the highly successful exposition. An early decision to not compete with Virginia's Jamestown Exposition in 1907 proved to be an excellent choice.[18]

Returning in November 1909, Olmsted wrote Sophia about the AYPE's aftermath. "The Park Commission has appropriated $10,000 to take care of our gardening work…& I suppose to mow the grass & keep the place neat—they do it by leasing that part of the university grounds as a public park—I mean they are thus legally able to spend park money on it."

No park gardener, however, could save the roses. "People are stealing the roses and other plants rapidly, I hear," he noted on November 29. "Mr. Dawson got here only a few days after the closing and was surprised that only one official & the stenographer were left. That one official remained to supervise the removal of exhibits. The last government official left today."

Secretary William Sheffield had gone to San Francisco (where he put in a good word for the Olmsted firm), and AYPE executive F.P. Allen already was in New York, job hunting. John Charles would later play a central role in Allen's hiring for the Panama-California International Exposition in San Diego (held in 1915–16).

Olmsted described the scene after the AYPE's final curtain call. "The government

bldg is standing still but the ornamental balustrades of the cascades, &c…gone…[T]he University is going to save the California, Oregon & Washington & New York bldgs besides the permanent exhibition bldgs, Art Auditorium, Machinery & heating & the wooden Forestry bldg & office."

"They built a drive to it last Spring from Washington Park," Olmsted reported, thus confirming that the City of Seattle had integrated the grounds into his planned boulevard system, so carefully sketched in 1903.

Visiting the site again, May 1910, he noted the winter's toll. "I took a car to the old exposition grounds. Most of the bldgs are gone but quite a number remain so it does not look as lonesome as I thought it would, particularly all the part near the old college buildings [in the original, northern part of the campus]. Some of the buildings are in use by the University and more will be used as they get money to fit them up…The grounds are kept up by the Park Comm'n…The public use them a good deal on Sundays as a park."

Some plants had survived through winter. "The flowers are sufficiently abundant to make a fine show especially pansies & roses. I noticed two palms against Machinery Hall that had apparently stood the winter—one all right and the other with half its leaves killed."

On May 29, among the remains of razed buildings, he picked up two exposition toys for his young daughters.

The AYPE's Music Pavilion. *Fairsted*

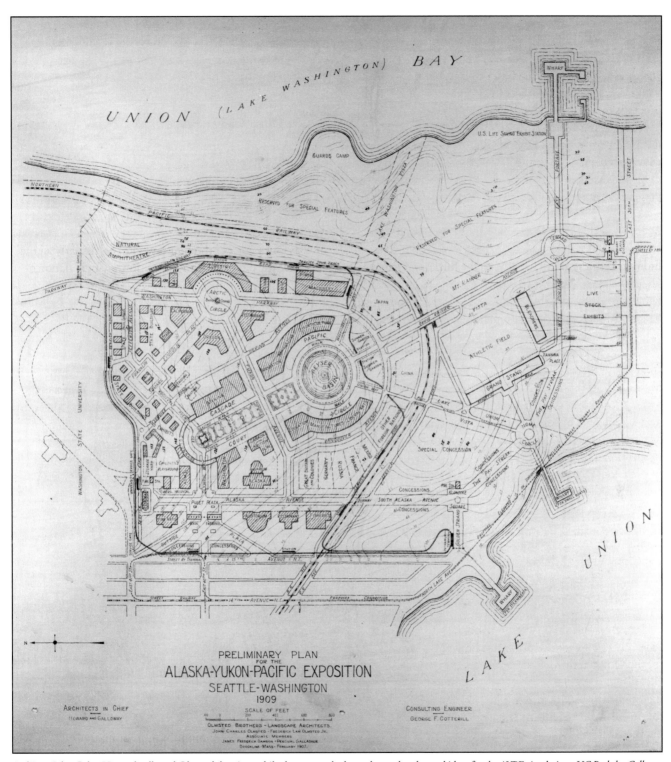

Architect John Galen Howard collected Olmsted drawings while the two worked together and exchanged ideas for the AYPE site design. *UC Berkeley College of Environmental Design*

While engrossed in this keepsake collecting, he heard a young lady ask her mother: "What is that man looking for?"

Rainier Vista: The Greatest Legacy

As Olmsted had planned, the view of Mt. Rainier loomed as prominent as ever after the exposition closed. He often described the peak with rapture when writing home, as on October 21, 1906: "I saw Mt. Rainier very distinctly particularly with [my] field glass. It is tremendous and being covered with snow looks at first like a cloud on a clear day…with the sun low in the west, striking it. It certainly is a grand sight."

Over the decades, the grand Rainier Vista would remain forever integral to the University of Washington campus, proving more lasting than the Union and Lake Washington vistas also created for the exposition. Three years after the closure, Olmsted worried about maintaining the latter lake vista when preparing his third, and final, campus expansion plan. "When I asked the draftsman to extend the vista lines it became obvious that we had planned the grandstand of the football field far into the space intended to be kept free for the Lake Washington vista," he wrote from Boston to Dawson, then attending university meetings in Seattle. "As the easterly grandstand might be 30' or 40' or possibly even 50 feet high, it would very seriously intrude upon the view," he reminded the staff.

"Inasmuch as we are making a very strong point of design that these vistas should be kept free of buildings for all time as far as the University is concerned, it seems to me we cannot consistently present a plan showing such a marked disregard of our fundamental idea…I hope you will find it acceptable to the President and others."

Though disappointments in their campus planning lay ahead after 1911, the Olmsted Brothers legacy still shapes much of the University of Washington today. In the final analysis, the AYPE defined a significant portion of the campus's future layout. Drumheller Fountain and the Rainier Vista remain a central focus, and John Charles' major axis, oriented to the southeast, defines the main campus.

Notes

1. The University of Washington was founded in 1861 on "Denny's Knoll," adjacent to downtown Seattle. As the business district expanded by the 1890s, however, the site proved to be too restricted. Consequently, a new campus site was chosen several miles northeast overlooking Union Bay on Lake Washington.

2. Following Olmsted's last visit in 1911 for a third campus plan, however, university committees rather than presidents or trustees soon took over the direction of campus planning. See subheading "University of Washington Plan Sidetracked" in Chapter 9.

3. Thirty-page report to Mr. A.J. Blethen, President of the Board of Regents, University of Washington, June 4, 1903, Olmsted job #346; Library of Congress.

4. Today, a walk from the western edge of the oval from Parrington Hall (then Science Hall) to the northeastern curve at both Lewis Hall (then the men's dormitory) and Clark Hall (then the women's dormitory), reinforces Olmsted's view that the space lacked proper human scale.

5. On this date, August 28, 1903, Frederick Law Olmsted Sr. passed away in Massachusetts, while John Charles was attending to summertime office work at Brookline.

6. Special Collections, University of Washington Libraries.

7. Olmsted job #2739, Alaska-Yukon-Pacific Exposition; Library of Congress. The AYPE is listed under Seattle Parks works on the National Association for Olmsted Parks (NAOP) master list. A copy of Sheffield's letter is held by Special Collections, University of Washington Libraries.

8. In 1914, the AYPE's former main architect, John Galen Howard, would write to his office: "I hate expositions that eat up all a man's vitality and then go up in dust…I didn't want the San Diego and I don't want the San Francisco show…all that either of them would be is pot-boilers." John Galen Howard Papers, Bancroft Library, University of California, Berkeley.

9. John Galen Howard, letter from the Hotel Butler, April 7, 1907, Ibid.

10. Olmsted's old Seattle associate, Charles Bebb, headed the Bebb and Mendel architectural firm when undertaking work for the AYPE.

11. Letter, November 12, 1906.

12. Olmsted job #2739, Alaska-Yukon-Pacific Exposition; Library of Congress.

13. After the exposition closed, Olmsted reported: "The Forestry Building, whose colonnade of grand logs was to have extended nearly half way around Nome Circle, was reduced to a portion only of the frontage of a much smaller building."

14. C.T. Conover, *Mirrors of Seattle: Reflecting Some Aged Men of Fifty* (Seattle: Lowman and Hanford, 1923).

15. John Charles Olmsted Papers, Special Collections, Frances Loeb Library, Harvard Graduate School of Design.

16. John Galen Howard Papers, Bancroft Library, University of California, Berkeley.

17. The John C. Olmsted and James Frederick Dawson reports are in the Library of Congress holdings, whereas John Galen Howard's reports are held by the Bancroft Library, University of California, Berkeley. Some originals and copies of office documents regarding the AYPE campus work are also archived by Special Collections, University of Washington Libraries.

18. Beset on opening day with unfinished buildings and partially muddy grounds, the Jamestown Exposition only gradually achieved spectacular results, though attendance was disappointing and significant financial losses accrued.

7

Spokane & the Inland Northwest

Possibly those Spokane people will want me to stop off on my return and tell them what they can do to improve their city. I was quite attracted by it in coming through on the train. They ought to preserve some of the river before it is too late, and also some of the pine-clad hills.
—October 19, 1906

Olmsted's initial Spokane work mostly resulted from two contacts—with park board president Aubrey L. White, and architect Kirtland Cutter. Aubrey White's interaction with Olmsted spanned the city's primary park-planning years. Moderately wealthy from a variety of entrepreneurial activities, White's unbridled enthusiasm and boosterism soon enveloped other influential friends of like persuasion into Olmsted's orbit, including the *Spokesman-Review* publisher William H. Cowles. Architect Kirtland Cutter's long collaboration with the Olmsted firm, on the other hand, had begun in Seattle after meeting John Charles by a Rainier Club fireplace in 1907.[1]

Aubrey L. White, parks booster and life-long friend of the Olmsted firm after the first meeting with John Charles in 1906. White's Hayden Lake investment came to nothing, but his decades-long Spokane parks support proved strong and effective. *Museum of Arts & Culture, Spokane*

Olmsted spent a third as much time in Spokane as Seattle. Nevertheless, he wrote more than 100 letters from Spokane, with additional references to his Inland Northwest work scattered throughout Portland and Seattle letters sent home. He submitted one overall park report for Spokane (in 1908), which afterward the city held under wraps waiting for bonds to sell and the sealing of real estate transactions before land prices escalated. Whereas the Seattle and Portland reports were announced with fanfare and received immediate media attention, Spokane's park proponents patiently waited several years for the right moment, in 1913, to trumpet Olmsted's advice.

In addition to providing direction regarding Spokane's 10 existing parks, the Olmsted Brothers recommended at least 20 additional new properties, weaving them together with Olmsted proposed boulevards. John Charles provided consultation on many of these park projects, and sketched precise plans for three of them—the then Adams (now Cannon Hill), Liberty, and Corbin parks. He also presented planning regarding landforms and land use in the city's Manito Park, an extensive South Hill greensward so beloved today. He likewise made recommendations regarding Coeur d'Alene Park in Browne's Addition in western Spokane, and proposed parkways along broad reaches of the Spokane River and Latah Creek, the latter a southern tributary joining the Spokane River just below the downtown area.

As in Seattle and Portland, Olmsted's private clients in Spokane were the economically flourishing elite who had mostly come from the east. Olmsted answered the requests of some of Spokane's first families—such as the Cowles, Davenports, Graves, and Whites—designing the properties of their dream houses on prominently situated lots. The Hayden Lake cottage development—located 30 miles away, just across the Idaho border—included prominent young Spokane residents seeking a summer retreat.

Private projects in Spokane typified much of Olmsted's work in the Far West—first, a client heard of his services by word of mouth or in newspaper accounts, and then quickly made contact. This would be followed with John Charles

Kirtland Cutter in front of the Western Union Life Insurance building on West Riverside Ave., which he designed and saw to completion in 1909. *Museum of Arts & Culture, Spokane*

making a site visit, with a report off a stenographer's type-writer following shortly. While much of brother Rick's time was spent teaching at Harvard, the Olmsted Brothers west-ern work was reaching a peak, which meant that the firm's mounting eastern projects already were beginning to suffer due to insufficient attention.

As Spokane flourished from the Northern Pacific Rail-road, real estate development, a rich agricultural and timber hinterland, and the Coeur d'Alene silver mines, prominent clients also held stakes in local water power production, trolley companies, and other ventures. Spokane was expanding by leaps and bounds south (the South Hill), west into Browne's Addition, and north across the river. Olmsted arrived at precisely these peak planning years. In all, Olmsted opened more than 30 separate files for Spo-

kane private clients and more than 12 individual Spokane park files.

The local cultural and arts scene, nevertheless, was as yet less advanced, a theme Olmsted returned to in his letters. The natural landscape, though, met with his wholehearted approval.

As private Spokane commissions kept coming in, Olmsted eventually found it difficult to sustain continuity without constant attention. The chill of winter visits, too, sapped energy from the usually bounding Olmsted. How-ever, his young office associate, Fred Dawson, flourished in the interior town. In fact, he eventually married into Spo-kane's social set and returned back east with his new bride.

Olmsted arrived just at the right time—when the com-munity's hopes and dreams from new railroads, mining, agriculture, and real estate were turning to reality. As with all economic booms, however, a downturn and slowing economy eventually came within a decade after Olmsted's last Spokane visits. He even lost some of his Inland North-west investments—most notably in the Hayden Lake development, where clients had insisted he take partial pay-ment in stocks for the project's design.

Spokane in the Snow

Olmsted previously had passed through Spokane by train, but his first projects in the city began on December 15, 1906, when returning east from working in Seattle, Port-land, and Walla Walla. After stepping off at the station, he quickly noticed the change in climate. "It snowed all day but so fine it only made a few inches…I did not drive about the city today because I could not have seen very far…I walked the street for an hour nearly—partly for exer-cise and partly to find warm mittens."

The following day, Olmsted took a tour of the snowy city in an automobile hired by Spokane businessman Aubrey L. White, today remembered as "The Father of the Spokane Park System." Olmsted's quick grasp of this Inland Northwest cityscape and the Spokane River was reflected in his long letter home that night. "The city was located here because of the waterpower but it has outgrown the water power and still it grows, being the largest city of what they call the Inland Empire."

He continued by comparing Spokane and Seattle. "It has, I understand, 75,000 population, and is 4½ miles

Following a great fire in 1889, Spokane's business elite quickly rebuilt an extravagant commercial district. *Museum of Arts & Culture, Spokane*

square. Seattle has, if I remember rightly, about 175,000 population. I see a great many hotels here, showing as at Seattle that there is a large transient population."

Just as in Seattle, money flowed through Spokane. "The prosperity of the country is in wheat, cattle, mines and latterly in irrigated small farms where alfalfa and fruits, milk and butter and eggs and vegetables are the principal products.

"The winters here are about like ours I should say but much less snow and it remains only a few days at most, and more clouds and fog. It is the snow which combined with the character of the soil makes the wheat so successful. The snow falls a little at a time and melts and soaks into the soil more than it flows off, so the soil is moist enough into summer down deep for wheat.

"Anything else dries up."

When describing the natural landscape of this part of the Inland Empire (today commonly called the Inland Northwest), he wrote: "The scenery is very picturesque with hills and valleys. The hills are mostly covered with pines all of one sort [Ponderosa] giving a remarkably monotonous effect. As they have only 19 inches of rain and scarcely any after June 1 no other tree seems to thrive naturally."

Of the settled gardens and the green verges nearby, he added: "In the streets and yards they have, as at Walla Walla poplars and yellow locusts, but the former predominate greatly. In shady moist ravines and along watercourses poplars and willows grow wild and there is a good deal of wild syringa which they say is very pretty in bloom."[2]

He described, too, the harnessed waterfalls adjacent to Spokane's commercial district. "The business center is south of the Spokane River and a little above the falls. In fact where it was easiest to build a bridge across the river. At that point the river is divided by rocky islands into three channels. The water power company has a dam about 12' or 15' high, as I remember it, and below that is a cascade. The total height used for power is 68 feet. The power is used for electric lighting and electric railways and besides those of this city, runs those of several small towns and vil-

lages. But in summer the power is so diminished that the company is building a big steam plant."

Hayden Lake Cottages

In mid December 1906, Olmsted spent only two days in snowy Spokane before leaving for Idaho with Aubrey White, "to Hayden Lake to plan a 'resort.'" In collaboration

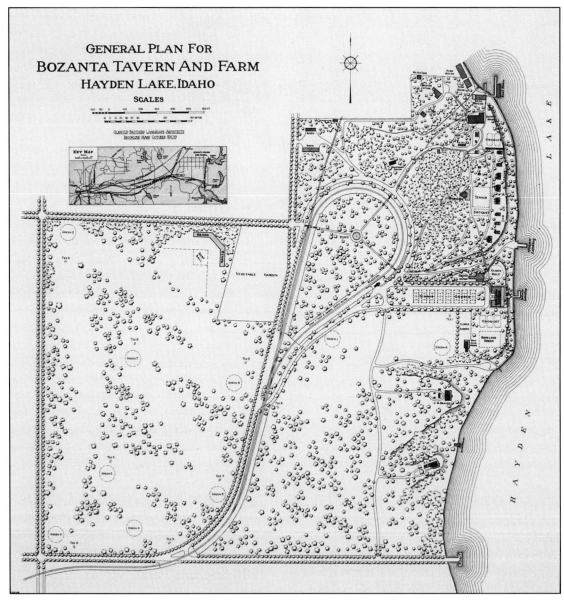

Olmsted Brothers' Hayden Lake general plan, October 1909. Agreeing to partial payment in Hayden Lake stocks that had little value, Olmsted and other investors lost claims but nevertheless kept their prestige for planning the well-regarded resort community. *Fairsted*

Rustic Hayden Lake "Wigwam" postcard, preserved in one of Olmsted's Brookline photo albums.
Fairsted

with Kirtland Cutter, Olmsted prepared preliminary plans for his private clients' lakeside community, with its new rail stop, located 30 miles east of Spokane.[3]

"Today I went with Mr. White and others to Hayden Lake. It is a picturesque lake something like Lake Placid with hills covered with tall pines and pretty high mountains beyond, but not far. The lake is 2242 ft. above sea level. I didn't notice on the map how high the mountains were. About half the east side of the lake has been taken out of the market by the U.S. government as a forest reserve which will make the lake especially desirable for summer cottages. Even a good deal of other land the owners have agreed that it will be for their interest not to cut the woods within 400 ft. of the lake as it may sell with the trees on for more than without the trees plus the profit on the trees. There is a saw mill at work at the outlet of the lake. At another place there is a steam pump pumping water for irrigating some prairie land W. of the lake. We went by electric ry. some thirty miles from this city. It ends in a loop near a resort consisting of 6 or 8 log cabin cottages, a sort of pavilion and a little house for dining room and kitchen.

"The cabins are furnished. One we were shown into had a sitting room with fireplace and there was a bedroom on each side. The son of the former owner said it rented for $125 for the season. He said they had four beds and two cots in it last summer. It had many cracks and gaps where flies and mosquitoes could get in. Now I must close and go

to bed. Ever your loving husband, [P.S.] It seems to me this is the last letter I shall write you this trip. I am to dine with Mr. and Mrs. Cutter tomorrow night. Wednesday morning I start for home."[4]

Envisions a "Great City"

The following fall, John Charles returned for a brief two-day Spokane stopover on his way to Seattle. On the night of November 19, 1907, he reported to Sophia that his Spokane park work suffered for two reasons. The railroads had since "taken the land" that he "wanted to reserve when I was here before," and sleep-deprived park commissioner Aubrey L. White "had a girl baby a few days ago." Consequently, Aubrey White ate breakfast at noontime while Olmsted finished his lunch. Then, "he drove me in his light buggy and good horse in the western part of the city."

Surveying the riverfront area and the steeper slopes of the South Hill, Olmsted noted that the north-facing wooded ravines made for better park sites. "It makes a marked difference in the vegetation whether the land is steep and slopes northerly or not," Olmsted wrote Sophia. "In that ravine [of the South Hill] on the south side [of the city], sloping north, a great many little spruces are springing up among the pines while on the sunny side are only pines. There is a good large spring in the ravine which makes it desirable for one of the parks."

He also recognized that the railroads—which took away planned park land in the flats of the main city area—were significantly contributing to Spokane's growing wealth. "Mr. White mentioned four more railroads of importance that are coming here, Chicago Milwaukee and St. Paul; North Coast, Great Western and another from Canada." Inspired during the horse and carriage ride that day, Olmsted ended his letter that night saying: "This is going to be a great city."

1908 Spokane Parks Report

Olmsted provided guidance for the entire Spokane park system when filing his city parks report in 1908 and during

An entrance to Manito Park announces, "See Spokane Shine." *Fairsted*

the new park design—put in a bandstand, prune out some Ponderosa pines, and add walks and take out roads.

He also had cast an eye on the Spokane River and its high bluffs extending for miles up and down its course, which at the time were largely uninterrupted by development. In 1908, he recommended saving as much as possible of these scenic forested bluffs, rock outcroppings, and river shorelines for parkways, natural preserves, and pleasure drives. (Remarkably, the city today is once again reclaiming its open lands, relying on the Olmsted report to further the goals never fully achieved in the heyday of the railroad land-grabbers. In regard to all the city park systems designed by John Charles, Spokane remains one of the most active in still achieving Olmsted-inspired additions.)

Manito Park

Manito Park—already on city maps in 1908 but barely developed—stood tucked away in the South Hill district of Spokane. The large property had been donated to the city

visits in following years.[5] The city, however, did not release the report in order to gather funding and to quietly achieve its aims without realtors and land developers jacking up property prices or otherwise interfering. The Spokane report was finally released to the public in 1913, along with updated comments from the recently-hired park director, John W. Duncan. Olmsted had recommended Duncan to the park board; the easterner eventually answered Olmsted's call around the time of the 1909 AYPE in Seattle.

In addition to advice regarding overall park directives and recommendations for riverfront and bluff-side sites, the report also included Olmsted's precise plans for three existing properties—Adams Park (since renamed Cannon Hill Park), Liberty Park, and Corbin Park. Site-specific drawings also were included for parks purchased or beautified since the submission of Olmsted's 1908 report.

Coeur d'Alene Park—a large square in the high-scale Browne's Addition neighborhood west of downtown—was already established, but barely distinguished. Olmsted, being characteristically thorough, gave timely advice on

Children's playground in Manito Park, from Olmsted's own Spokane photo album. *Fairsted*

with a proviso that water be brought in—for the park and surrounding homes. It clearly was one of the centerpieces (then, as now) of the Spokane park system. Still in the infancy of its development, Manito's vast greensward with crags, wetlands, a menagerie, and oddly-sited huts received special attention in Olmsted's 1908 report. He suggested eliminating the zoo, adding playing fields, and tearing down an unsightly employee hut.[6]

Because of its fine location close to a handsome and well-financed residential development, the long-term success of the beloved park was assured. Even then, however, Olmsted advised the city to expand its broad boundaries. The final touches to Manito's brilliance today are due in

From its earliest days, Manito Park was one of Spokane's favorite outdoor gathering places. *Fairsted*

part to Olmsted's man, John W. Duncan, hired away from Boston's park office. Left unrecorded, however, is the exact advice exchanged during John Charles and Fred Dawson's luncheon with the recently-arrived Duncan on April 28, 1910, at Spokane's Pennington Hotel.[7]

"We had Mr. Duncan, the Park Superintendent here, formerly asst. superintendent on the Boston Parks, to lunch. It was very slow. Also a smoke. And he told us about park matters here." Having spent the morning engaged with private client Jay P. Graves and his architect, Kirtland Cutter, regarding Graves' Waikiki estate out in the country north of Spokane, Olmsted was anxious to keep a quickened pace, but mealtimes often slowed his work days.

Nevertheless, John Duncan, a Scotsman by birth, provided continuity and stayed on as Spokane's superintendent for 32 years, retiring in 1942 at age 77. One of his most visible remaining legacies is the sunken Duncan Garden in Manito Park, designed like many Scottish estate gardens in a grand formal manner.

Adams (Cannon Hill) Park

Olmsted told Sophia that Adams Park, located not far west of Manito Park, was as one of his favorite designs. (Since renamed Cannon Hill Park, it endures to this day. Planners still view it with pride for its perfectionist planning.) Carved out of an unsightly 13-acre brickyard, with water trickling in sections of the property, Olmsted took these

two landscape features—the deep cut, and the presence of natural-flowing water—and created a pleasure park for the surrounding homes, with a wading pool and a small lake. Prospects initially had seemed dim on February 9, 1909, however, when he revisited the site to specifically design its interior.

"Adams Park…is a most discouraging piece of land for a park almost all of it having been excavated some 8 or 10 ft deep for clay for bricks, but it was left in the most irregular and chaotic shape, which will mean a lot of grading to put it in shape. There are no trees except some little pine trees which have sprung up since the brickyard was abandoned.

One of the stone bridges in Cannon Hill Park, originally known as Adams Park.

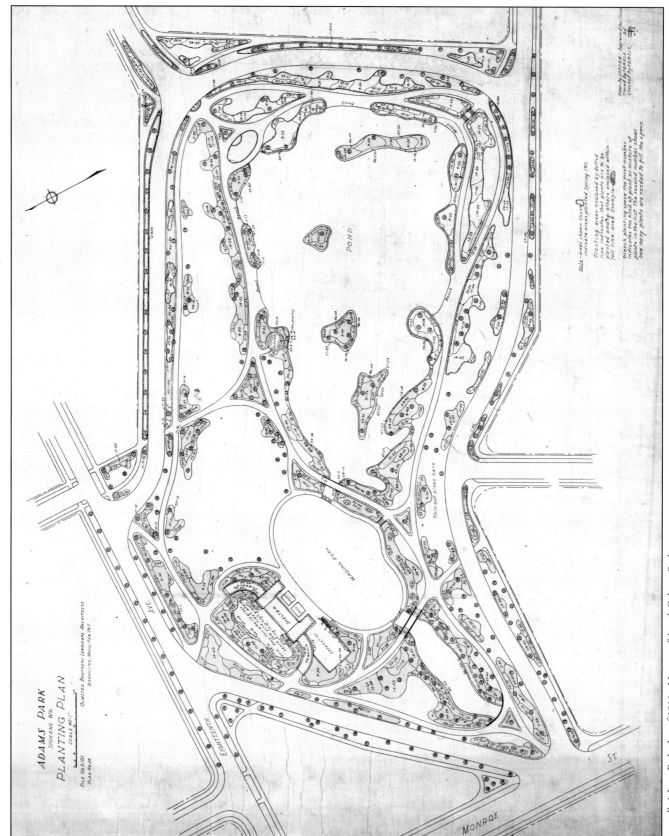

Olmsted's Adams Park plan of 1911. *Museum of Arts & Culture, Spokane*

There are no views as it is in a hollow…My arctics proved to be just what was needed to wade in the snow."

Ice skating on the pond in winter and summertime strolls under overarching trees helped make this a popular smaller park. Today, it is a well preserved and authentic legacy of Olmsted's three specifically designed parks in Spokane. Adding to the Olmsted firm's touch—as in New York's Central Park—stone bridges span walkways near the pond.[8]

When initially assessing the site, he judged whether facilities for toddlers or teenagers should be provided. He concluded in his report to the city: "The arrangements in this park should be refined and pretty and adapted to quiet recreation, on the assumption that the larger boys of the neighborhood can easily walk as far as Manito Park for ball games and other sports."

Safety, too, was considered in the planning. "The lake should be shallow so as to serve as a wading pool and for safety when used for skating."

Today, as with many of Olmsted's park designs, wide green patches bordering the perimeter sidewalks and streets integrate with neighboring homes, maintaining a natural appearance in the park's immediate surroundings.

Liberty Park

East of town and farther removed from built-up areas, Liberty Park came off Olmsted's drawing board at the same time as Adams Park, but it suffered a different and more drastic fate. Property in Liberty Park later became ripe for the taking as the city's boundaries eventually expanded east and automobiles came into general use. Spliced almost in half by Interstate 90 in recent times, this vast park exists, as a whole, only in Olmsted's May 1909 sketch, published in the 1913 Spokane Parks annual report.[9]

Its original 24.5 acres, as Olmsted reported in 1908, was "so much broken into hills and valleys with abrupt slopes and prominent projecting ledges that it is capable of uncommonly picturesque landscape gardening development. Unfortunately, however, these marked topographical features will make it difficult and costly to improve properly for the active sports of the constantly increasing numbers of children of the neighborhood…It would be appropriate and pleasing to have a lake in the valley which occupies the middle of the park, and this lake may be made shallow enough for wading and for toy boat sailing in summer and for skating in winter."

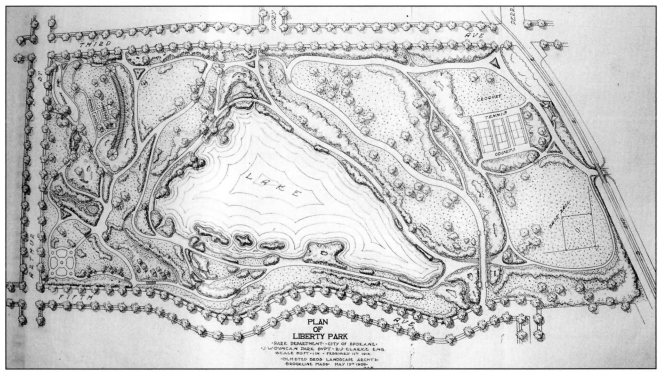

Olmsted's Liberty Park plan of May 1909, as published in 1913. *Museum of Arts & Culture, Spokane*

A Liberty Park view in Olmsted's photo album, with reluctant subjects looking on when the photographer snapped the shutter. *Fairsted*

Olmsted meticulously captured the essence of the original property by taking his own photographs. They reveal Olmsted's entire vision for the park, taking into account the smaller features, the property's overall size, the views, and the proximity to homes. The rock work, the steep sided features, and the park's level center all came together in Olmsted's well panned design.[10]

Eventually with only 2½ acres surviving "redevelopment," but after another 8 acres later were added, Spokane park historian Sally Reynolds noted in a 1995 report to the city: "Reflecting Spokane's economic decline in the mid 1960s, the park fell into disrepair…Now bisected by Interstate 90, the old site still contains the pergola ruins now owned by the state highway department, portions of the old park have attracted community interest for park reuse."[11]

Corbin Park

Corbin Park located north of the Spokane River, on the other hand, remains as established in Olmsted's day—a mile-round oval of handsome proportions, entirely intact and surrounded by vintage cottages.[12] Here, the surrounding neighbors greatly influenced the park's design, which Olmsted rarely allowed to happen.[13]

Spokane park historian Sally Reynolds reported that park commissioner Aubrey White "warned Olmsted that it would be necessary to please the Corbin Park Improvement Association. Adamantly opposed to any form of children's play area, or even a bandstand that might attract a crowd, the homeowners wished the park to be a passive 'beauty spot.' Olmsted acquiesced, designing only two narrow cross-park roads, and a series of graceful curved walks, a central fountain and limited planting beds surrounded by lawn."[14]

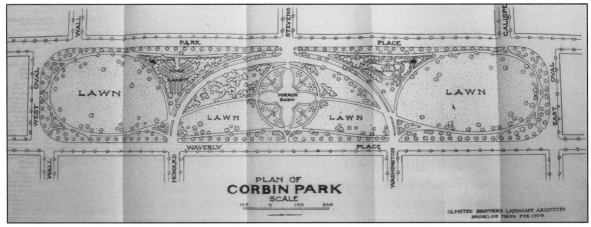

Olmsted's Corbin Park plan of February 1909. Today, the perimeter's leisurely strolling path appears almost intact, as Olmsted envisioned it a century ago. *Museum of Arts & Culture, Spokane*

In the 1913 parks report, Superintendent Duncan said of Corbin Park: "Much work was done during the past two seasons in the improvement of walks and drives and plantings…with two seasons' growth, this has made Corbin Park one of the beauty spots of the city."

The park area today remains quiet and neighborly as intended. It retains its perimeter path, broad grass lawns, and a dotting of trees. The nearby bungalow homes are knitted to the park—as intended.

Private Clients

Intermixed amongst his Spokane park planning, Olmsted found time for private clients willing to pay for specialized personal advice on estates then in the planning stages. A tangle of financiers, land brokers, and boosters, however, also crossed paths with Olmsted. This is chronicled in a recent Spokane history—the following excerpt shows the speed with which developers were stumbling over one another to carve out the South Hill for sale.

Jay P. Graves—an Olmsted client and one of Spokane's flamboyant entrepreneurs, land developers, and promoters. *Museum of Arts & Culture, Spokane*

"To Olmsted, [Aubrey] White expounded that [Jay P.] Graves's 'land company is worked in conjunction with his electric railway company, being composed in the main of the same stockholders. The idea is to get hold of dead but promising land secretly and as cheaply as possible, then to lay out some streets with better grades and build an electric railway through the property, advertise it and sell off lots at good prices and as rapidly as possible.' White himself thought of building a home" in the Rockwood extension then being developed by Graves[15] (who likewise was one of Olmsted's private clients).[16]

After his first solo visits, Olmsted on later trips brought along associates to finish the planning he began in Spokane. This included Fred Dawson, his expert plantsman from the Olmsted Brothers staff, who immediately found favor with Spokane clients.

John Charles, so shy and formal—attributes appropriate in the longer settled cities of Seattle and Portland—acknowledged Dawson's social success in rambunctious Spokane. "Mr. Dawson does better than I can (in the conversational line)," Olmsted wrote his wife after a dinner party with the Davenport clients on May 14, 1908. "Mr. Davenport admires Dawson's energy," Olmsted observed.

John Charles' private garden design for the home of restaurateur and hotel-developer Louis Davenport, followed by a subsequent design for Jay P. Graves' estate, "Waikiki," on the Little Spokane River well north of the city, gave Olmsted a chance to exhibit his skills in the Spokane area apart from park work. On a larger scale still, Olmsted's work for land developers in the south part of Spokane—in the Manito Park addition, and the Rockwood and Lincoln Heights districts—rounded out the private client projects in the next few years.

Louis Davenport's House and Garden

A particularly remarkable commission came from another collaboration with Kirtland Cutter who was designing an elaborate home on a rocky South Hill promontory for respected restaurateur Louis Davenport. Later noted for operating the spectacular Davenport Hotel, Louis Davenport already had prospered with a popular restaurant on

Louis Davenport, one of Olmsted's first private clients in Spokane. *Museum of Arts & Culture, Spokane*

the same downtown block. Olmsted often dined at Davenport's establishment, reporting to Sophia about menu selections and people met at the table.

Davenport's 3-acre grounds would exhibit an embodiment of Olmsted's various landscaping talents, though the project began tentatively. On January 24, 1908, in a letter from Seattle's Savoy Hotel, he informed Sophia: "Last night Mr. Davenport of Spokane came in and talked about his place. He seemed pretty cautious as to employing us but I judge he practically decided to do so."

Dawson Marries Spokane Socialite

Fred Dawson was the fourth son of the gregarious and successful Jackson Thornton Dawson, plantsman at Harvard's Arnold Arboretum. Dawson's expertise was in plantings, rather than design, which helped fill out the talents of the Olmsted Brothers team. Both John Charles and Fred Dawson had watched their famous fathers succeed to high expectations, and both had adopted their fathers' traits and talents. These were applied when the Olmsted Brothers began working in the West.

Dawson's socializing skills with Spokane's first families were so successful that he eventually brought back a bride from Spokane. He married Hazel Lease on June 4, 1913, at an extravagant wedding celebration in the Campbell House in Browne's Addition. (John Charles regrettably was not in attendance, having ended his Northwest trips a couple of years before.)

The bride, Hazel Lease, was Helen Campbell's cousin who lived in the magnificent Campbell House, built in 1897-98. (Today, the Cutter-designed Campbell House is owned by the Eastern Washington State Historical Society and museum, and is open for tours.) The new bride returned east with her husband to the Boston area, where Fred Dawson had grown up near, and in, the Arnold Arboretum.[17]

The Amasa and Helen Campbell House, shortly after its completion in Browne's Addition west of downtown. *Museum of Arts & Culture, Spokane*

Hazel Lease, at an upstairs window in the Campbell House. *Museum of Arts & Culture, Spokane*

Fred Dawson, 1901. *Dawson Family*

The scented setting for the wedding, evening of June 4, 1913. *Museum of Arts & Culture, Spokane*

Hazel (left) and Helen at the Campbell estate. For Spokane's elite, "Oriental" themes often were common at social gatherings and for interior décor. *Museum of Arts & Culture, Spokane*

The Davenport mansion stood on the South Hill overlooking downtown Spokane to the north. Cutter & Malmgren designed the elaborate home and teamed with Olmsted to plan an equally elaborate garden. Here, Kirtland Cutter inspects the property from his buggy. *Cutter, Museum of Arts & Culture, Spokane*

Olmsted provided an assessment: "It is only a small place 3½ acres I think he said and the grading and construction will not be heavy I judge but he wants to do quite careful and elaborate planting, so I shall turn it over to Mr. Dawson after the preliminary visit and preliminary plan."

From Seattle, John Charles proceeded east toward Spokane to finish his park report later that month. Upon reaching Spokane, however, snow and cold temperatures prevented a survey of Davenport's property, but later visits finally produced a full design.[18]

"It is a commanding site, but very little of the land is available for building on because it is such a steep hillside and deep, steep sided ravine," Olmsted wrote Sophia on May 13, 1908, regarding Davenport's "new place." The

following night, after another session at the site along with Kirtland Cutter, Olmsted and Fred Dawson dined in the "private apartments" of Mr. and Mrs. Davenport above their restaurant in town. "Mr. Davenport…likes Donald the gardener we sent him, and finds Hussey the surveyor we sent him all right so he is so far apparently well satisfied."

Months later—during a Spokane visit in mid-February 1909—Olmsted became dissatisfied with a delivery of trees to the property. "I went out for a stroll to Mr. Davenport's place. He is in S. California. Saw his gardener. He has moved a lot of good big fir trees, many of them 25' or 30' high. They cost about $20 to $30 each as they had to be hauled 8 miles.

A team of horses bringing in giant trees for the Davenport grounds. Olmsted advised against the massive project, suggesting that if the contractors failed, the landscape architect would take the blame. *Museum of Arts & Culture, Spokane*

"They are at present prettily draped with snow. I hope they will succeed. If they don't it will be bad for our reputation even though we advised Mr. Davenport it was a very risky and questionable thing to do.

"But people do not distinguish advisors from contractors," Olmsted complained to his wife that night. "They attribute to us the same responsibility for the work that they would to a contractor…It snowed quite hard this morning but stopped before noon."[19]

With the Seattle exposition opening in just a few months, the Olmsted firm in early 1909 was hard pressed to fulfill the many city and client demands in the Northwest. The day

Workers posing on some of the massive stonework at the Davenport estate. *Cutter, Museum of Arts & Culture, Spokane*

after John Charles observed the trees at Davenport's property, Olmsted Brothers' employee Harold Blossom came through by train. He was on his way to Seattle to help Dawson finish up the exposition work. Blossom lingered for a quick review of the Spokane jobs.

"Blossom from our office arrived and has been with me until…near ten [p.m.]. I walked up to Mr. Davenport's place with him and walked about…in the snow till 5:15. Then we were standing in the street discussing [a nearby] great 6-story brick hospital, the erection of which has greatly injured [the view from] Mr. Davenport's place, when Donald his gardener came along. Then he joined us and we walked through

The Louis Davenport home in the snow. Years later, the property was razed during a Spokane medical complex expansion. *Museum of Arts & Culture, Spokane*

various streets and down to Davenport's restaurant." (Olmsted's observation that the hospital "injured" Davenport's home was right on the mark—years later, the grand house fell to the wrecker's ball and the elaborate garden was destroyed to make way for hospital expansion.)

The next day, February 15, Olmsted provided Sophia with an overview of his day's activities with the travel-weary Harold Blossom. "I have been all day showing Blossom four of my jobs here so he can attend to some of the drawings later if it should be desirable. We were late at breakfast as he was sleepy and did not get up early and we took nearly an hour before starting out so I could explain those and other matters. Then we went to Liberty P[ar]k. The snow was from 4 to 6 inches deep in spite of…rain earlier in morning and it thawed all day so the walking was very bad and I got my feet wet both morning and afternoon in spite of arctics, the uppers of which are not waterproof, and besides it was slow walking because of slipping and getting a poor foothold. We walked from Liberty Park to Mr. Brown's place [a client].

"Then we walked from there to the Manito cars and returned to hotel to change foot gear and have lunch. As he wanted broiled chicken, lunch was very slow. Then we went to Adams Park and around it and finally to Corbin Park by which time it was pretty dark. After again changing foot gear Donald [the gardener] came and talked quite a while. Then we had supper…[Blossom] left about 9:30

p.m. for his train. This visit of his just took a whole day of his time but maybe later he can be of a good deal of benefit in working up details."

John Charles reported more client news: "Mr. Brown telephoned about 3 more possible clients, owners of small places here. I gave price for prel. visit and prel. [plans] but I doubt if they will care to pay the price. If they do—more delay."

Destiny

Olmsted's Spokane legacy includes the work he did on the grounds of Jay P. Graves' 1,000 acre Waikiki estate, situated on a bluff overlooking the Little Spokane River. Graves, a prominent railroad, mining, and real estate entrepreneur, had Cutter and Malmgren design his grand Tudor or English Revival mansion, built in 1911–12, while the Olmsted Brothers planned 8 acres of grounds and gardens.

Eventually, a real estate bust hit Spokane, Graves fell on lean times, and his grand property proved too expensive to keep up (the Olmsted firm had billed the client with limited success). The estate was sold in 1937 to pay debtors. Graves searched for new prospects to recoup his fortune, but failed to match his earlier luck and success. He died in 1947 at his winter retreat, the Huntington Hotel, in Pasadena, California.

Today, Waikiki is the largest of the old estate homes remaining in Spokane County. Though most of the

Jay P. Graves' "Waikiki"

Jay P. Graves' "Waikiki" home and grounds, today a popular Gonzaga University retreat center. Both John Charles and Fred Dawson worked on the Graves commission. Note enclosed garden, left, where Olmsted's little summerhouse has one of the best valley views from the bluff today. *Peter S. Hockaday*

outbuildings are gone and the acreage has been reduced, the fine mansion and its immediate grounds are intact. Waikiki now serves as a retreat for Gonzaga University.

The business interests of parks advocate Aubrey White also declined, in part after a housing sale snapped up by Graves. Nevertheless, he remained in the public eye, energetically acquiring more park properties for the city after Olmsted's visits. In 1921, he moved to "Montvale," the country estate of his wife's family on the Little Spokane River, and consequently lost his park board seat because he no longer was a city resident. He remained active, however, as the *Spokesman-Review* garden and civic development correspondent (1926–46), constantly promoting parks until just before his death in 1948. As a writer, White was able to keep Spokane's cherished parks and gardens in the limelight.

John Charles had regretted the fact that expansive new railroad yards and structures had preempted his plans for the broad, spectacular Spokane Falls area. Many years later,

however, once transportation and industrial activities there declined, the city was able to recapture the Spokane River's magnificence. Removal of the tracks and revitalization of the waterfront area occurred during the planning for Spokane's Expo '74. The rushing river with its many falls and rapids were the main attraction of a grand new park, much as Olmsted originally envisioned.

A modern historian, J. William T. Youngs, has recorded this transformation. "Spokane had all but forgotten the falls," until the area's revival became a key goal of the World's Fair planning. "Riverfront Park in Spokane, the location of Expo '74, is within a five-minute walk from downtown stores and offices. Moreover, the site encompasses the city's waterfalls, arguably the most arresting river landscape in the midst of any American city."[20]

Due to Olmsted's work and Aubrey White's energy (and the latter's self proclaimed "powerhouse" of influential townspeople), Spokane today retains one of the largest percentages of park acreage for any city in the country.

Whitman College, Walla Walla

On November 22, 1906, President Stephen Penrose of Whitman College wrote to the Rainier Club, where Olmsted was wrapping up his winter work in Seattle. "I have been informed by Mr. Will H. Parry [an associate of Olmsted's Orcas Island client, Robert Moran] of Seattle that you are expecting to return east within a few days. Would it be possible for you to stop in Walla Walla for a day or two en route and look over the town and grounds of Whitman College with a view to advising us concerning the approximate cost of preparing plans for properly beautifying the city park system and the College campus."

President Stephen B.L. Penrose of Whitman College. As a Williams College graduate, Penrose also knew the Massachusetts countryside so familiar to Olmsted. *Whitman College*

Penrose offered to pay traveling expenses and told Olmsted he hoped to tie together campus and town park planning. "As chairman of the Committee on Parks and Highways I am anxious to secure the most competent advice in regard to the improvement of the town, and know that we would be most fortunate if we found it possible to secure your services as landscape architect."

After receiving Olmsted's positive reply, Penrose urged a slight delay in his visit until Penrose could personally show Olmsted around the campus. Penrose finished his December 2 response with a memorable line: "Congratulating ourselves upon being able to secure your services, I am Sincerely Yours, Stephen B.L. Penrose."

In a December 4 letter to Olmsted, who by then had left Seattle and moved on to Portland, Penrose added: "In case you wish to dictate your report on the ground my private secretary, an excellent stenographer, is at your service." Knowing he could only spare a few days for the Walla Walla work, Olmsted appreciated this most generous offer of Miss Taylor's services, especially after having difficulties with stenographers when finishing up his Portland reports.

Traveling to Walla Walla for the first time, Olmsted eyed local landscapes as usual. "My train followed the Columbia River for some distance. It was mostly a sandy waste with sage brush. They say it will soon be wheat fields and orchards as extensive irrigation schemes are on foot. Then we struck easterly up through rolling sage brush lands which gradually give way to wheat fields. It seems strange that with nearly 3 months drought and only 18 in. of rain the rest of the year wheat will grow, but the soil seems to be able to absorb what rain does fall and give it up gradually to the roots which can go down deep for it. The only trees growing naturally here are along water courses and in specially moist places and they are cottonwoods and willows but I am told maples and elms grow all right if they are watered the first year. They keep lawns only by watering twice a day in July and August. All shrubs also are watered."

Penrose kept Olmsted waiting for 20 minutes that morning before attending to the noted landscape architect. "Even then he was called off several times so I just had time to make a slow tour around the campus when it was 12 and he invited me to lunch." Penrose redeemed himself, though, providing much attention later that day, and the following day.

Penrose, the long-serving Whitman College president, was an 1885 graduate of Williams College in Massachusetts. Thus, he shared eastern connections with Olmsted. Both men had attended Yale—Olmsted as an undergraduate, and Penrose as a Divinity School graduate. There also was a personal connection. On December 10, John Charles wrote Sophia informing her that Mrs. Penrose "knows Aunt Bertha very well and the family. She says Aunt Bertha always writes her for her birthday every year."

After touring the campus grounds for two days, Olmsted immediately wrote his report while facts were fresh in mind, and while the president's stenographer was at his service. An 11-page report came swiftly off the president's office typewriter, one of Olmsted's quickest submissions while out west. The report immediately won approval.[21]

Penrose and Olmsted shared a preference for the long view. Later in December, President Penrose informed the Board of Trustees: "You will notice that this report practically outlines the development of the College for the next fifty years."

Penrose further stated: "When these plans are carried out, Whitman College will have become outwardly worthy of its name and its influence in the life of the northwest, and its internal work and spirit will be likewise quickened. The aim of the College should be to become as rapidly as possible a

Stenographers

Before leaving on the first Northwest trip in 1903, Olmsted informed Sophia regarding the firm's expanding projects: "I wish we had another energetic partner." Three years later, he might have said: We need a traveling office assistant! While in Portland, just prior to taking a train for Walla Walla, woes caused by a hotel stenographer and other local typists are revealed in a letter to Sophia written late on December 7, 1906, from the Hotel Portland.

"I have had a 'time' with my reports. The two I dictated yesterday I did not get off until about 7:30 this evening. One of them I corrected partly after breakfast. Then I had to go...to Mrs. W.S. Ladd's...got back here and finished correcting the Ladd [client] report by 1 and left it on the stenographer's desk to correct. She had not got the Lewis report ready—Told me to come at 5 p.m. for it. She said she wouldn't do any more of those long reports they tired her so! I went after lunch to a big office bldg across the street and enquired of the elevator boy for a stenographer. He told me of one in the bldg. She wanted to take it on the typewriter while I dictated. I refused as it is slow and tedious doing a long report that way. Then she took it shorthand and told me to call at 6 as it would then be ready...Then about 3 I went to another stenographer whose address I had learned of...I dictated the Mr. H.S. Corbett report to her until about 4:30.

"Then I came back [to] the hotel stenographer and caught her just as she was leaving and corrected the Lewis report while she was finishing it. By the time I had got those two mailed it was nearly six and I hurried across the street and just caught the stenographer with her hat and coat on about to leave and she had only one page done! She said it was time to go home and wanted to finish in the morning—I begged her to stay and after some discussion she agreed to.

"Then she wanted me to dictate the report all over again to her while she did it direct on the typewriter. She said if I would it would only take 20 minutes! I said I could not possibly remember all I had said and would be sure to omit important ideas. I insisted upon her at least reading from her stenographic notes. It then developed that she could not read her own notes! She had delayed me by writing out long hand many words and asking me to spell them—Well I was disgusted but I dreaded the effort of memory to dictate it all over again. So she started in and about every 4th or 5th word she stopped at and I had to guess what it might have been and dictate something. Every few minutes she had some excuse...I persisted until 7:15 when I decided to let her stop...I felt a little sorry for her or I should have kept her until 8. I dare say it was beastly irritating."

In Walla Walla, however, these complications would be avoided, thanks to the capable Miss Taylor, the Whitman College stenographer in President Penrose's office.

---

place where the solidest and noblest kind of an education can be gained amid the most inspiring influences."[22]

The Walla Walla *Daily Union* reprinted the Whitman campus report in its entirety on December 18, 1906. With fanfare, the newspaper already had announced Olmsted's arrival in town a week earlier: "Famous Artist Views Grounds."[23]

The report advised Whitman College to keep the vast center of the campus open, only landscaping it with a broad lawn and high-branched trees (the college has since precisely followed this advice). Along College Creek—meandering through the campus—shrubs, vines, and other low-growing vegetation would provide a balance to the open part of the campus (Olmsted's creek-side recommendations also have been followed). "Lakum Duckem" is the affectionate name for a dunking pond for ducks as well as underclassman during traditional tugs of war.

John Charles again presented his simple campus design principles. "In the placing of buildings there are two or three things which are very important to be borne in mind. First...[buildings] should be oriented all alike. Second—There should be a reasonable degree of harmony in architectural style and color and nature of materials of exterior walls. Third—The entrance should be systematically arranged not only with regard to convenience but to dignity, so as to relate one building with another."

Modern-day view of a portion of the Whitman College main quad, remaining as Olmsted envisioned.

Walla Walla Parks Plan

On December 12, Olmsted next turned his attention to Walla Walla's park plan, as requested by President Penrose. The *Daily Union* also trumpeted this assignment: "Landscape Artist Takes in the City" was the headline on December 13, 1906. "Delegation Shows John Olmsted the Natural Beauty of Walla Walla."

Miss Taylor's typing once again made Olmsted's report writing faster and more efficient than in Portland. "The most notable topographical and landscape feature of the city is Mill Creek, and of the same character on a smaller scale are the numerous other creeks which give rise to the

Indian name for the city. I strongly advise that every possible advantage be taken of these attractive natural features by laying out parks so as to include them. There are many cases where even a comparatively narrow strip along a creek will be an exceedingly desirable investment for the city," Olmsted wrote to the park board on December 14.[24]

Olmsted need not have rushed, however. A month later, on January 23, 1907, Walla Walla park board president John W. Langdon informed him: "The city has not yet made public your report owing to other business and the severe cold weather we have been experiencing. Some of the Council declaring that 'it is too cold to talk about parks and shrubbery.'"

Pioneer Park, located several blocks southeast of Whitman College, remains today as one of Walla Walla's showcase places, thanks to Olmsted's advice. When the city had debated releasing this water department land, he advised keeping it. The old-fashioned bandstand in the park is a holdover from the earlier era of Walla Walla park planning.

Walla Walla's college trustees and park commissioners had only this one visit from the landscape architect. Likewise, Olmsted only made a few side trips for a Kennewick land developer, as big of a commission as that was. However, these diversions further eroded John Charles' time for extensive Spokane work, which was waiting for his first attention during those cold December days in 1906. Over the decades, nevertheless, Walla Walla proponents have succeeded in following through on Olmsted's advice at Whitman College, Pioneer Park, and for the creeks meandering through the town.

University of Idaho, Moscow

In June 1907, President James Alexander MacLean of the University of Idaho escorted Olmsted around the Moscow, Idaho, campus and asked for written advice. Located just seven miles east of Washington's new land grant college in Pullman, the University of Idaho (opened 1892) occupied a gradually rising slope to a hill on the campus's south side. The following year, Olmsted produced a 25-page written report with a handsome sketch.

President MacLean, like Whitman's Penrose, was another eastern-educated transplant serving as a college president out west. As a Columbia University graduate student in New York during the previous decade, MacLean had studied near Central Park. MacLean now sought the same kind of landscaping maturity for the fledgling University of Idaho campus.

Unlike the 1906 Whitman College consultation, which began and finished within one week, the University of Idaho conferences, reports, and advice continued for a decade.[25] Finally, in dramatic fashion, the Olmsted plan would resurface decades later when the campus's main green came under threat.

Olmsted's advice and recommended principles were now a familiar refrain. "It is of fundamental importance that a general effect of harmony be evident in the design of the principal group of buildings. This is a matter as to which most of the universities are open to severe criticism. It is difficult to understand how architects can consciously become responsible for such breaches of good taste…It is hoped that the board [of regents] will insist upon reasonable uniformity of exterior materials and architectural style in buildings hereafter erected."

Expand, Olmsted advised, to the east toward town, to wrap in the landscape view between the town and college. The university instead started to spread west and north, with only a patchwork to the east toward town. Tree plantings, nevertheless, filled in the bare patches existing in 1907, presenting a more harmonious landscape on the town side.

Olmsted's most lasting advice would pertain to the Administration Building grounds, near the core of the campus. Keep a greensward clear of buildings and roads, Olmsted advised in 1908. In 1913, when campus engineers confessed to constructing a road for convenience, cutting across the Administration Building's lawn, Olmsted objected strongly.

President James Alexander MacLean of the University of Idaho (1900-1913). *University of Idaho*

"Our principal objection to this…drive is that it cuts up the main front campus. In other words, the grounds would be more enjoyable to the great majority if kept as an informal park of grass and scattered trees, unbroken in the middle parts by a drive…Of course the case of a university is very different from that of some other institutions. The great majority who pass through the grounds do so on foot and their convenience must always receive first consideration."

Olmsted also objected to the recent planting of trees lining this rogue road. He was objecting to the manner of the roadway planting, rather than the well planned dispersal of trees elsewhere in the original Olmsted Brothers designs. "We strongly advise against the planting of rows of trees along the university drives. The drives are laid out on informal curves and the grading is intended to be gentle and naturalistic in style, while rows of trees would be very markedly stiff and formal, and so entirely out of harmony with the naturalistic style."

The new university's Administration Building stood in a mostly barren, undeveloped setting. *University of Idaho*

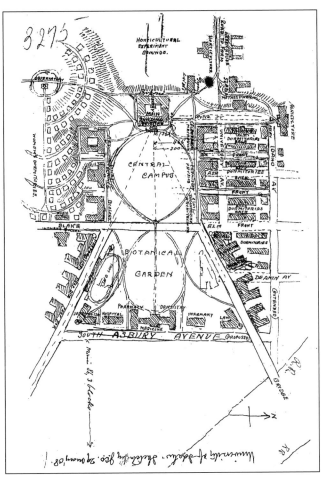

University of Idaho campus plan, sketched by Olmsted at Seattle's Hotel Savoy in May 1908. *Library of Congress*

with Olmsted about the University of Manitoba grounds. But with MacLean and Olmsted together once again, they produced the final words on the 1908 University of Idaho campus plan. Olmsted's field notes confirm this fortunate timing.

"I took advantage of the fact that President MacLean of the University of Manitoba had previously been president of the University of Idaho when he called about 11:30 A.M. in connection with plans for the University of Manitoba to look at the plan of the drive which I had received from Professor W.L. Carlisle [Carlyle], acting president of the University of Idaho, and to give the benefit of his knowledge and advice as to the plan of drives and walks."

One last University of Idaho president, E.H. Lindley, wrote the Olmsted firm on April 23, 1920, but only to ask for original plans from past years, and to boast of Idaho's Olmsted connection. "You will be interested to know that [Lt. Governor] Dr. Charles Moore has recently visited us and expressed great pleasure in knowing that your firm had furnished plans for our campus." It was the last correspondence from the University of Idaho to the Olmsteds.[26]

In the spring 1988 edition of the University of Idaho alumni magazine, architecture professor Nels Reese told of a proposed alteration in the Administration Building grounds design, which appeared a half century after Olmsted's work. The controversy centered on a plan to erect a new library. In defense of Olmsted's greensward, "the chairman of the Department of Art and Architecture, Theodore J. Prichard, threatened to resign if the library were built on

The roadway, indeed, was abandoned by 1920, and towering trees today follow the curve of concrete once used by automobiles. Without Olmsted's intervention and logic in 1913, the road might yet cut across the campus green where chestnuts arch over a favored campus pathway.

Credit also is due President MacLean, who in 1913 had left Moscow to become president of the University of Manitoba. Now a Canadian client of the Olmsted firm, MacLean traveled to Boston in June of that year to confer

A modern view of the old administration building, showing a preserved greensward as Olmsted intended.

Olmsted Brothers, Inland Northwest (projects started, 1906–30s). Job numbers (#) and names of files opened by the Olmsted firm. Compiled from Beveridge, *Master List* (1987), and Lawliss et al., *Master List*, 2nd ed. (2008), with additions from Johnson, *Olmsted in the Pacific Northwest* (1997).

Civic planning/improvement
#3471—White, A.L. and Associates, Spokane
#5430—Coeur d'Alene Civic Club, Idaho

College/school campuses
#3201—Whitman College, Walla Walla
#3275—Idaho, University of, Moscow
#5389—Otis Orchards School House, Spokane
#5497—Boise Board of Education, Idaho
#5939—Whitworth College, Spokane

Country club
#3108—Hayden Lake Improvement Co., Idaho

Hotel/business
#3734—Western Union Life Ins. Co., Spokane
#5943—Davenport Hotel, Spokane

Monument design/cemeteries
#3588—Woodlawn Cemetery, Spokane
#5502—Bolster Memorial/ White, A.L.
#5813—Riverside Park Co., Spokane
#8084—Cemetery in Spokane
#8047—Greenwood Cemetery, Spokane
#8077—Wenatchee Cemetery, Wenatchee

Parks/parkways/recreation
#3095—Spokane Parks
#3096—Liberty Park
#3097—East Latah Parkway
#3098—Summit Boulevard
#3099—Corbin Park
#3100—Down River Parkway
#3101—Adams Park
#3102—Manito Park
#3103—Rockwood Boulevard
#3104—Garfield Road
#3107—City Plan Committee
#3230—Walla Walla Park System
#4074—Williamson, Volney

Private residential clients (Spokane locality)
#3109—White, Aubrey L.
#3350—Paine, James L.
#3354—Brown, David
#3360—Richards, J.P.M.*
#3427—Davenport, L.M.
#3550—White, Mrs. A.L., "Ranch"
#3552—White, Aubrey L.
#3557—Gould, David E.
#3587—Coman, T.E.
#3638—Martin, F.N.
#3639—Pfile, J.W.
#3641—Finucane, F.J.
#3736—McGoldrick, J.F.*
#3813—Cowles, W.H.
#3879—Graves, Jay P., "Waikiki"
#4005—Ham, D.T.*
  (also #3357—Spok./Wash. Impvt. Co.)
#4006—Ryland, A.S.*
#4007—Grant, A.E.*
#4059—Jones, C.H.
#4085—Galland, S.
#4086—Witherspoon, A.W.
#5096—Mason, Fred H.*
#5261—Turner, Senator (George)*
#5262—Traver, Alice*
#5455—White, A.L., "Browne's Add."
#5490—Sherwood, J.D.
#5499—Twohy, D.W.
#5800—Hansen, C.T.
#5801—Porter, J.D.*
#6188—Mathews, C.L.*
#6506—Humbird, J.T.
#8040—Rooney, F.P.
#8055—Davenport, L.M.
#8059—Gordon, Mrs. B.L.
#8067—Leuthold, W.M.
#8068—Goodwin, E.S.
#9370—Powell, William

Private clients (other localities)
#3211—Fletcher, A.H., Walla Walla*
#3217—Webb, John, Walla Walla**
#3239—Langdon, John W., Walla Walla**
#8043—Anderson, C.C., Boise, Idaho

Subdivisions/suburban communities
#1142—Rockwood
#3357—Spokane and Washington Impvt. Co.
  (also see #4005—Ham, D.T.)
#3557—Northern Pacific Irrig. Co., Kennewick
#3707—Western Trust, Rockwood Park Add.
#3814—White and Graves
#3910—White, Graves, and Newberry
#5341—Security Trust Co.
#5957—Peyton Investment Co.
#9667—Jones, Arthur D., Co.

---

*Catherine Joy Johnson's inventory in *Olmsted in the Pacific Northwest* indicates private clients making "inquiry only" in these job files.
**Johnson identifies as "voice consultation"—"VC."

the green just north of the Administration Building. The fact that funding for the new building did not materialize settled the issue…The green in front and to the north of the building…remains intact. This cherished feature of the campus is a direct result of Olmsted's plan—and later passionate defense of it…the campus green, now free of bisecting roads, with its surrounding buildings in the historic Gothic style, has become the University of Idaho's crown jewel."

Notes

1. For a detailed overview of Kirtland Kelsey Cutter's career in Spokane and Seattle, and later in California when Fred Dawson drew him there, see Henry C. Matthews, *Kirtland Cutter: Architect in the Land of Promise* (Seattle: University of Washington Press/Eastern Washington Historical Society, 1998). For a briefer treatment focusing on Spokane, see Henry C. Matthews, "Kirtland Cutter: Spokane's Architect," in David H. Stratton, ed., *Spokane and the Inland Empire: An Interior Pacific Northwest Anthology* (Pullman: Washington State University Press, rev. ed., 2005).

2. Olmsted had just arrived from Walla Walla, where he was asked to prepare Whitman College and city parks plans.

3. Olmsted job #3108, Hayden Lake Improvement Company; Library of Congress.

4. Letter, December 17, 1906.

5. Olmsted job #3095, Spokane Parks; Library of Congress.

6. Olmsted job #3102, Manito Park; Library of Congress. For a historical overview, see Tony and Suzanne Bamonte, *Manito Park: A Reflection of Spokane's Past* (Spokane: Tornado Creek Publications, 1998).

7. The Hotel Spokane was Olmsted's favorite overnight stop in Spokane although the Pennington Hotel was an alternate in later years. Meals however were mostly enjoyed elsewhere—at Davenport's restaurant or at the Spokane Club with member Aubrey White.

8. Adams Park plan, October 1911, Olmsted job #3101; Library of Congress.

9. Olmsted job #3096, Liberty Park; Library of Congress.

10. The Liberty Park photographs are permanently preserved at the Frederick Law Olmsted National Historic Site in Brookline.

11. Sally Reynolds, Report to Spokane Park Commission, 1995.

12. Today, joggers keeping track of their distance with stopwatches and global positioning devices report that the perimeter path is almost a mile around—just as it was in Olmsted's day.

13. Olmsted job #3099, Corbin Park; Library of Congress.

14. Sally Reynolds, Report.

15. See John Fahey, *Shaping Spokane: Jay P. Graves and His Times* (Seattle: University of Washington Press, 1994).

16. Olmsted jobs #3103, Rockwood Boulevard, and #3879, Jay P. Graves, August 1911, "Waikiki"; Library of Congress.

17. Helen Campbell diaries and Campbell House wedding photos (June 4, 1913), Eastern Washington State Historical Society archives, Museum of Arts and Culture, Spokane.

18. Olmsted job #3427, L.M. Davenport; Library of Congress.

19. Letter, February 13, 1909.

20. J. William T. Youngs, "Thinking Globally, Acting Locally: Spokane's Expo '74, the Environmental World's Fair," in David H. Stratton, ed., *Spokane and the Inland Empire: An Interior Pacific Northwest Anthology* (Pullman: Washington State University Press, rev. ed., 2005).

21. Olmsted job #3201, Whitman College; Library of Congress.

22. Whitman College archives.

23. The December 11 *Daily Union* article remains enclosed with a letter sent to Sophia from the Hotel Dacres, Walla Walla; John Charles Olmsted Papers, Special Collections, Harvard Graduate School of Design.

24. Olmsted job #3230, Walla Walla Park System; Library of Congress.

25. University of Idaho planning and sketch, Olmsted job #3275, University of Idaho; Library of Congress. For an overview history of the University of Idaho, see Keith C. Petersen, *This Crested Hill: An Illustrated History of the University of Idaho* (Moscow: University of Idaho Press, 1987).

26. Two months before, John Charles Olmsted had died at his hilltop home, Cliffside, in Brookline, after 45 years of campus, park, and estate design work.

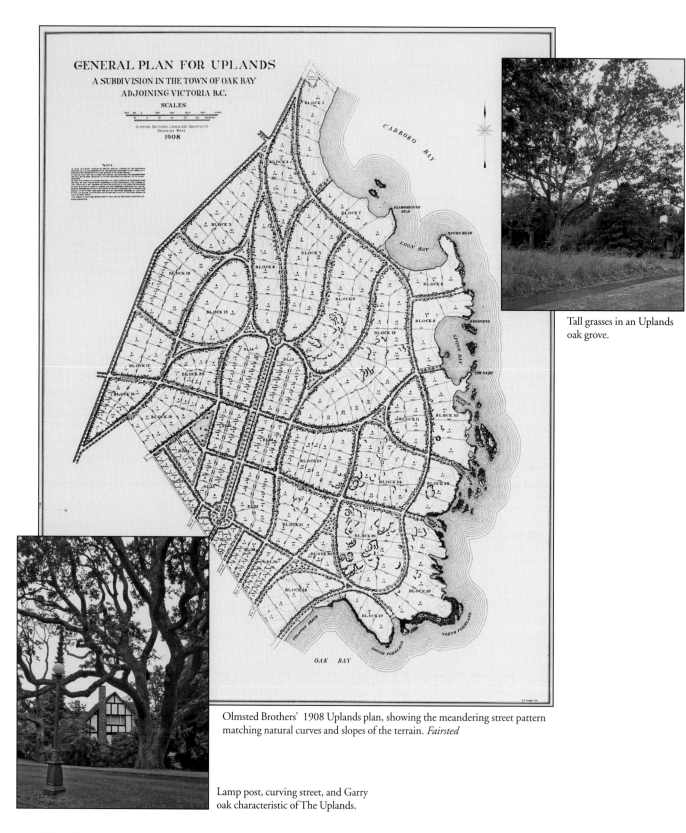

Tall grasses in an Uplands
oak grove.

Olmsted Brothers' 1908 Uplands plan, showing the meandering street pattern
matching natural curves and slopes of the terrain. *Fairsted*

Lamp post, curving street, and Garry
oak characteristic of The Uplands.

8

Vancouver Island—The Uplands

People here have always been asking whether I have seen Victoria & say it is a beautiful town. Now, the opportunity has come for me to do so.—April 3, 1907

*B*eginning in 1907, The Uplands of the Oak Bay vicinity, northeast of Victoria harbor, was a landscape architect's ideal commission—the planning of an expansive upscale neighborhood nestled by the sea. John Charles wrote Sophia on April 3, 1907, from Seattle just before his departure for Vancouver Island. "It is remarkable how many parts of the country I am getting familiar with. I begin to feel like a commercial traveler in that respect, but fortunately do not have to be always pushing in where I am not invited nor always trying to sell someone something they do not want!"

Reflecting on his expected 7½ hour journey on the steamer *Princess Beatrice* between Seattle and Victoria, Olmsted again drew parallels between eastern and western waterways. "If it should happen to be a clear mild day, the return trip would be interesting because, besides seeing the varied coasts on both sides—something like Penobscot Bay only hills & trees on a much bigger scale, one should see the fine snow-clad mountains in the distance both sides."

The trip north, however, would be at nighttime. A letter home captured details of his lodging during the voyage and his arrival in Victoria. "I had a good little stateroom with doors opening both onto the saloon and out on the narrow deck passage. There was a nice little ventilating window above the door which had glass in it but would be awkward to leave open for ventilation. I was awakened at daylight by the rolling in the Straight of San Juan de Fuca, but got asleep again. We got to Victoria I think about 6 or so… until 7 when…[a] Doctor would come aboard…I believe they are excited about Cerebro-Spinal Meningitis by which there have been 4 deaths among the students of the University of Washington at Seattle…the customs inspection on the wharf only took a few seconds. There I was joined by Mr. W.H. Gardner and went with him to [the Driard]

hotel and breakfasted with him. We spent the morning out on the property…lunched at the [Union] club …conferences occupied the afternoon and then we went to Mr. Andrew Wright's for dinner." Clearly, the traveling Bostonian had little time to rest.

Both clients at The Uplands—developers W.H. Gardner and Andrew Wright—allowed Olmsted the freedom in planning to follow the lay of the land, rather than prepare a rigid grid pattern, which was the fashion of the day.

After returning to Seattle a couple of days later, John Charles wrote to Sophia from the Rainier Club on April 6. "The land I am to plan was bought of the Hudson Bay Co. being a cattle farm. The Co. has got rich with its land. But the piece I am working on is beautiful and a pleasure to plan."

Set in a rolling countryside filled with fine, gnarled Garry oaks, hedges of snowberry, and ledges with views of Mt. Baker and the Cascades, the extensive 465-acre Uplands development had clients willing to wait for a perfect plan.[1] Summoned this first time in early spring 1907, Olmsted returned on five more occasions to put proposals onto paper.

On his third trip to Vancouver Island—in November 1907[2]—he wrote Sophia from the Union Club after lunch with the clients, reporting continuing excellent progress. "Everything about this business seems to be going smoothly and I enjoy the work because it is a beautiful property and is going to be improved in a good fashion,"

Mt. Baker

During the November 1907 visit, Olmsted moved from the old Hotel Driard downtown out to the Oak Bay "suburbs" to stay at the "quite English" Oak Bay Hotel "on the beach."

Olmsted's Uplands clients "induced me to move" he noted on November 13. The "glorious" view from the Oak Bay Hotel veranda gave Olmsted his Uplands' inspiration.

Returning again in January 1908, he described the magnificent view of Mt. Baker over on the American mainland. "Mt. Baker has been in sight all day and is glorious especially this afternoon with the sun shining full on it. I set the Kodak on the floor of the veranda which was too low and brought a brick post up too prominently. The mountain is 10,613 ft. high and perpetually snow clad and has glaciers. The crater is only 20 ft. across and is hot. Old people remember when it was active. It is over 100 miles away but looks only 50 or 60."

Along with the distant sight of Mt. Rainier from Seattle and Mt. Hood from Portland, John Charles had magnificent views of the Cascade and Olympic Mountains to gladly take into account for major Northwest urban areas.

His January 1908 call to British Columbia had been quick and unexpected, as he then was in the midst of filing park and private client reports in Seattle. He had rushed to Victoria to see for himself The Uplands plat before cows knocked the stakes down. He reported to Sophia: "The surveyor says the stakes are in…the cattle are rapidly knocking them down by using them to scratch on or pick their teeth with."[3]

His subsequent walkabouts on The Uplands property rarely failed to report sightings of Mt. Baker or interesting land forms. "In the upper part of the property it is dry and sheltered and very well adapted to winter residences. In most of the lower part it is ledgy and wet at this season and near the shore it may be considered too exposed to be comfortable in winter. Still the views are delightful… strolling about there in the more open & wet part it was a little chilly. I wish we could live in such a beautiful locality," Olmsted uncharacteristically tempted his wife in a January 26, 1909, letter.

Today, The Uplands sidewalks sit well back from the streets and are carefully placed to just one side of the roads, just as Olmsted planned. Swaths of smooth grass—uninterrupted by fussy planted shrubs or "bedding out"—border the streets, which are lined by old-fashioned lamp posts. Community design controls remain in effect, allowing only compatible construction.

In places, patches of Garry oak woodlands, while endangered in lowlands elsewhere, stand serenely in The Uplands.

The oak groves are surrounded by tall grasses allowed to grow naturally, as do masses of snowberry, all intentionally retained. Planted triangles and curving streets add variety to the overall landscape scene. Olmsted's intended effect is remarkably intact to this day. He anticipated by many decades the trend for conserving natural vegetation and had less trouble convincing his Victoria clients to do so than in other Northwest communities.[4]

Though Olmsted gave The Empress Hotel a mixed review in January 1909, British Columbia's formal and reserved social style was more to his liking.

Impressions of The Empress

His last visits coincided with the transformation of Victoria's Inner Harbor into a refined tourist stop when he stayed at The Empress Hotel, newly-built by the Canadian Pacific Railway. The magnificent hotel, however, received his mixed review on January 24, 1909, being so new and needing trees out back and vines up the sides. A visit in wintertime, however, was bound to produce a gloomier picture than during other seasons in Victoria.

"This hotel wasn't open when I was here a year ago—It is good looking outside & handsomely designed inside but quietly decorated. It has thick walls and I guess is fireproof as hotels go. But it is too cool for me. Only a tiny corner next [to] the pipe has any heat of the radiator in my room so I am writing in the palm room. The halls and rooms are astonishingly spacious after the Savoy [in Seattle]. It fronts the harbor which is a fine idea but the back looks out into a low place surrounded by poor factories, stables & cheap untidy little houses. There is plenty of ground behind so trees can be eventually grown up to hide the beyond. I have spent the afternoon proof-reading my Uplands report."

The traveling in January 1909 also revealed growing steamship competition on British Columbia waters. "This is the first time I have made the trip all by day—all daylight I mean. The steamer is built for night service but competition has reduced the fare to 25 cents and at that price they can get more passengers by day. The steamer now stops here instead of going on to Vancouver but they have night steamers between Seattle and Vancouver—that is a dollar. It's remarkable to get such a ride as from 8:30 to 1 on a fine large fast steamer for 25 cents."

Quiet Social Life

Olmsted's professional and social interactions—partnerships started and lasting friendships formed—were fewer in Victoria. Here, architects were less in number and his time spent on The Uplands plan normally precluded distraction by private client inquiries, in which he only lightly dabbled. For Olmsted, of course, plenty enough of those associations already existed back in Seattle.

Nevertheless, Victoria's British style and manners suited John Charles' formality. He spent more hours here than in most cities enjoying formal dinners and "Sunday afternoon salon" discussions, including with clients Andrew Wright and W.H. Gardner and the noted architect Samuel Maclure.

Over dinner at the Wrights shortly after first arriving in Victoria, John Charles was urged by Mrs. Wright to sample a locally-made "Rogers" chocolate cream. Olmsted "fell a victim."

Within a day, he purchased a box or two and sent them quickly off to Sophia and his sister back home. "I bought a box of chocolates for you this morning & will mail it tomorrow…It is a little immoral…but I do not often sin in this way you will acknowledge…[The Wrights] told me the man & his wife make every bit of candy themselves that they sell at their store," and "they are so particular to have it the best, and they won't sell any that's the least stale and won't take orders for more than they can make. Even at Christmas."[5]

Charles Rogers, the confectioner, originally was a pioneer coming from Massachusetts. Beginning in 1885, he and his wife built up their Victoria-based chocolate busi-

---

Olmsted Brothers, Vancouver Island (projects started, 1907–30s). Job numbers (#) and names of files opened by the Olmsted firm. Compiled from Beveridge, *Master List* (1987), and Lawliss et al., *Master List,* 2nd ed. (2008), with additions from Johnson, *Olmsted in the Pacific Northwest* (1997).

College campus
#5902—British Columbia, University of, Vancouver

Parks/recreation/suburb development
#6059—Victoria Park, Truro
#9348—British Pacific Securities Ltd., Vancouver

Private residential clients
#3419—Dunsmuir, Lord ("James"), Victoria*
#5381—Marpole, Clarence M., Vancouver
#5815—Rogers, B.T., Victoria
#9273—Taylor, A.J.T., Vancouver
#9400—Taylor, Austin, Vancouver
#9401—Taylor, A.J.T., Vancouver
#9402—Taylor, A.J.T., Vancouver
#9403—Taylor, A.J.T., Vancouver
#9461—Aubeneau, Henry, Vancouver*

Subdivision/suburban community
#3276—Oldfield, Kirby & Gardner/Uplands, Victoria

---

*Catherine Joy Johnson's inventory in *Olmsted in the Pacific Northwest* indicates private clients making "inquiry only" in these job files.

---

ness from humble beginnings to world-wide fame. (Today, Rogers chocolate creams are available only in Canada and select locations.)

Few architects of note crossed Olmsted's path for work-related or social association in Victoria, as he rarely sought extra Vancouver Island work. His brief collaboration with Victoria architect Samuel Maclure quickly came to nothing, except social calls. When Olmsted met with Maclure's client, Sir James Dunsmuir, the latter decided to only "take under consideration" the famed landscape architect's employment for a new residence in the planning stages.

"I think this means that he will not decide favorably," John Charles quite rightly predicted on January 17, 1908.[6]

James Dunsmuir, son of Craigdarroch Castle builder Robert Dunsmuir,[7] had by then moved to Government House to represent the Queen in British Columbia.

A Sunday afternoon "salon" call to Maclure's residence a few days earlier, however, gave Olmsted an even better view of Mt. Baker—this time from a picture window at the architect's house. "He has a full view of Mt. Baker from his landscape window and it was glorious."

The conversation, too, was to John Charles' liking. "Talked about art & acting and books so it was pleasanter for me than the ordinary afternoon tea."[8]

Mild Weather and Manicured Gardens

The mild weather and spring-like vegetation in winter astonished Olmsted, as he explained to Sophia in January 1908. "The grass is green and the pasture fairly good. I picked two wildflowers which I was going to send you…It is strange to see so much green herbage in midwinter."

He found it remarkable that the hotel gardener mowed grass during winter. "Here a man was running a lawn-mower on the hotel lawn today. To be sure it did not look very much in need of mowing."

Of the manicured winter gardens in Victoria, Olmsted was equally enthusiastic. "This town is much more like Brookline than any other in the West because of the attention paid to planting hedges and shrubs, trees, vines and flowers. Also they have oak trees many of which are preserved in the yards, so it looks entirely different from Seattle."[9]

For a fleeting moment, Olmsted perhaps even suggested that he and Sophia might pull up winter stakes and consider a Vancouver Island home at The Uplands. "It is a beautiful property. I should be happy to live there, but it would be hard to make a choice. I think on the whole a sheltered cove for boating would be my choice although then I should not have Mt. Baker in view as it is from the southern (exposed) and the high part of the property. I should like to have taken some photos to show you but they were not needed professionally."[10]

An ownership change in 1911 brought a hasty but "pleasant" return to The Uplands and a revised plan for a client named David Rogers—not to be confused with Charles Rogers, the Victoria chocolatier.

Notes

1. Larry McCann (University of Victoria), various research, and *John Olmsted's Masterpiece: The Uplands and Suburban Development in Western Canadian Cities, c. 1900–1950* (book in progress).
2. Victoria's Union Club later moved to another location, across from The Empress Hotel.
3. Letter from the Savoy Hotel, Seattle, January 8, 1908.
4. Olmsted job #3276, Oldfield, Kirby, and Gardner, The Uplands; Library of Congress.
5. Letter, April 6, 1907.
6. Olmsted job #3419, James Dunsmuir; Library of Congress.
7. British Columbia coal baron Robert Dunsmuir had started the magnificent 39-room Craigdarroch Castle in 1889, but died before its completion. His sons Alexander and James finished the project. The stone walled mansion remains a major Victoria tourist attraction today.
8. Letter January 13, 1908.
9. Letter, January 15, 1908.
10. Letter, January 14, 1908.

Final Northwest Visits

I am leaving Mr. Dawson to go on with my work. It is very gratifying to be able to do so.
—June 13, 1911

ohn Charles' last visits to the Pacific Northwest all came in three brief but work-filled stopovers in 1911. Intending to return to the Puget Sound area in the following year, his health suddenly gave out in February 1912, ending his long cross-country travels at age 59.[1] He never again set foot in the Northwest, and only once returned to the Pacific Coast when his physical condition improved somewhat. In 1916, he inspected the Palos Verdes development plan in California, a major project that proceeded soon thereafter.

Thus, after 36 years in the business, he no longer was able to venture so far, or so often, from home. Nevertheless, he kept up his correspondence—and loyalties—to old Northwest clients. Fred Dawson stepped in, too, as Olmsted intended, and remained active in the Northwest for the next three decades.

John Charles continued to engage eastern clients, work that hardly slowed. Often enough, he also traveled for them, when some of his vigor returned. In fact, the firm's eastern business benefited from Olmsted's now continued presence in the East.

In these last years, public recognition still came Olmsted's way; for example, "Park Expert in Lexington," read a Kentucky newspaper banner in early May 1916.[2] "John C. Olmstead [sic] Comes to City to Inspect Local Playground System…Is Not a Stranger…Has Executed a Number of Landscape Contracts in the City," the headline continued.

Colman Park beach, just off Lake Washington Boulevard. *FSOP*

"He came here in 1905 and platted Woodland Park, a park on South Upper Street that was never built, the Henry Clay estate and the Experiment Station grounds…Mr. Olmstead was employed this year after the board had gotten into communication with him and found that he would do all the necessary work for a complete survey for $250…

"He was at Dayton [Ohio] at the time, looking after eighteen separate contracts, several of which were for John H. Patterson, president of the National Cash Register Company, and others for the Dayton High School, a 400-acre industrial village, several golf clubs, the monument to Robert H. Patterson, grandfather of John H. Patterson, and formerly of Lexington, and a number of other contracts. Mr. Olmstead has been employed by Mr. Patterson and the Cash Register Company for a number of years…the firm has been park and landscape advisor to the city of Louisville [Kentucky] for twenty-three years, and has laid out the entire park system of that city."

San Diego, 1910–11

In 1911, with hand-picked superintendents keeping park plans on track—Emil Mische in Portland, John W. Thompson in Seattle, and John W. Duncan in Spokane—John Charles could rest assured that Olmsted Brothers' principles would hold in the Northwest, at least for now. In regard to private clients, Olmsted had sent capable eastern gardeners to finish up estate work in Spokane for the Davenports and at American Lake for the Thornes. In addition, he had continued consultations with Fred Dawson, his young Pacific Coast assistant. Meanwhile, in the winter of 1910–11, Olmsted spent most of his time working in California.

From San Diego on March 24, 1911, he wrote Sophia: "A year ago—half a year ago I had no more idea of passing a winter here [in California] than I had of doing so in New Zealand." Using the U.S. Grant Hotel as his home base during a half year of San Diego exposition planning, he supervised two office employees and an Olmsted sister, Marion, who decided to relocate to warm California. "It isn't the climate of San Diego that holds me out here, but work," he wrote Sophia six weeks later after receiving telegrams urging his presence for Pacific Northwest and Riverside, California, jobs.

The Golden State's fair weather, however, hardly camouflaged the cloud over the planning for the Panama-California International Exposition, scheduled for 1915–16. Site selection in San Diego suffered from a tug of war between differing local and design interests. The conflict finally wore down Olmsted's patience (which he normally held in abundance).

"The climate is so nearly perfect here that it is a pity my pleasure has been spoiled of late by…political conditions," he told Sophia on June 1, 1911. After advising the San Diego exposition organizers to hire F.P. Allen, Seattle's AYPE executive director, Olmsted later regretted the move. It caused factions to align with Allen's point of view regarding site selection, instead of Olmsted's.[3]

Against this backdrop, John Charles' brief train trips to Northwest cities seemed a welcome break. For the first time in a half-dozen years, however, Olmsted did not spend a portion of the winter in the Northwest. Preoccupied in 1910–11 with the increasingly contentious San Diego planning, he only came north twice in the spring of 1911, and once from the East in the autumn, to attend to a Washington State Capitol proposal, a third University of Washington campus plan, The Uplands project, and for other consultations.

He also renewed old acquaintances with Seattle park board members and met the new commission president, J.D. Trenholme. In 1910, Olmsted's key ally, Edward C.

Seattle's park board in 1911 included a new president, J.D. Trenholme, for Olmsted to greet. E.C. Cheasty, like old friends E.F. Blaine and Charles Saunders, no longer were on the commission. Long-time supporters Ferdinand Schmitz and J.M. Frink still served, however, and remained in Olmsted's corner. *Seattle Municipal Archives*

Cheasty, had been suddenly ousted as president of the park board by the new mayor. This had left John Charles temporarily without a leading confidant and booster. He had to make political and social rounds again to maintain the Olmsted Brothers strong ties to city leaders. Cheasty had pulled Olmsted aside to pour out the sorry political details. The Fort Lawton design and the symphony-in-the-park plans—Cheasty's pet projects—were on hold, for now.

Washington State Capitol, Olympia

After meeting with Washington Governor Marion E. Hay on April 13, 1911, Olmsted reported to his wife: "Upon arrival at Olympia, I went to the Governor's office and had to wait some time. Had a talk with him & he called in…[architect Harry] White who walked over the site with me…read a pamphlet about the proposed Capitol…Attended a meeting of the Board and discussed some features to be considered in a plan of the grounds and stated my price. The Governor said he would call a meeting on Monday to decide the matter."

The Olmsted Brothers did get a Washington capitol grounds job in 1911[4] (as they did for capitol campuses in other states before and after). However, the work turned out to be limited; not until the late 1920s did the firm fully get on board with a more complete design for the Washington capitol campus. Construction of the buildings at the site began in 1912, with the Temple of Justice being the first completed (1920), followed by the Insurance Building, a power and heating plant, and finally the grand Legislative Building (finished 1928).

It was in February 1912 that John Charles' health unexpectedly gave out, just as he was making plans to come out west to confer with the capitol commission. He had telegrammed from Brookline on January 29: "Will visit Olympia Feby. 22nd and should be glad to confer with Commission informally at that time."

On February 14, however, the Olmsted firm sent an urgent night-time telegram: "Mr. John C. Olmsted unable to visit Olympia on account

of surgical operation. Mr. Dawson will be there however about February twenty-second and would like to confer with members of your Commission."

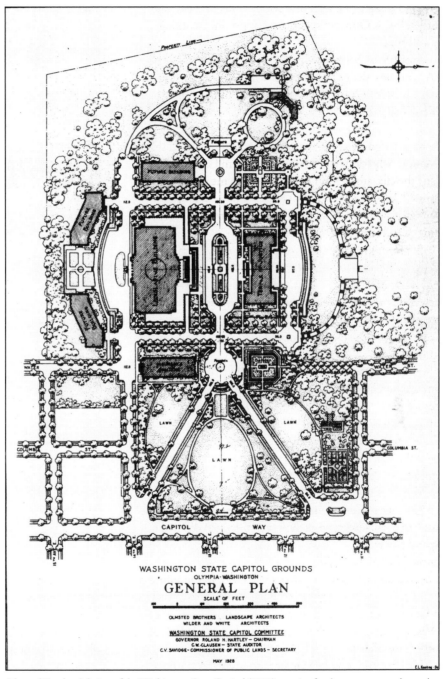

WASHINGTON STATE CAPITOL GROUNDS
OLYMPIA · WASHINGTON
GENERAL PLAN
SCALE OF FEET

OLMSTED BROTHERS   LANDSCAPE ARCHITECTS
WILDER AND WHITE   ARCHITECTS
WASHINGTON STATE CAPITOL COMMITTEE
GOVERNOR ROLAND H. HARTLEY – CHAIRMAN
C.W. CLAUSEN – STATE AUDITOR
C.V. SAVIDGE – COMMISSIONER OF PUBLIC LANDS – SECRETARY

MAY 1928

Olmsted Brothers' design of the Washington State Capitol (1928) remains for the most part unchanged today, with grand open spaces for lawmakers and constituents alike. *Secretary of State Archives*

Olmsted's site plan differed from that of the New York architects, Walter Wilder and Harry White, who had been chosen the year before to work with the Olmsteds in siting the Temple of Justice. On January 25, 1912, Olmsted had sent two watercolor sketches to Olympia, expecting to persuade Governor Hay and the capitol commission to defer in locating the Temple of Justice south, rather than north, of the future capitol dome.

In John Charles' absence, however, Fred Dawson was unable to persuade the commission to select the southerly location, or, in fact, to even keep the Olmsted firm on retainer. Enclosing a check for $2,000 in fees, Dawson on February 28 broke the news to Olmsted's brother Rick in correspondence from Seattle. "I am sorry to have to inform you that I was unable to persuade the Washington State Commission to retain us. I worked for three or four days on the matter, both here in Seattle and in Olympia."

Dawson said he might have succeeded "if the commission were not at loggerheads with each other politically and if the Governor had taken any initiative in running his commission and in supporting us…Please accept my finest wishes for your brother's recovery and comfort."

In later years, however, as the capital buildings were completed, a Seattle state representative in Olympia would champion the Olmsted Brothers cause again. Charles W. Saunders—the former Seattle park commissioner, now architect-turned-politician—helped secure a second capitol site job for the Olmsted firm, which in a more stable political climate had more lasting effect than the earlier work.

Perhaps Saunders remembered John Charles' letter of January 30, 1912, which outlined Olmsted's strategy for the meeting he never attended. At the time he informed Saunders: "It seems to be useless to send telegrams, letters and plans and as you say the only way that there is any chance of getting any good result would be by personal interview."

State legislator Charles Saunders, representing Seattle at the state capitol in Olympia in the 1920s. His service earlier on the Seattle parks board provided Olmsted with one of the firm's first loyal supporters. Later still, in the 1930s, he would tip off the Olmsted firm to a planned arboretum, for which the firm eventually submitted its plan. *Washington State Capitol Archives*

Seattle, April and June 1911

Just hours after meeting with the governor in Olympia on April 13, 1911, Olmsted had proceeded on to settle into a Seattle hotel. In the evening, he reported receiving word by wire "that the…University had accepted our proposition for a revised plan…I shall call there on Monday."

With two major jobs now on the horizon in the Northwest, but with little time to prepare detailed proposals or "state his price" with complete reflection, Olmsted's letters took on a clipped, hurried tone. He stayed in Seattle only six nights in April and another eight evenings in June (plus another four days in October). These were among his shortest stays in Seattle, pressed as he was with work elsewhere.

On June 3, on his second trip up the coast from California in 1911, Olmsted stopped overnight at the University Club in San Francisco to visit family relative Fritz Olmsted and also see how San Francisco was faring after the great earthquake and fire of 1906. "The city is well built up…a rich community," he wrote Sophia that evening.

Two nights later, he passed briefly through Portland during the Rose Festival. The Westover Terrace plan for Lewis and Wiley remained the Olmsted firm's main private work in Portland. The city on the Willamette, however, now was a more appealing place than in 1903, thanks to civic leaders who championed Olmsted's perspectives.

During his two 1911 springtime visits in Seattle, Olmsted attended UW regents and Seattle park board meetings, and strolled Woodland Park with Park Superintendent John Thompson, still on the job after Olmsted recommended him for employment seven years earlier. Olmsted also found time to take in two theater productions, one of his few indulgences while traveling.

His June letters home, as always this time of year, reassured Sophia of his return in time for their traditional Deer Isle, Maine, gathering on July 4. "I am leaving Mr. Dawson to go on with my work. It is very gratifying to be able to do so. Otherwise I might have been obliged to stay here a week or two longer," Olmsted wrote on June 13.

Spokane's Adams Park. Today, the small lake is considerably reduced in size but yet retains as natural a look as possible in any artificial landscape. Unclipped reeds and other plants are allowed to fill in the shoreline, as Olmsted intended, for less formality than seen in most city parks.

Liberty Park postcard from Olmsted's Spokane album, showing rustic stairs and woodwork commonly seen in a number of early 20th century parks. *Fairsted*

In a Brookline album, the "Log Cabins among the Pines" indicates Olmsted's planned Hayden Lake resort community had reached fruition in Idaho. *Fairsted*

Kirtland Cutter designed Bozanta Tavern, the clubhouse and centerpiece of the Hayden Lake development. *Fairsted*

Modern views in Walla Walla's Pioneer Park. During a one week visit in December 1906, Olmsted was charged with preparing a parks plan for the city as well as for Whitman College. The reports were written, dictated, and typed on the spot, thanks to the capable assistance of Miss Taylor in President Penrose's office.

VIEW OF
VICTORIA, B.C.
SHOWING RELATIVE POSITION OF
THE UPLANDS

The Uplands—aerial view with Victoria, Juan de Fuca Strait, and the Olympic Mountains in the distance. *Fairsted*

The Uplands on Vancouver Island remains today much as Olmsted envisioned, with gnarled Garry oaks predominating, streets with rounded center islands and graceful curves, and native vegetation preserved in neighborhood commons.

A double turn in the Lake Washington Boulevard.

The automobile soon invaded Olmsted's newly-designed boulevards, allowing scenic drives for families able to afford this new mode of transportation. Between Olmsted's first 1903 visit to Seattle, and his last in 1911, the automobile gradually replaced the streetcar as preferred transportation to visiting far-flung parks. *FSOP*

A modern view of Sophia's family home "Cliffside" at 222 Warren Street in Brookline, where John Charles spent his last years. Olmsted's earlier residences, "Fairsted" at 99 Warren and a rental at 16 Warren, also remain intact. Cliffside stands next door to the hilltop home of the renowned architect H.H. Richardson, who in the 1880s influenced Olmsted Sr. to move from New York to Boston.

Dawson Carries On

Fred Dawson, who so ably assisted John Charles during the AYPE years, indeed carried on the firm's Northwest work at this time, and intermittently for years to come. Dawson, who had spent his childhood at Harvard's Arnold Arboretum, would represent the Olmsted Brothers with distinction, building on the prestige that John Charles enjoyed out west.

He took a hand at The Highlands in Seattle and for client contracts in Spokane and Tacoma (but less so in Portland). He worked on the state capitol planning in the late 1920s and, finally, the Washington Park Arboretum during the 1930s.[5] The example of his plantsmanship and adherence to Olmsted principles became rooted amongst the next generation of landscape architects in Seattle.

The arboretum was one of the final pieces in Olmsted's plan for Seattle, though its development had proceeded at a snail's pace. The suggestion for an overall Washington Park design had been cast aside by the city in 1903–4, over John Charles' objections. Instead, the park would be created in phases, rather than as a complete whole, leaving the land where the arboretum later was created without an Olmsted Brothers master plan, at least for the time being.

In the 1930s, the time had come, and Dawson's expert plantsmanship was a convincing credential for gaining the new arboretum project. In Seattle, however, there now were new decision-makers who were rather unfamiliar with the Olmsted Brothers. The fact that an Olmsted employee needed to present a portfolio in the 1930s was a sign of the changing times. Dawson did not disappoint; he conducted his arboretum work with the usual Olmsted Brothers patience and perseverance.

When traveling out west with John Charles before 1911, Dawson had provided Olmsted with good companionship. In time, Rick Olmsted also would assume some western work after his older brother's health gave out. Rick, however, mostly stayed to the south in California, working with Dawson in planning the Palos Verdes Estates after John Charles' visit there in 1916.[6] Dawson, meanwhile, also handled Northwest clients, while the firm kept their offices in Boston and Palos Verdes in business.

The Uplands

In the autumn of 1911, Olmsted arrived in Victoria for what would be his last visit to British Columbia and shortly to Seattle and Portland as well.[7] Olmsted again absorbed himself in The Uplands project. On October 2, he noted that a "Mr. Street," an Englishman "one year here," had been hired by the developers "to do some landscape gardening at Uplands on the little park triangles."

On October 3, Olmsted noted that he "enjoyed seeing Uplands again," when writing from the Empress Hotel on his last day there. "But I do not see how I can much influence the details of carrying out my general plan as I am too far away and cannot come often enough."

The great distance from Brookline combined with Olmsted's concern for retaining "natural" landforms were cause for worry. "If they [the developers] were willing to employ one of our men on a salary it might be a good thing but I doubt if they will go to that expense," Olmsted noted in the October 3 letter.

"They have engaged Mr. Street, a local landscape gardener, to do some landscape work. I am afraid he will do too much showy decorative work on the little parklets. His is a man of good address & no doubt knows enough of horticulture for practical purposes but I fear his taste may not be simple enough & natural enough."

Nevertheless, John Charles' steady hand and confident, yet opinionated, advice held sway through the next decade. Today, The Uplands' triangles are filled with wildflowers and other native flora, in keeping with Olmsted's "natural" approach.[8]

Seattle and Portland, October 1911

From Victoria on October 3, John Charles informed Sophia: "I am leaving at 5 p.m. for Seattle, a day ahead of my schedule, which is good as I felt I needed more time at Seattle." This visit would last a mere four days, and there was much unfinished business still on the drawing board.

In John Charles' last letters from Seattle, it is clear that the horse and buggy era had given way to the automobile age. John W. Thompson, the parks superintendent, now had a chauffeur drive Olmsted from park to park. "It is fine the time the auto saves," Olmsted wrote after a whirlwind day taking in West Seattle's Schmitz Park, lunch at the Rathskeller, meeting the new park board president, and then quick visits that afternoon to Frink Park, Lake Washington Boulevard, Mt. Baker Park, and back again to Frink Park.

Beautiful Seattle. A Typical Residence Street, The Cascade Mountains in the distance.

Photo by Nowell & Rognon.

First Hill Residence District, Seattle, Wash.

Photo by F. H. Nowell

Fine residential developments often bordered Seattle's premier parks. A duplicated view shows elegant homes south of the Volunteer Park water tower. *Bryce Seidl Collection*

Olmsted's last four days in Seattle were filled with client demands enough to exhaust even the most-traveled businessman. Many of the encounters between automobile field trips were on familiar ground, such as conferences with the university regents, but he also met new park commissioners.[9] A 10 o'clock evening meeting with a Victoria client ended one of his last days in Seattle.

A shift in travel plans—booking for Portland instead of Spokane—saw him in his few spare moments studying train schedules. On this final trip, he had no assistants along to deflect the workload. It was just John Charles, working at his peak in accommodating each client request, while eastern work waited in the wings.

After arriving in Portland and tending to Westover Terrace, Olmsted boarded a train east and described the trip in his typical travelogue fashion. "I took the 10 a.m. train so as to see the Columbia River scenery, which is fine. The

best of it is passed in two hours or so from Portland. Then it becomes dry and very dusty. It seems odd to pass into so completely different a climate & scenery so suddenly. At Umatilla we left the Columbia."[10]

Olmsted, however, worried about not giving Seattle's parks enough attention during the visit, which was most unusual during his years out west. After arriving at the Hotel Utah in Salt Lake City—where the Olmsted Brothers were engaged in planning the state capitol grounds[11]—he noted that as soon as park maps arrived, he might "look over [Seattle] parkwork more carefully than I had time for this trip."

Indeed, the Olmsted firm's public and private work in the Northwest would soon somewhat slow up, due to the fact that John Charles could no longer travel out west, and because of a changing economy when America entered World War I later in the decade. Nevertheless, the Olmsted Brothers continued to thrive with extensive projects across the United States. By 1917, the firm had 47 employees, and up to 60 in the 1920s.

When John Charles left the Northwest for the last time, he was well-versed in the region's seasons, landscapes, mountain and shoreline scenery, wild places, and natural vegetation—even admiring frost-covered sagebrush in the interior. Love of these things left an indelible impression on him, and it remains visible today in the projects he came out west to complete.

University of Washington Plan Sidetracked

The revised University of Washington plan—the firm's third and last for the Seattle campus—would suffer from Olmsted's absence after 1911, and perhaps because Fred Dawson did not fully press efforts to meet political and other demands. By 1914, President Thomas Kane—who had enthusiastically steered every Olmsted design through the regents' meetings—was no longer at the helm. Now with an interim president from the geology faculty in charge, some university committee members saw an opening to reshape John Charles' final campus plan.

Architect Carl F. Gould, on the board reviewing Olmsted's work, within a year got the campus planning job himself. Unlike earlier partnerships with Seattle architects, collaboration with Gould never materialized for the Olmsted firm. Carl F. Gould had founded the UW architecture department in 1914, and in the next two decades became prominent for designing not only campus buildings, but numerous other private and public structures in the Pacific Northwest, normally in collaboration with Olmsted's gregarious old acquaintance, Charles H. Bebb.[12]

One university letter would point to Fred Dawson's lack of immediate attention in regard to the UW campus plan. "I have regretted very much that Mr. Dawson was not able to stay with us sufficiently long to get full force of different suggestions which were made by the members of our faculty," the president's assistant wrote the Olmsted Brothers in September 1915.

John Charles' drawing was lost, and the new UW president, Henry Suzzallo (1915), asked the firm for the final campus sketch. "In behalf of President Suzzallo I wish to thank you for the copy of the plan and to assure you that it will be placed on exhibition with the other plans and studies which have been made of the campus," secretary Stevens wrote the Olmsted Brothers.

A campus exhibit in 1915 included the Olmsted plan displayed alongside, presumably, new faculty sketches. Two undated drawings, done under the auspices of the faculty committee, survive in the university archives and tell the changing story. The first is titled, "Sketch No. 1 Modification of Olmsted Plan. Rainier Axis. University of Washington." The second and most telling, without making reference to Olmsted at all, is the one labeled, "Sketch No. 2. Suggestions to Committee Plan. University of Washington." By then, Gould was in full charge of what would be called the "Regents' Plan," thus cementing the post-Olmsted era.

In 1914, the changes from Olmsted's landscape-based campus planning to designs done by the engineering and architecture faculty had been almost immediate. The review board, however, trod lightly when suggesting the slightest changes in Olmsted's campus proposals.

"The committee is of the opinion that the situation in regard to the Olmsted plans is one of some delicacy," engineering professor E.O. Eastwood wrote acting President Henry Landes in January 1914. The Olmsted plan was "impracticable," the faculty committee agreed, yet the media fallout from dropping Olmsted's directives would hurt the campus's image. "It seems clear that a considerable body of citizens outside the University are advocates of the Olmsted name and reputation as publicity assets and would probably oppose with unpleasant vehemence any proposal to throw aside the plans."

Instead of telling the regents it intended to drop the Olmsted plan, the committee asked Landes to only inform them "to appoint a committee…to sit with a committee… to consider the immediate building programme of the University in its relation to the Olmsted plans."

The committee's first motion—"That the present arrangement with the Olmsted brothers for the development of the grounds be terminated"—should and would remain unannounced. "By such quiet discussion we are of the opinion that we can achieve the end in view with little unpleasant publicity and attendant bad feeling, and for that reason we recommend that you take up the regents at present only [one] of the…recommendations."

In October and November 1914, letters in quick succession had landed on the desks of committee members and the acting president, resulting in a flurry of decision-making. "Mr. Carl Gould has just been to see me and he is anxious to see the work resumed for the laying out of a definite plan," acting President Landes wrote Professor Eastwood on October 26.

Just two weeks later, Eastwood in the engineering department noted: "Mr. Carl F. Gould, who is now giving instruction in the University, is a member of the Faculty Committee and, in our judgment, is the best qualified architect in this community for undertaking this class of work." A sum of $600 was suggested for Gould's expenses.

A year later, on September 16, 1915, in response to the UW request for another set of Olmsted Brothers' drawings, Dawson wrote to the university: "We regretted that the new Board of Regents and the members of the Faculty did not see fit to confer with us about the plans of the Campus at the time a committee was appointed to report on this subject."

While graciously admitting defeat, the Olmsted firm kept the door open for further consultation. "We understand that Mr. Carl Gould has prepared a plan for the Campus which has been adopted and that some of the new buildings are being erected in accordance with this adopted plan. If the Committee or your President should so desire we should be glad to be consulted in regard to the plan of the University Campus. If you have a reproduction of the plan which was adopted will you be good enough to send

John Charles Olmsted is buried alongside Sophia in the White family plot at Walnut Hills, so near the homes he lived in on Warren Street in the village of Brookline, Massachusetts.

us a copy of same? Very truly yours, Olmsted Brothers." The letter was signed in Dawson's hand.

Thus, Olmsted's 1911 campus design had become a showpiece for consultation, rather than the directive it was intended to be.

End of an Era

In March 1920, when news of John Charles' death on February 24 reached Emil Mische in Portland, he quickly sent off a letter to Seattle Park Superintendent John W. Thompson. "Dear Thompson:—Just had word from F.L.O. [Olmsted Jr.] that J.C.O. passed away. That is a national loss as well as a personal one and I know you will share with me the personal and profound feeling of sympathy and regret…Hastily yours, Mische."

The next day, Thompson wrote the younger Olmsted in Brookline. "It was with great sadness that I read the report of the death of your brother John. I am more than pleased, however, that on my last trip east, in September, 1919, I had quite a long talk with your brother. I

knew he had been ill for a long time, but his cheerfulness and patience were wonderful."

Within a year, Thompson lost his top parks job in Seattle, after 17 years of representing and carrying through on Olmsted ideals. The old guard in Seattle—led by Charles Saunders—tried valiantly and publicly to reverse a new trend toward allowing engineering expertise to overtake plantsmanship as top parks planning requirements. From Boston, Fred Dawson again sent John Charles' 1909 Seattle report to the current park board president, outlining the Olmsted Brothers' perspective. In the early 1920s, however, minds were made up in city government.

Writing to the firm's old influential friend, Charles Saunders, in May 1921, Fred Dawson made clear his pleas against the coming change. "It seems to be against all good sound judgment for the Park Board of Seattle to select a trained civil engineer, who has no training or experience and probably no liking for park work, to take charge of the parks of the City of Seattle."

The city's parks "are now among the most beautiful in the United States…[A] technical engineer…can not help but let the vegetation, which is the most important part of any park, become second to roads, bridges, buildings, and other structural features," Dawson noted.

"The parks of our great cities are built for…the purpose of giving to the public a place to seek recreation of mind and body, where they may go and forget their anxieties and worries, and where they can enjoy the peace and quiet that nature provides in our fields and forests and parks. Parks were not created for any business purpose or for any public thoroughfare that requires the technical training and experience of an engineer, and therefore they should never be under the care of such a person."

Despite Dawson's reasoned pleas, change did come. Nevertheless, numerous fine parks, boulevards, and gardens laid out by the Massachusetts' men still remain today, as lasting reminders of John Charles Olmsted's dedication and love for the Pacific Northwest.

Notes

1. For 1912, only two Olmsted letters survive from when he was traveling—February 6 and 7 during a trip in Ohio. Shortly after, he was stricken down by his health problems, preventing further business travel for many months. Reviving after a year, his next letters written on the road begin on March 17, 1913, during visits to New York and Philadelphia; John Charles Olmsted Papers, Special Collections, Harvard Graduate School of Design.
2. Newspaper article enclosed with letter to Sophia, May 4, 1916, from the Phoenix Hotel, Lexington.
3. Olmsted job #4501, San Diego Exposition; Library of Congress.
4. Olmsted job #5350, Washington State Capitol; Library of Congress.
5. Olmsted job #2699, Seattle Arboretum; Library of Congress.
6. Olmsted job #5950, Palos Verdes Estates; Library of Congress.
7. During the autumn 1911 trip, Olmsted also took a jaunt into Canada by train. The Northwest's climate he knew so well was ever in mind as a reference, as noted in a remark to Sophia about the weather in Winnipeg, Manitoba: "It has been a Seattle light rain and mist here today."
8. Larry McCann (University of Victoria), various research, and *John Olmsted's Masterpiece: The Uplands and Suburban Development in Western Canadian Cities, c. 1900–1950* (book in progress).
9. Don Sherwood Parks History Collection, Seattle Municipal Archives.
10. Letter from Pendleton, Oregon, October 8, 1911.
11. John Charles conferred with Utah's governor. Olmsted job #5357, Utah State Capitol; Library of Congress.
12. The Suzzallo Library, completed in 1927, is included among the UW campus buildings designed by Gould. For a biography, see William T. Booth and William H. Wilson, *Carl F. Gould: A Life in Architecture and the Arts* (Seattle: University of Washington Press, 1995).

Afterword

John Charles Olmsted's Northwest Legacy

David C. Streatfield

*Professor of Landscape Architecture, Urban Design
and Planning, and Adjunct Professor of Architecture,
University of Washington*

John Charles Olmsted—the lesser known of three family members in the Olmsted firm—first visited the Pacific Northwest during Easter week 1903. He was 50 years old and recently married with two small daughters. His last visit was a brief trip to Victoria, Seattle, and Portland in October 1911.

In nearly a full decade, he played a major role in transforming the region's rapidly changing urban landscapes—through the planning and design of expositions, public parks and park systems, university and college campuses, the Washington State Capitol grounds, and a series of private client projects including residential subdivisions, gardens, and estates.

These commissions occurred during a period of explosive urban growth fueled by the Alaska/Yukon gold fields, the extractive wealth of the Puget Sound country and the Inland Northwest, and massive increases in population, manufacturing, and commerce. Leading citizens in the region sought—in the Progressive Era—to change the frontier character of their cities into places that would clearly express new civic pride.

Civic beauty also had a positive economic value and, indeed, was considered an inducement for future growth. It was an opportune time to invite the foremost firm of landscape architects to assist in beautifying and transforming the region's cities.

When park commissioners in Portland and Seattle first invited the Olmsted Brothers to plan their respective park systems, they naturally assumed the mantle of Frederick Law Olmsted Sr. had fallen on the shoulders of his son, Frederick Law Olmsted Jr. Yet despite the fact that the younger Olmsted was the first professor of landscape architecture at Harvard University and was appointed to the McMillan Commission to plan the Washington D.C. Mall, he was a far less experienced designer than John Charles

Olmsted, his older half-brother. By virtue of nearly three decades of working in the Olmsted firm, John Charles was one of the most accomplished American landscape architects trained in the late 19th century.

He played a major role in the design of the Fenway in Boston, and planned the first children's playground, Charlesbank, in Boston. Yet despite these accomplishments and his position as a founding member and first president of the American Society of Landscape Architects, he had lived in the shadow of his father and younger brother. His new work in the Far West, however, would change this. *Greenscapes*, of course, is the story of how John Charles became the best known Olmsted family member in the Pacific Northwest and the Inland Empire.

The many letters and documents reproduced in *Greenscapes* are drawn from extensive archival collections held at Harvard University, the Library of Congress, and the Frederick Law Olmsted National Historic Site in Brookline, Massachusetts. This extensive documentation enables us today to establish John Charles' legacy in the Northwest. The major facets of this legacy can be examined in three broad categories.

First Legacy: Regional Documentation

John Charles' detailed field notes and his letters to Sophia, written practically every day when away from Brookline, provide a most revealing record of what he saw, who he met, and what his opinions were. He was the first member of the Olmsted firm to spend time in the Northwest. (His father had prepared an unexecuted scheme in the Tacoma area but apparently never visited the site.) John Charles' impressions of Northwest landscapes entailed deep appreciation, and his astute observations remain today as a valuable regional historical record.

His delight in the lushness of the vegetation recalls his father's similar reaction on the Isthmus of Panama. In the Northwest, John Charles marveled at the size of old growth trees, and the beauty of the understory and mosses. These reactions are all the more interesting because he was a sophisticated easterner trained by his father to value, above all else, New England pastoral scenes as an almost universal standard of landscape beauty. Nevertheless, some Northwest landscapes made him recall the East—visits to the San Juan Islands, for example, caused homesickness for his family's summer residence at picturesque Deer Isle, Maine, which he deeply loved and his father had loathed.

Letters to his wife also provide a splendidly revealing, and sometimes unflattering or even comical, social commentary concerning some of the prominent individuals he met. John Charles was a private and somewhat introverted individual, but also rather snobbish. He clearly felt most at ease with people having a similar social background, thus he wrote favorably about a number of men who became congenial companions while he stayed at the Rainier Club in Seattle. But his pen also described people and situations he considered uncouth, as when writing about a barely tolerable dinner gathering in Seattle. He told Sophia there was "considerable standing around in entirely unheated rooms with the doors mostly open and being introduced to various men whose names I either did not hear or promptly forgot." This involved "introductions to many more people to whom I had little to say."

His keen powers of observation also captured the character of many prominent, brash, and hard driven individuals in the Northwest, such as industrialist Robert Moran on Orcas Island, the well-known Judge Thomas Burke of Seattle, flashy entrepreneur Jay P. Graves of Spokane, and the demanding Kerr clients in Portland.

Second Legacy: Art of Northwest Planning and Design

John Charles brought to the Northwest for the first time the sophisticated services of a large and efficient landscape architecture firm. At Brookline, he had modernized the office when introducing the use of the telephone and telegraph, maintaining meticulous records, taking photographs to record project progress, and building models to present complicated design proposals, such as for the large

formal garden at Thornewood, on American Lake south of Tacoma. He was the consummate professional landscape practitioner of his day.

John Charles and his younger brother, of course, continued the consulting practice established by their father, which was important in successfully maintaining their extensive nationwide practice. While the firm provided expert overall design in landscape planning, they did not necessarily provide (or were contracted) for the detailed, on-site, follow-up services. This had its frustrations. Thus, it often was necessary to ensure that the execution or the supervision of proposals would be undertaken by responsible local individuals, such as in the case of the firm's recommended people who became park superintendents in Portland (E.T. Mische), Seattle (J.W. Thompson), and Spokane (J.W. Duncan).

John Charles was often critical of elements included in the later detailed execution of projects. For example, he said this about Interlaken Boulevard in Seattle: "What between economy of land and construction, and trying to suit the ideas of individuals, the boulevards are narrow, crooked and with unscientific boundaries." He continued: "The lines of the drives were in many cases conspicuously stiff and formal, consisting of simple radial curves and straight lines as is customary in railroads, instead of gracefully varying curves as is customary in the best parks." He also presented to the city his criticism of horseshoe curves in Colman Park.

Overseeing large, complex projects from 3,000 miles away at the firm's Brookline office also caused difficulties. Furthermore, Olmsted wrote drafts of many reports while staying in hotels or clubs, or when traveling on a train. Plans were sent across vast distances via the mail, and important messages came by telegram. The distances and the sheer volume of the firm's work sometimes caused serious delays, especially in tending to private clients.

Nevertheless, Olmsted brought a new standard of excellence to the Northwest. His carefully written reports clearly stated the rationale for a proposed design. They were extremely proficient in nature and even today serve as models of professional precision.

He prepared reports with the unquestioned assumption that the designer-planner was an expert, whose judgments should not be questioned. Olmsted was willing to vigorously defend well-held park planning principles. For example, he viewed the center part of a park as inviolate. In Seattle, he successfully defended against proposals for building a new art museum in the middle of Volunteer Park. His same argument caused the firm to withdraw completely from San Diego's Panama-California Exposition when architect Bertram Grosvenor Goodhue proposed locating exposition buildings in the center of Balboa Park.

Olmsted's approach to designing large public projects was invariably based on a long term vision. The Bailey Peninsula (now Seward Park), which in 1903 lay south of the Seattle city limits, is an example. Olmsted saw the potential value of this natural area in an expanding parks system and continued to argue for its incorporation before the peninsula was consumed by residential development. He likewise patiently waited to incorporate privately owned parks into the Seattle system, such as Ravenna Park. He also believed that the long term viability of a park system was best attained by having an independent park board. In Seattle, after his initial encouragement, the city voted in a separate park commission in 1904.

The successful practice of large-scale landscape design also depended on close relationships with architects. Perhaps the most critical was Seattle's Charles Saunders, originally from Cambridge, Massachusetts. He viewed Olmsted as a fine example of the cultivated, well educated easterner who would bring polish to evolving Northwest cityscapes. As secretary of the Seattle park board, Saunders proved to be a tireless supporter. John Galen Howard from Berkeley, California, the principal architect for Seattle's Alaska-Yukon-Pacific Exposition, was another professional with whom Olmsted had especially warm relations. Howard later noted that he never before experienced a better or more fortunate working association.

Third Legacy: Regionalism

Frederick Law Olmsted Sr. had believed in the international nature of landscape architecture, espousing a strong affinity for New England pastoral landscapes, which were similar to the English style. Thus, none of his Midwest commissions attempted to evoke the character of the native prairie, unlike in the later "prairie style" work of Jens Jensen. Commissions in California, however, forced him to reconsider, and to recognize the necessity of creating a different regional design tradition in the semi-arid West.

John Charles likewise grappled with these issues, such as in the unexecuted scheme for San Diego's Panama-California Exposition done in the early 1910s. In the Northwest, indeed, he created a new regional design idiom; thus his work is comparable to the accomplishments of other regional designers, such as the Midwest's Jensen and "landscape gardener" Ossian Simonds.

Olmsted's new distinct regional mode conceptually treated open spaces in parks and gardens as "clearings in the forest." The retention of large native trees and the wild understory emphasized the inherently Picturesque character of Northwest landscapes. These forest clearings, with their distinctive vegetation, were subtly enhanced by the sensitive grading that characterized all of the firm's work.

Even the more monumental projects, such as the Portland and Seattle expositions, were designed to incorporate spectacular regional settings with expansive views of mountains and bodies of water. Rainier Vista at the University of Washington campus, despite later alterations, remains today as one of the Northwest's most memorable created landscapes. It unites foreground and middle distance with the unique snow-clad profile of Mt. Rainier.

Embodying a Broader Context

John Charles never returned to the Northwest after his last brief visit in October 1911. A few months later, he became ill and suspended his work in the Far West, being unable to undertake long train journeys. Overwhelmed by frail health, and the stress as senior partner in a firm with an extensive national clientele, he declared: "I'm leaving my western work in Dawson's able hands."

Olmsted's aide, Fred Dawson, carried on nobly, supervising numerous domestic commissions, a new state capitol campus plan, the Palos Verdes development in California, and the Washington Park Arboretum. The state capitol and arboretum projects were obtained through the vigorous intervention of John Charles' old Seattle friend, parks supporter, and politician, Charles Saunders.

Though Dawson had been trained by John Charles, his work would exhibit a subtle change. Affable, well liked, and amendable to client requests, he proved more willing to compromise than John Charles had been. He initiated a change from the Picturesque design mode favored by John Charles to what Dawson, a knowledgeable plantsman, called the Gardenesque, or garden-like manner, which entailed using many exotic plants.

In the early decades of the 20th century, the Olmsted Brothers continued to complete a large number of landscape commissions of great diversity and complexity. But with time, the legacy of the regional design principles laid down by John Charles became largely forgotten and its original manifestations often obliterated.

But after the mid 1970s, John Charles' achievements again affected the work of a generation of later designers in different ways. For example, Richard Haag's design for the Gasworks Park in Seattle, apart from its innovative retention of an old unused industrial facility, had a conscious relationship to the older Olmsted parks. Realizing that Seattle's picturesque parks were mostly unsuited for large raucous gatherings, Haag designed Gasworks Park to accommodate such needs and thereby relieve pressure on the Olmsted parks.

Today, the Olmsted legacy influences proponents of large-scale, open-space planning. And today's detailed designs better incorporate the natural beauty of native vegetation, and views of mountains and bodies of water. While no evidence suggests that John Charles had any real understanding of the complex ecological interdependencies that dominate contemporary practice, one suspects he surely would have approved of it as a means of protecting regional identity.

Appendix A

1903 Portland Parks Report[1]

Excerpts

* * *

JOHN CHARLES OLMSTED   FREDERICK LAW OLMSTED, JR.

OLMSTED BROTHERS

LANDSCAPE ARCHITECTS

BROOKLINE, MASS.

December 31, 1903.

Honorable George H. Williams, Chairman, Board of Park Commissioners, Portland, Oregon.

Dear Sir: We have the honor to submit our report upon existing parks and a proposed system of parks for the City of Portland.

In preparing our minds for this duty we were occupied more or less every day during three weeks in going about and examining various parts of the city and of the surrounding country and in conference with Colonel L.L. Hawkins and Mr. Ion Lewis, of the Park Commission, and other interested citizens, and we were taken upon a number of long and interesting drives by Colonel Hawkins, besides making various excursions by ourselves. We were provided with good maps and other printed information, and took numerous photographs as an aid to memory in the subsequent study and digestion of our observations and wrote out very full notes of what we saw and were told.

INTRODUCTION.

1—Importance of Municipal Parks.

Leading writers and other authorities in modern municipal development agree that no city can be considered properly equipped without an adequate park system...

2—Duty of Citizens Toward Parks.

...[E]very inhabitant of a city owes to it, in return for benefits and advantages derived from it, certain duties not specifically compulsory according to law. Among such duties is that of aiding in every possible way to make the city more beautiful and more agreeable to live in and work in, and more attractive to strangers...

3—Parks and Park Purposes Should Be Defined in Advance—Park Units.

...The units of a park system generally recognized are city squares, play grounds, small or neighborhood parks, large or suburban parks, scenic reservations, boulevards and parkways.

City squares are comparatively small, ornamental grounds, usually dominated by surrounding buildings... They are usually flat or simple in topography...much used by people who although they pass through them are bound elsewhere and, in other ways, they are more distinctly ornamental incidents of daily city life and of urban conditions than are larger parks. Hence they are usually...improved formally and symmetrically and often with prominent architectural and sculptural features. They may even be...without trees, flowers or grass...yet command the admiration of people...an indication of their essential qualities and fundamental differences from parks proper. Few cities have anywhere near as many ornamental squares as they should...

Play grounds are primarily selected and improved for particular forms of recreation and only such beauty and ornamentation is allowable as will not unduly interfere with their usefulness...As the noise...makes them somewhat objectionable to neighbors it is often best to combine them with public squares in such a way as to partially separate and screen their strictly utilitarian parts from adjoining streets and buildings...or to locate them in parks proper in such a way as to avoid undue injury to the main purposes of the park as in the case of Jackson Park, Chicago.

Urban or neighborhood parks include public pleasure grounds of a variety of sizes and styles. They may be formal in general design and informal in some details like the public park at Dijon, in France, or they may be as informal as the designer can make them, like Morningside Park, in New York, or, as is generally the case, they may be informal in general design but more or less filled with formal and artificial details like the Public Garden in Boston...the local park is the more useful to the daily life of the citizens since its restricted size and cost enable the city to distribute them...in close proximity to densely populated sections...It may not be possible to wholly screen out surrounding streets and houses, yet it will usually make them more enjoyable for visitors to do so to some extent...Drives are often inadvisedly introduced into such parks. Unless there is some fine outlook to which it is desirable to lead people in carriages, as in the case of The Front, in Buffalo, or some bluff or river bank or lake or other landscape feature which cannot be viewed from carriages in adjoining streets, or unless there is a concert grove at which it is desired to provide for visitors in carriages, or unless the local park be part of a continuous chain of parks and parkways, or unless there is some other good reason, a drive is an undesirable intrusion in a local park. Such a park is worth far more for visitors on foot especially children of the neighborhood than it is for visitors in carriages who may be presumed to be better able to visit the larger suburban parks...

Rural or Suburban Parks. These parks are intended to afford to visitors that sort of mental refreshment and enjoyment which can only be derived from the quiet contemplation of natural scenery...The fundamental purposes of a rural park requires the shutting off from the interior of the park as completely as possible, all city sights and sounds... it requires that most of the area be devoted to that beautiful but comparatively tame type of scenery which is composed mainly of flat or gently sloping or undulating surfaces covered with smooth, close turf surrounded with an abundance of shade trees. The beauty of this type of scenery is ruined by the introduction of numerous incongruous and artificial features. Straight lines of drive or walk or water surface, rows of trees, buildings, monuments, fountain jets, flagpoles, and particularly formal flower beds are usually injurious to and often destructive of simple rural beauty with is appropriate to this class of parks.

Scenic Reservations...usually differ from parks proper in being rougher, wilder and less artificially improved and are usually more remote...Municipal reservations are sometimes selected to preserve one or more notable landscape features of moderate size, such as, for instance, the gorge of the Genesee River north of Rochester; the Blue Hills southeast of Boston...and Mount Royal of Montreal.

Boulevards and parkways are important parts of a complete park system. For convenience, formal city pleasure drives may better be called "boulevards," while informal pleasure drives may be more specifically designated "parkways"...Eastern Parkway and Ocean Parkway, in Brooklyn, are instances of liberal and complete boulevards, in which there is a broad central drive devoted exclusively to pleasure driving and a narrower drive on each side intended for access to adjoining private properties as well as for ordinary street traffic and separated from the middle drive by double rows of trees with promenades between them. Drexel Boulevard, in Chicago, is another type of boulevard (more popular with real estate men) in which there are two sidewalks each with a row of trees, two broad driveways and a broad central ornamental strip. The parkway called in part Fenway, in part Riverway and in part Jamaicaway, in Boston and Bay Ridge Parkway or Shore Drive, in Brooklyn, are examples of informal parkways in which adjoining or included local scenery or distant views are more important than the decorative turf strips and shade trees.

4—The Parks of a City Should Be Parts of a System.

...Many cities have one or more parks in which their citizens may justly take pride, but comparatively few of these cities have what can properly be called a comprehensive, well-balanced and well-developed system of parks, a system which will compare favorably as to completeness with, for instance, the system of public schools, or the system of fire protection and other principal departments of the city government.

The backwardness of municipal park systems is not so much due to lack of public intelligence and public spirit, as to the defective development of the love of beauty, as compared with a well-developed appreciation of practical, utilitarian progress.

5—Park Systems Should Be Comprehensive.

A park system should comprise all the various units which go to form a complete system. Some cities, Savannah, for instance, have a liberal provision of public squares, but few, if any, play grounds, parks and boulevards; some, New Orleans, for instance, have boulevards and parks, but few, if any, play grounds and neighborhood parks; some, Washington, for instance, have public squares, boulevards and parks, but few, if any, play grounds; some, Chicago, for instance, have parks and boulevards, but few public squares and local parks; some, Philadelphia, for instance, have parks and public squares, but few connecting boulevards and play grounds.

6—Park Systems Should Be Well Balanced.

…It not infrequently happens that the sections of a city in which the population is most dense and most in need of squares, play grounds and local parks, are almost wholly devoid of these advantages because no well-balanced system has been devised and carried out while land was sufficiently cheap and comparatively unoccupied so that now the expense is prohibitory.

7—Parks Should Have Individuality.

…[Parks] are liable to repeat each other too much. The West Side parks of Chicago resemble each other to regrettable degree. Each has its little, crooked lake, its green house and flower beds, its little lawns, its curving level drives and walks, its bridges and statues, its plantations mainly of the same selection of trees crowded and slim and only partially screening out surrounding houses. Only of late years has a bicycle track and speedway been introduced into one, a bathing establishment and an athletic ground in another. In New York and Boston and Rochester, and many cities largely, perhaps owing to the topographical differences the parks are strongly individualized.

8—Parks Should Be Connected and Approached by Boulevards and Parkways.

A connected system of parks and parkways is manifestly far more complete and useful than a series of isolated parks.

Delaware Park, in Buffalo, is an example of a park with handsome boulevards forming approaches from the city and connecting it with Humboldt Park in one direction, Gates Circle in another, and Delaware Avenue and The Front in another. Washington Park, Chicago, also has its two imposing approaches in Drexel Boulevard and Grand Boulevard and its boulevard connection with Jackson Park and the West Side Parks. The broad avenues of Washington are admirable examples of boulevards because the houses are kept back from the sidewalks by turf strips upon which houses cannot be built, although porches, bay windows, and other projections are very properly permitted, and also because they have ornamental circles and squares at turning points and often begin or end at important buildings.

9—Parks and Parkways Should Be Located and Improved to Take Advantage of Beautiful Natural Scenery and to Secure Sanitary Conditions.

Only recently has it begun to be realized what enormous advantages are gained by locating parks and parkways so as to take advantage of beautiful natural scenery. The most expensive large parks, Central Park and Prospect Park, were located without taking advantage of the magnificent natural landscapes of the rivers and bays which distinguish New York and Brooklyn. There are many similar cases…

…[B]rooks or little rivers which would otherwise become nuisances that would some day have to be put in large underground conduits at enormous expense, may be made the occasion for delightful local pleasure grounds or attractive parkways. Such improvements add greatly to the value of adjoining properties…

10—Park Systems Should Be in Proportion to Opportunities.

A city having many or extensive opportunities…may wisely mortgage its future wealth much more heavily by the issue of long-term bonds for the acquirement and preservation of beautiful natural scenery than a city relatively devoid of such opportunities…[I]mprovements tend to draw to the city wealth, the taxation of which may more than repay the city for the outlay…

11—Parks and Parkways Should Be Acquired Betimes.

It is particularly urgent that a city having beautiful local scenery adapted for parks and parkways should secure the land betimes lest these natural advantages be destroyed or irreparably injured by the owners...To take an extreme case one has only to consider how utterly impossible it would now be for the city of New York to secure on Manhattan Island another such park as Central Park...There is still a large vacant area west of the Boston Park called The Fens...twenty six years ago, only...$4,300.00 an acre... now…$86,000 an acre.

12—The Land for Park Systems Should Be Paid for by Long-Term Loans.

There is a very commendable disinclination on the part of legislatures to pass laws authorizing long term municipal loans...But the case of loans for purchase of land, especially land for a park system is very decidedly different from that of loans for most other municipal improvements... [I]t should be borne in mind that the land is an asset that will be worth more in almost every instance...Moreover, as a general rule, the special increase in the assessor's valuations of adjoining private lands and in the improvements subsequently erected upon them, will yield increased taxes sufficient to meet the interest and the annual contributions to the sinking fund of the park-land loans...[E]xperience indicates that the limits for park-land loans may safely be set very much higher than for other municipal loans…

13—Park Systems Should Be Improved by Means of Loans, Special Assessments and Annual Taxation.

The experience of the larger cities has been that by far the most satisfactory and profitable results have been obtained by improving their parks as rapidly as such difficult and complex work can wisely be affected, usually in from three to five years after the acquisition of the land...

14—Park Systems Should Be Improved Both Occasionally and Continuously.

...The loans for improvement of parks and still more decidedly those for the purchase of land should be authorized during good times and expended during hard times... [I]t makes tremendously for economy to purchase lands during hard times when land owners often are more eager to obtain cash than to hold on for a possible future profit and it is far more advantageous to employ common labor for park improvement during hard times either to prevent or to diminish the sufferings of the poor and to get the work done at minimum wages.

15—Park Systems Should Be Improved According to a Well Studied and Comprehensive General Plan.

...[T]here are in every city many more persons who consider themselves competent to direct the expenditure of public money on parks without plans prepared by experts than there are persons who would be willing to direct the expenditure of similar amounts on a large city hall, and yet...the ability to design landscape is very much rarer...

…The absence of such a general plan or a failure to comprehend and follow it will result in the hodge-podge of incongruities so often seen in parks...

16—Park Systems Should Be Governed by Qualified Officials.

...[A] complete park system for a city is one of the most difficult and responsible duties that ever comes to a city government...

Experience proves that the most successful government of important park systems is by a small board of unpaid park commissioners...The Board should be financially independent of the city government...The Board should not meet normally oftener than once a month else the ablest and most desirable men who are therefore the busiest men, may decline to serve...most matters, except matters of taste, can be referred to committees...

The president of the park commission should be an able administrator…[and] have traveled enough to have gained a general knowledge of the characteristics that...make the parks of other cities beautiful…

…[I]t is of the utmost importance that the rest of the Board be men of refined taste...[T]here are probably more [women] in a given city who have had the time and inclination to cultivate an appreciation of the beautiful in nature and art…A single commissioner may be very proper in the case of the police department, the fire department and others where efficiency is the main consideration and beauty incidental, but park beauty should always be the controlling consideration, and the two or four members of the Board who were selected primarily because they were believed to be good judges of beauty in park matters are certainly much more likely to judge safely all matters of appearance than is one man who has been selected for his business ability…

17—Park Systems Should Be Improved and Maintained by Specially Trained Men.

...Unfortunately the number of men who know how to make and maintain beautiful parks is very small...Even those park commissioners who know and appreciate beautiful landscape when they see it are rarely able to select and adapt a particular type of landscape to the particular land with which they are dealing. Perhaps they can appreciate good acting or good music, but they would be unable to write the play or compose the music...Many of the civil engineers employed on park work do more even to injure naturally beautiful scenery, because their operations in grading and road building and bridges are apt to be larger, and more conspicuous, and so expensive that once done, it is practically impossible to change them and because most of their training has been in smashing beautiful landscape with railroads, streets, dams and bridges and other constructions, all of which might at the same time, or at moderate additional cost, be made beautiful in form and location, even if without ornament...Civil engineers are not to be blamed for this. Their education and experience has compelled them to it... If a park commission cannot find artistic gardeners and artistic civil engineers, the next best thing is to "catch them young"—those who have innate artistic feeling—and help them to become such.

18—Park Systems Should Be Managed Independently of City Governments.

...Parks, like public libraries and art museums, must meet the public needs in the main, else they will lose their power for educating the people to better things, but they should be managed by wise and public-spirited men who have high ideals and will strive to gradually and considerately improve the public taste...

Parks should not be brought into politics not only for the important business reasons that apply in all departments of municipal administration, but for the more important reason that the essential requirement of parks is that they should be naturally and artistically beautiful and because politicians as a class give small consideration to matters of art and beauty of natural scenery...The schools may not be beautiful, but yet may serve all practical purposes; bridges may be and usually are hideous, but we can use them and hope for better things some day, but if parks are not beautiful, they are very nearly useless...

[second part of report]

[Following a brief discussion of Portland's topographical conditions, city growth, landscape features, and recommended property acquisitions, the report next presented "A Comprehensive System of Parks and Parkways for Portland," with "Detailed Description of Suggested Systems." These extensive specifics—two-thirds of Olmsted's report—included particular recommendations and proposals regarding numerous city squares, playgrounds, parkways, boulevards, reservations, and shorelines, in addition to at least 18 individually-named existing and proposed parks, such as Macleay Park, Forest Park, Mount Tabor Park, and Sellwood Park. Following here are several brief excerpts.]

PRINCIPLE LANDSCAPE FEATURES.

...The most notable landscape feature that is conveniently accessible to the greater part of the population is obviously the river itself. Unfortunately the requirements of commerce prevent any considerable area being set aside for park purposes in connection with the river until one reaches Ross Island, above the city, and Swan Island below the city...

From almost all parts of the city that are fairly open and from all the high hills extremely beautiful views are commanded of the distant snow-clad mountains and especially of the five great snow-clad peaks: Mount St. Helens, Mount Adams, Mount Hood, Mount Rainier and Mount Jefferson.

The city is most fortunate, in comparison with the majority of American cities, in possessing such varied and wonderfully strong and interesting landscape features available to be utilized in its park system...

ROSS ISLAND PARK.

Another landscape feature of considerable importance to the city, the value of which in this respect is realized by but few people, is Ross Island and adjoining islands. If these islands can be obtained at a reasonable price by the city, their acquisition will unquestionably prove in the long run a very profitable investment. Although the islands are almost wholly covered by the annual floods, they are not injured by this to any appreciable extent, and during the summer, when people most resort to pleasure grounds of this character, the ground will be in fit condition...and the groves of trees on this island will be a source of pleasure to all who live, or have to pass, within sight of it on both sides of the river...

SWAN ISLAND PARK.

Swan Island is less desirable as a pleasure ground than Ross Island, because further from the center of population and more often and more completely flooded, but it is equally valuable as a beauty spot in the landscape from considerable portions of the city. If this island can be purchased at a moderate expense, it should be secured. It would undoubtedly prove a very valuable asset to the city hereafter…

"GUILD LAKE."

…The base of the [west] hills forms almost a straight line and runs nearly northwest from the mouth of Marquam Gulch Canyon to the mouth of Balch Creek Canyon, and continues in the same general direction for some miles further down the river. Up the river for some distance beyond Marquam Gulch, there is a narrow margin of moderately flat land between the hills and the river...Down the river from Balch Creek much of the space between the base of the hills and the river is occupied by Guild Lake and other lakes so that there is little opportunity for the city to expand in this direction...

…In the main this lake presents an attractive natural landscape feature, well adapted to be converted into a park. It is, however, a fair question whether this area may not eventually be dyked and drained and filled and used for manufacturing and other commercial purposes...It seems inadvisable to press the matter at present...[2]

---

1. *The original 123-page typewritten version of the highly acclaimed 1903 Portland Parks Report is archived in Olmsted job #2640; Library of Congress. The reprinted version from the* Report of the Park Board *(Portland, 1903)—complete on a more consolidated 63-page format—can be accessed on-line, or found in regional archival collections.*

2. *See Michael C. Houck and M.J. Cody,* Wild in the City: A Guide to Portland's Natural Areas *(Oregon Historical Society, 2003), for a modern-day, comprehensive overview of the city's contemporary parks, boulevards, parkways, city squares, and natural areas. In regard to the wildlife-rich Ross Island locality, Houck and Cody note: "The best way to explore the islands is by canoe or kayak." Swan Island has met a sadder fate: "There are still those alive today who can remember when Swan Island was truly an island."*

Appendix B

1903 Seattle Parks Report

Overview and Excerpts

Compared to the Portland parks report, the Seattle assessment was more precise and practical regarding park and parkway properties, and less philosophical concerning overall landscape principles. It was submitted in the summer of 1903, soon after Olmsted spent all of May and the first few days of June investigating the Seattle area with the park commissioners.

With fewer distractions than in Portland (where the upcoming Lewis and Clark Exhibition consumed much time), Olmsted could focus entirely on the parks system when in Seattle. Also, quiet time back at the Brookline office that summer—so soon after his Puget Sound trip—proved convenient for writing the Seattle report.

Adopted in October 1903, Olmsted's blueprint for parkways linking shorelines and lakes, the new university campus, and city parks still holds true today, despite some gaps in the broad boulevards as envisioned for connecting neighborhoods.

Beginning in Seattle's southeast environs, John Charles laid out a boulevard system running from Bailey Peninsula (now Seward Park), north along Lake Washington, slightly inland through the Denny-Blaine land holdings, and north through narrow, logged-over Washington Park to the university campus above Union Bay. The system continued north and west to Ravenna Park (but not through its handsome deep ravine), following the creek to Green Lake. Along with suggestions for the Green Lake shoreline, Olmsted recommended a "pleasure" drive inside Woodland Park and a steep sweep of parkway to the Ballard lowlands and beyond, but this hardly materialized.

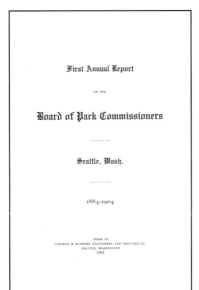

First Annual Report

OF THE

Board of Park Commissioners

Seattle, Wash.

1884-1904

PRESS OF
LOWMAN & HANFORD STATIONERY AND PRINTING CO.
SEATTLE, WASHINGTON
1905

Along Seattle's western shoreline, Olmsted's Magnolia Bluff boulevard did finally become a reality years later, along with Fort Lawton pleasure drives, despite initial suspicion from the U.S. Army.

"Branch" parkways along, for example, the crest of Queen Anne and Beacon hills, and through the deep woods of Interlaken ("Volunteer Parkway"), also were proposed and carried through with some success in following years, after some forthright prompting from Olmsted in subsequent reports. Much of these "branch" and main boulevards followed old narrow bicycle routes, which Olmsted advised keeping or enlarging, or discarding in favor of better grades for heavier traffic—i.e., teams of horses or automobiles.

In a few years, with the city's annexation of Ballard, West Seattle, and southeast shoreline communities, these additional localities also came in for review and recommendations in subsequent reports.

Olmsted's detailed, exacting, and encouraging vision came through in the latter pages of his 1903 report, which resulted in many successful specific park plans. But he also did not hold back his sharp criticisms of aspects of existing park lands, as is clearly evident in a number of the following excerpts.

Volunteer Park—"The boundaries of this park are not satisfactory...This park is situated on the summit of one of the high hills of the city, and at present commands fine distant views; but the park is so little above adjoining private property that houses, and particularly trees to be planted on the properties and in the streets, will in time completely shut out all distant views...

"At present formal beds are scattered promiscuously in portions of the ground...There should be an association of formal flower beds with some strong architectural features of formal design...separated from the informal portions of the park...The number of fir trees should be greatly reduced...There being no rugged topography in this park, and as it will be surrounded by highly finished style of city development, it will be best to adopt a neat and smooth style of landscape gardening throughout, thus harmonizing the park with its surroundings...Another reason for eliminating most of the fir trees from this park is that they are associated in the mind with wild surroundings, and hence are not quite appropriate on clipped lawns."

Kinnear Park—"The park [on a steep bluff southwest of the Queen Anne Hill summit] is pleasing in detail and extremely valuable, owing to the fine views which it commands over the Sound. It is a good sample of the miles of similar bluff parks which it is hoped the city will eventually have. Such parks will always be a great benefit to adjoining residential property...The shrubbery which has been added in the park is perhaps open to the criticism that it is too miscellaneous, and that it repeats practically the same assortment used in Denny Park, and in many of the principal private grounds of the city...As before stated, each park should have an individuality of its own...in the planting as well as in the constructive features."

Denny Park [donated years earlier by the pioneering Denny family]—"This park contains about five and one-fourth acres and has already been improved...all coniferous evergreens would better be eliminated at once. The little deciduous trees are much too numerous, and would better be thinned out to some extent at once, and considerably more within ten years. The shrubbery plantations in general are too miscellaneous in composition...The proportion of very large-growing shrubs should be reduced, and the shrubbery plantations should be composed mainly of low-growing, compact, neat and healthy shrubbery. A distinctly informal style of design having been adopted, all rows of plants, and especially formal beds of tender bedding plants, should be avoided...A more complete system of catch-basins and underground drains should be provided for the walks, which are now subject to excessive wash."

Lincoln Park [Broadway at Pine, Olive, & Howell; renamed Cal Anderson Park]—"More than half of this park is occupied by the city reservoir, with its surrounding walk...There is not a tree or shrub upon the whole park. The ground south of the reservoir having been graded... has come to be used as a ball field, much to the annoyance of neighbors...The great building of the High School being only half a block west of this park, it would be a great advantage to add to the park the six lots of land which separate the two. The southern part of the park should then be laid out according to a purely formal design, the east and west axis being on the center of the High School, and the north and south axis on the center of the stone gatehouse of the reservoir...The design should provide suitable short-cut walks, and these should be shaded by rows of trees. Instead of using the elm, maple and other common street trees, it would be well to distinguish this park by using much smaller growing trees, such as the Hop Hornbeam."

Woodland Park—"A large portion of this park is covered with the remains of native woods. Most of the largest and best trees have been cut, but what remain are amply sufficient to preserve the typical characteristics of the woods which originally clothed all the region...The park is unfortunately crossed by the electric railway, and there does not seem to be any real necessity for this serious injury to the park...every effort should be made to minimize the objectionableness of the railroad in the park...carried throughout the park mainly on a wooden trestle. This results in a great increase in the noise incident to the running of cars.

"Except in the woods and on steep slopes, much of the ground in the park should be covered with grass, especially for some distance back from the lake [Green Lake], as this will be one of the most attractive places for crowds to ramble and sit under the trees.

"The lower portion of the park is too beautiful and the limited area will be too much needed for the accommodation of crowds of visitors to justify the sacrifice of any part of it to the purposes of a menagerie. There should be no enclosures for deer or elk or other pasturing animals in the lower part of the park. There being less natural beauty in the upper portion of the park, since it is flat and has no view, and has been mainly cleared of the original forest, it would be comparatively unobjectionable, if it be thought desirable, to devote part of this portion of the park largely to a collection of hardy wild animals [now Woodland Park Zoo].

"Sufficient space should, however, be provided for field sports, and also for a formal garden when this can be afforded."

Washington Park—"Considerable parts of Washington Park and of the land which it is proposed to add to it have been cleared...portions of the park are covered with the remains of the original forest, but only in places are there groups of very large firs and cedars. These groups, and in general the undergrowth in and about them, should be carefully preserved, but elsewhere a considerable part of this park should be partially or wholly cleared and the surface covered with grass...to provide lawns and open fields for the use of large numbers of people...

"The existing natural growths along the brook, in a strip having a width of from 50 to 200 feet, should generally be carefully preserved, and also an irregular strip along the boundaries, to serve as a border plantation.

"The large logs and stumps should be left in the wooded areas containing good-sized or large fir trees and cedar...A considerable area along the border of Union Bay should have the trees upon it thinned to a comparatively open grove effect...this will be one of the most popular parts of the park. As the ground is swampy near the lake and where the brook enters it, it may be advisable to fill in some places...

"For many years the existing summer flow of the brook, derived mainly from springs, will no doubt be adequate, but in time, when the adjoining lands become more fully occupied, this source of supply will be diverted by sewers and otherwise, and it will become necessary to supply the brook from the city water mains. It will not, however, require a very large amount of water to keep the brook in good condition, so long as care is taken to keep it as shady as possible. Pure water which is densely shaded is rarely objectionable, but the purest water, if it is shallow and of limited extent, is liable to become foul if exposed to the sun."

Beacon Hill Park [renamed Jefferson Park]—"This is a tract of unimproved land, about 115 acres in extent, lying east of the pipe line road on Beacon Hill. All of the original forest trees that had any market value have disappeared... and the stumps and logs...are gradually being taken away for firewood...

"The northern part of the park being wider, and containing more nearly level land, would best be cleared and graded and smoothed and covered with grass for ball [today, golf] games. A good deal of the existing wild growths should be preserved along the borders to frame in and beautify the ball field.

"If the proposed Beacon Hill Parkway is accomplished... the road should eventually be widened so that there will be at least two separate driveways, one for the ordinary commercial traffic and the other for pleasure driving...There does not appear to be need of other drives in this park.

"The southern portion of the park should be made to contrast with the larger open northern part, by having little or no grass, the surface being clothed with low, ground-covering plants. There may be long winding masses of trees and shrubbery...Some walks may be carried through under the groups of trees, but most of the paths should be carried through the openings between the masses of trees and shrubbery, so as to...command the distant views of Lake Washington."

Olmsted also reviewed Somerville Park, a Queen Anne Hill tract, another Beacon Hill park, and ended the 1903 report with advice regarding Pioneer Square in downtown Seattle. "This small triangle should be reserved for the site of an important monument...The monument should be an important architectural feature...[and] most appropriately be in commemoration of the early settlers."

Appendix C

1908 Spokane Parks Report

Overview and Excerpts

"Mr. Olmsted has completed his report for the City of Spokane up to the 109th page but is writing some concluding pages," Brookline wrote the impatient Aubrey L. White on April 13, 1908. Indeed, a few days later John Charles sent his detailed report to Aubrey White, Spokane's park commission president.

White responded immediately on April 27: "I acknowledge receipt of copy of the report made for the city of Spokane Park system...the magnitude of your recommendations made me gasp."

To Aubrey White, credit is given for initially engaging the Olmsted firm and then tirelessly seeing that Olmsted's recommendations were carried through—from the report's delivery in 1908 until its publication (and with passage of bonds to pay for park expansion) in 1913.

Olmsted not only provided Spokane with suggestions for in-town parks, but expanded the scope to include more distant landscapes along the river bluffs and plateaus not yet platted—a rare opportunity to capture "large park" lands while the properties were still inexpensive. Four large parks were singled out and given full treatment in the report—Gorge Park, Upriver Park, Downriver Park, and Latah Park.

He next presented the city fathers with extensive multi-paragraphed suggestions (and criticisms) for Spokane's existing parks—Manito Park, Coeur d'Alene Park, Liberty Park, Corbin Park, Audubon Park, Cliff Park, Adams Park, and four other parks. (The Olmsted firm later sketched exact designs for Liberty, Corbin, and Adams/Cannon Hill parks—each sketch was included in the city's 1913 published report.)

A year after the 1908 report, Olmsted provided an equally important gift to Spokane. He hand-picked and delivered to the city the next park superintendent, John W. Duncan, who in the next 32 years carried through much of the parks report recommendations.

In 1909, Duncan—an assistant Boston park director (and president of the Park Superintendents Association)—came west with other eastern park administrators to visit Seattle's AYPE. Olmsted urged Duncan to stop by Spokane during his travels. "He is...young, energetic and capable," Olmsted Brothers wrote Aubrey White on July 26, 1909.

Within the year, Duncan arrived to permanently stay in Spokane, and three years later wrote a review introducing Olmsted's 1908 report when it was included in the city's 1913 publication. Duncan revealed his worth in these new western surroundings: "During the past three, and especially the last two years, the maintenance has been kept at an excellent standard and extensive improvements undertaken. These improvements have been the building of drives, greenhouses and flower gardens in Manito Park; the grading, planting and completion of Cannon Hill Park; the grading, building walks, planting of Cliff Park... the remodeling and planting of the slopes at Liberty Park... the remodeling and planting of Corbin Park." Duncan also listed another 11 park and parkway improvements.

In concluding the 1908 report—and perhaps the reason why park president White would "gasp"—Olmsted outlined broad design concepts for Spokane to consider in overall city planning. It was one of the earliest city planning documents completed out west, and a lengthy reply to White's initial simple request.

Olmsted began: "You asked us to make some suggestions as to improvements in the city plan of streets and in regard to municipal esthetics generally." The report then went on to give advice regarding diagonal avenues and crooked trolley lines: "The present routes of street railways in this city...might almost be called a disgrace." In regard to railroads: "The Northern Pacific...was located when the city was very small and with insufficient consideration of the true interests of the future city."